Managing Sustainable Development Programmes

Managing Sustainable Development Programmes

A Learning Approach to Change

GÖRAN BRULIN
LENNART SVENSSON

Routledge
Taylor & Francis Group

LONDON AND NEW YORK

First published in paperback 2024

First published 2012 by Gower Publishing

Published 2016 by Routledge
4 Park Square, Milton Park, Abingdon, Oxon OX14 4RN

and by Routledge
605 Third Avenue, New York, NY 10158

Routledge is an imprint of the Taylor & Francis Group, an informa business

British Library Cataloguing in Publication Data
Brulin, Göran.
    Managing sustainable development programmes: a learning approach to change.
    1. Project management. 2. Sustainable development.
    3. Knowledge management.
    I. Title II. Svensson, Lennart, 1944-
    352.3'67-dc23

Library of Congress Cataloging-in-Publication Data
Brulin, Göran.
    Managing sustainable development programmes : a learning approach to change / by Göran Brulin and Lennart Svensson.
        p. cm.
    Includes bibliographical references and index.
    ISBN 978-1-4094-3719-2 (hardback) -- ISBN 978-1-4094-3720-8 (ebook)
        1. Sustainable development. 2. Sustainable development--Case studies. I. Svensson, Lennart, 1944- II. Title.
    HC79.E5.B7794 2011
    338.9'27--dc23

                                                                                2011042808

ISBN: 978-1-4094-3719-2 (hbk)
ISBN: 978-1-03-283692-8 (pbk)
ISBN: 978-1-315-59364-7 (ebk)

DOI: 10.4324/9781315593647

Contents

List of Figures and Table

Figures

Table

Foreword

The Regional and Social Funds face large and demanding challenges. They should contribute to the supply of competence, strengthen vulnerable groups in the labour market, and support innovation, entrepreneurship, regional development and growth. All these were emphasized as important tools for realizing the EU strategy for Europe 2020 of a more innovative, smarter and more inclusive Union.

Different evaluations show extensive activities and results. The programmes have involved some 100,000 individuals and a number of exciting results have been documented. Nevertheless, we cannot be satisfied with results achieved so far! We believe one area for development is that projects could make a better contribution to long-term sustainable development.

However, being responsible for programmes, we have taken a number of initiatives to ensure quality in the implementation of programmes and their many projects. Learning and ongoing evaluation are run at a number of different levels, by implementing organizations, in programmes and projects. The requirement that we should contribute to building up evaluation competence has led to the start-up of a number of university courses and the professionalization of the role of evaluators and interactive researchers. This book is one more piece in the puzzle of improving this work. Based on proven experience and scientific foundations, the authors point out the mechanisms required for programmes and projects to contribute to sustainable development. They show the importance of collaboration between different actors. Joint knowledge formation in project implementation ensures reciprocal learning and feedback from the experiences gained. Active ownership means that the knowledge gained is fed back into core activities and provides energy for creating regional growth and employment.

The book itself is one example of the contribution made by the Structural Funds to development through better project work. Success in project-based development work requires a deeper understanding at different levels, and among different actors (covering those responsible for programmes, project case handlers, project owners, steering groups, project management, participants et al.), of how projects should be run and organized. The book contains a critical review, analyses and a range of examples that can provide useful assistance in such a learning process. The authors are themselves responsible for the data, analyses and conclusions presented in the book.

Åsa Lindh
Director-General
ESF Council

Göran Theolin
Deputy Director-General
Swedish Agency for Economic and Regional Growth

About the Authors

Göran Brulin is senior analyst at the Swedish Agency for Economic and Regional Growth (goran.brulin@tillvaxtverket.se). He is responsible for ongoing evaluation of the European Regional Development Programmes. He is adjunct professor in local and regional innovations at Linköping University and associated with HELIX VINN, Centre of Excellence (see www.liu.se/helix). His research interests include interactive local and regional development, organization of work, business administration and management, and economic sociology.

Lennart Svensson is professor in sociology at Linköping University and a member of the research management team at HELIX VINN, Centre of Excellence (see www.liu.se/helix). He is also research manager at APeL, an R&D centre for workplace learning and the framework for different development projects (see www.apel-fou.se). His research field has covered local and regional development, workplace learning, interactive research, networks, partnerships and project work. He is author or co-author of more than 30 books.

Running Programmes for Sustainable Development

What Is the Book About?

Large amounts of resources are put into different programmes to create greater innovation capacity, entrepreneurship, new jobs and competence enhancement. How should these programmes, aiming at new routes, be organized to achieve lasting effects? This book aims to show how public programmes in regional growth and sustainable development should be designed, steered and evaluated in order to produce a return from the initiatives taken. The starting point is primarily the experiences gained from the EU Structural Fund programmes in Sweden, both the Regional Fund and the Social Fund. During the programming period 2007–2013, several thousand projects have been implemented, an investment amounting to more than 3 billion Euros in Sweden, 83 billion in Europe. Our firm conviction is that the Swedish way to manage and evaluate these programmes should work as a starting point for a discussion about a more rational and effective implementation of programmes. There is an urgent need to critically examine how to conduct public development programmes (see European Commission 2007a).

The book and its conclusions are based on a strong critique of traditional programme implementation, the belief in the all-powerful project manager, a linear programme logic, as well as strong focus on planning, activities and short-term results. We take instead an approach where we show how active ownership and steering, collaboration between different actors and the dynamics of developmental learning can be used to provide multiplier effects. Learning through ongoing evaluation is regarded as the binding element enabling continuous improvements and above all knowledge formation gained from previous experiences. We wish to explain the mechanisms leading to sustainable development work, that is to say, what is it that enables activities in programmes and projects to continue after financing has ceased and project management has completed its work.[1]

A programme consists of a group of related projects with different stakeholders. The ambition is often to achieve strategic change. Goals often include different values – economic, political, social and environmental (Maylor 2010: 60). Projects grow in scale, cost and complexity (Stokes 2009). The complexity of a project has to do with size, technical difficulties, conflicting environmental and political constraints, a large number of stakeholders, and so on (Remington and Pollack 2008). Second order project management deals with large and highly complex projects, which are often organized as a programme. What does it mean to be a project leader in such a programme – in terms of competencies, position in the project organization, mandate, and so on? These questions will be dealt with in this book.

The programmes we have studied aim to combine growth and innovation[2] with individual development and employability. This combination of growth and welfare is part of a strategy for sustainable change. Changes at different 'levels' – the individual, organizational and societal – are seen as necessary and mutually reinforcing to accomplish a sustainable change. A system perspective is necessary and this involves a large number of stakeholders (Cavanagh 2012).

This book is not about Sweden. It is about the organization of large and complex projects that are publicly funded and is illustrated by what we consider to be interesting examples from Sweden which are of general theoretical and practical interest. We think it important to get a better understanding of which strategies and approaches enable outcomes and values from projects to become sustainable (cf. Thomas and Mullaly 2008: 365). The examples we use originate mainly from the EU Structural Funds for regional growth (the European Regional Development Fund – ERDF) and employment (the European Social Fund – ESF). There are 27 member states

---

1   The book is the result of close cooperation with programme implementers, project management, project participants, coordinators, evaluators and representatives from structural fund partnerships. It has been written in cooperation with Per-Erik Ellström, Sven Jansson and Karin Sjöberg. Sven Jansson has also been responsible for the draft of Chapter 6 and, in cooperation with Göran Brulin, worked out the learning system in Chapter 3. Jan Ottosson, Staffan Bjurulf, Martin Nyqvist, Ingela Wahlgren, Filis Sigala, Ingmar Paulsson and Lena Lindgren have all provided important views on contents and conclusions in the book.

2   Innovation includes cultural, social and economic aspects. Numerous practical examples from 60 countries, presenting multiple perspectives and models, can be found in Von Stamm and Trifilova 2009.

running thousands of programmes and projects in EU Structural Funds in order to improve the labour market, innovation and growth.

One reason for mainly using projects in the Regional and Social Funds in Sweden as an empirical base for our research is that Sweden is promoting and developing a model for learning through ongoing evaluation. It is an approach for securing higher quality in projects and a mechanism for creating strategic change. This attempt from Sweden is unique with respect to the other 26 member states of the EU, but there is growing interest from other countries in Europe. Sweden has also been able to deal with the financial and economic crisis successfully through a partnership approach between the unions, employers and the state. This strategy for finding a joint solution to the crisis in Nordic countries can explain the positive economic development in these countries, increasingly referred to as 'Tiger economies'. Scandinavian countries are well-known examples of mixed and pluralistic economies in which the state plays a major role in regulating the economy. These countries are also characterized by a high degree of participation and public–private cooperation between different actors (Gustavsen 2010). The Scandinavian 'tripartism' (between the state, companies and unions) can be seen as an important element in a strategy for sustainable change.

But the book does not deal with country-specific conditions for change and innovation. Instead, we have studied how large and complex projects can be more effective and sustainable in order to find more generic answers (cf. Thomas and Mullaly 2008: 364).

What Do We Want to Analyse?

In order to specify in greater detail this question, we must clarify the starting points, our perspective on development and the goals for such types of public programmes. In order to be able to examine the complex problem of how programmes and projects can be run more or less well, we need to discuss different theoretical approaches and some important concepts. To do this, we report a number of conclusions based on research from different programmes from the two funds. In later chapters, we will return to this and build on these conclusions.

For Sweden, entry to the EU means that responsibility for growth and employment has been regionalized. Increasingly it is the regions that should drive growth, innovation, competence and employment questions. The rationale of the EU Structural Funds is that they should work as an additional 'lubricant' in relation to regular initiatives. Both the Regional Fund and the Social Fund should change, improve and strengthen different regional growth and employment policies. The programmes and projects should be innovative and 'additional' in terms of supplementing regular activities. For this reason, it is particularly important that they are as development oriented as possible. In other words, it is not the initiatives themselves which are the main goal of the Structural Funds, but rather the long-term effects which the programmes should achieve.

The visions and goals of the Structural Funds are set at a high level. Programmes and projects should increase innovation capacity, create a more inclusive working life and lead to greater growth, as set out in the EU strategy for Europe 2020. They are a part of the Union's cohesion policy and they should provide a social corrective to the negative effects of the internal market (Tarschy 2003). At the same time as programmes should facilitate structural transformation, they should also support renewal and the creation of better jobs, with increased skill content, good working and employment conditions, as well as a labour market that does not exclude specific groups and where environmental factors are taken into account. In this way our questions come within the scope of what is usually defined as sustainable growth and sustainable working life, namely working life and growth where different interests are balanced and where human resources and the physical environment are not consumed. The terms 'sustainable growth' and 'sustainable working life' provide a reference framework for our analysis, but the focus is on the conditions for sustainable development in programmes and projects. So what does this mean?

A distinguishing characteristic of sustainable development work is not that it focuses primarily on activities and short-term results. Quite the contrary: long-term multiplier effects, not least in other development activities, are of special importance. We should step back and clarify how we view these concepts and how they are linked together.

What Is Sustainable Development Work?

Distinctions between activities, results and effects in development work or in a project are often made in programme theory (Brulin and Svensson 2011). The usefulness or the value of development work can be assessed from different starting points. This can cover the following:

1.   number and types of activities implemented and their results;

2.   short-term results of activities;

3.   long-term effects, that is, if results are applied and become an integrated part of an activity or contribute to strategic impact (of agreements, rules, laws, policies, steering documents or public debate). If programmes and projects kick-start learning processes and knowledge formation in other development activities, then we can speak of long-term multiplier effects, that is, where effects are formed, value added and leveraged obtained.

To be more concrete, we can apply the reasoning above on the usefulness of a project to the two programme areas in the Social Fund. In programme area 1, namely competence development for employees and business owners, *outcomes* usually involve participation in education and the experiences and usefulness that participants find in these initiatives. It is relatively easy to report the number of participants and how many were satisfied with the activities. Participating in education, however, does not itself guarantee learning that leads to results. In order to be able to discuss the *results* of an education, an individual should have learned something – not just theoretically, but also something that can be applied, that is, the individual should have enhanced their competence. Nor is learning any guarantee of long-term *effects*. If participants are not able to use their knowledge and if the workplace does not function as a learning environment, then results (learning) will not be transformed into long-term effects (more effective activities). Ideally, education (an activity) should lead to learning which provides broader and more responsible work tasks (a result), which in its turn contributes to developing the activity, that is, by it becoming more innovative and competitive (an effect).

We can apply similar reasoning to the Social Fund's programme area for initiatives for social cohesion and inclusion, called Priority 1. The target groups in Priority 1 are those who are furthest from entering the labour market. The activities arranged by the projects for these groups can deal with education and other support measures for vulnerable individuals. The outcome of activities can be assessed by the proportion who complete the programme, and the proportion who are satisfied with the measures. Results deal with the actual usefulness for participants, that is, in terms of increased competence and employability, but also strengthened resources such as increased self-confidence, increased ambitions and access to networks. Long-term effects in this context mean that participants have got a firmer footing on the labour market such as work of a particular kind or running their own business.

Long-term multiplier effects in other development activities are particularly important for projects in the Regional Fund. Prioritized projects in the areas of regional innovation environments and entrepreneurship/ business development are expected to initiate learning and development processes that lead to greater capacity to innovate and also entrepreneurship. Similar to 'ripples on the pond', experiences and knowledge from projects are disseminated to contribute to greater dynamics in regional growth processes. Evaluating multiplier effects is difficult since causal relationships are often unclear.

How, for example, does one value the fact that the Mid Sweden University, through a Regional Fund project, succeeded in acquiring primary responsibility for the government's special initiatives in innovation offices at four universities? Together with two municipalities and a co-financier, the Mid Sweden University built up an innovation project with the aim of providing coaching on research-based ideas for innovations. The idea of the project was to get researchers, students and other personnel to change attitudes, cultures and approaches to the creation of innovation. As a result of the government launching seven innovation offices in its bill on research and innovation, the Mid Sweden University could, on the basis of the knowledge base and organization built up in the Regional Fund project, implement and take primary responsibility for the innovation offices in three universities. Investing programme funds to kick start such multiplier effects involves high risks. There was an obvious risk that the innovation project would not have any long-term effects. When the project was launched, nothing was known about the initiative at the innovation offices. Success in contributing to long-term multiplier effects in many respects involves timing, policy intelligence about the surrounding world and, quite simply, luck!

The problem in evaluation contexts is that it is very difficult to really pinpoint the contribution that a project makes in creating a multiplier effect. The project 'Establishment of a node for outdoor educational activities in a municipality' was based on research into educational methodology, which was implemented in conjunction with a university. The goal of the project was to increase entrepreneurship and the number of businesses in the area of games and outdoor educational activities. This involved determining whether business could be created on the basis of a cultural heritage of games and outdoor educational pedagogy that Vimmerby, after the author Astrid Lindgren, is associated with. However, it turned out to be difficult to mobilize companies in Vimmerby to contribute to greater entrepreneurship in outdoor pedagogy. On the other hand, the project has had a clear effect on

Linköping University's successful initiative in exporting pre-school education around the world – from Peking to Los Angeles. The association with Astrid Lindgren through this project has helped the university to embark on the export of pre-school teacher training. In similar ways, different pre-school companies hope that the project will enable them to export their pedagogical approaches. Evidently the project has contributed to entrepreneurship, but possibly not in the way intended from the beginning. Running such types of projects is to some extent similar to how venture capitalists operate. The financier is involved in a number of processes based on creating value from a knowledge base or an idea – and it is not possible to state in advance if this can be created, as goals and instruments change during the process of adding value. It is important that venture capitalists continue to take care of the 'companies' as well as possible. This involves continuously evaluating activities and initiatives to determine whether they lead towards goals that will fulfil expectations for creating value-added.

With the help of the concepts above, we have formulated the question more precisely as to what sustainable development work is, and pointed out some of the dilemmas and challenges it entails. Sustainable development is something that can lead to joint learning and long-term effects, where activities or results are regarded as instruments for achieving this, and not as goals in themselves. It can be said that sustainability depends on how these different components of development work are linked together. Activities such as undertaking experiments and trying out new approaches are crucial in development processes. Since most activities in a project cannot be successful, a large number of attempts and experiments are required to achieve innovative solutions. The results which are the consequence of successful activities show what is successful in the short term in development work. At the same time we know that short-term results do not automatically lead to long-term effects.

This applies particularly to multiplier effects which often occur in unexpected and surprising ways. Experiences and results from projects must be transformed and applied to new contexts if they are to develop their own life and become autonomous. For results to be sustainable when projects have been completed, they must survive adaptation to new (internal and external) conditions and requirements. Our analysis of the sustainability chain concentrates on the relationship between results and effects. We make this restriction as the lack of knowledge is greatest within this area. What the linkages between results and effects look like, and how they are organized, are questions we will take up later in the chapter.

Using the concepts above, we have shown that projects can lead to results and long-term effects in the most surprising ways. At the same time we can also find an explanation as to why different kinds of development work, especially when run in project form, are seldom sustainable. An important explanation is the dominance of the kind of project logic that focuses on isolated activities and short-term results. In a project application, an undertaking may have been given to carry out 40 company visits in a project, and after 20 visits project participants already realize that they have what they need to be able to work towards long-term sustainable development. Despite this, there is a feeling of having to complete the company visits in order to fulfil the undertaking. Since public funds are used to finance programmes and projects, the managing authorities and the EU Commission have set up a number of indicators and rules to ensure that projects are carried out correctly. The problem arises from overloaded indicators and steering by rules that often lead the project in the wrong direction, that is, towards short-term results and a large number of activities. It is in this context that learning through ongoing evaluation plays an important role – right in the middle of this 'jungle' of short-term requirements – by continuously evaluating projects to ensure that they are steered in the direction of the overarching goals and provide learning and long-term effects.

In the following sections, we will present some explanations as to why development work is seldom sustainable. This is a question which has often occurred in our contacts with those responsible for programmes, coordinators, project managers and evaluators. We do not claim to have ready or complete answers, but we satisfy ourselves with two of the more common ones, the dominance of project logic and the focus on short-term aspects.

PROJECT LOGIC DOMINATES

In publicly funded projects and programmes, there is a great risk of focusing on planning, implementing activities and reporting their outcomes. The primary motive is to implement the programme, allocate funds, administer projects, and control and report what has been done. Long-term sustainability and multiplier effects can easily fade into the background. Why does this happen so often?

In externally financed development work, projects and their reporting logic are often developed to cover economic and administrative responsibility and to rapidly distribute funds. Funds are to be used and correctly accounted for. Those responsible, together with project case handlers, are forced to focus on immediacy and necessity, and not on the long-term and strategic aspects of a programme. Managing project funds in a correct way is a necessity, but when this becomes excessive there is a risk that the fundamental aim, that is, creating results and long-term effects that represent a part of sustainable development work, is not achieved. A project manager in an EU project referred to the risk of ending up in the 'activity trap' where short-term requirements for implementing activities in line with the project plan replace the ambition of creating long-term effects in terms of new jobs. He was referring to activities that can easily become ends in themselves and which are not clearly linked to long-term effects.

How have the Regional Fund and Social Fund handled this dilemma between outcome and effects in a project? There is no simple answer to the question, and the answers, of course, can vary between regions and over time. The ambitions in the formulations of the programmes have, however, been clear. The focus is on learning and long-term effects! At the same time, indicators and systems for rule steering often lead in the direction of short-term results and activities.

The question is how these programmes can manage something that has been so difficult in earlier initiatives. As a result, new conditions have been created – in the Social Fund a comprehensive system for support and learning for projects, and in the Regional Fund a comprehensive system for ongoing programme and project evaluation. In the Social Fund, there are four support projects that aim to raise quality in projects and thereby contribute to better results and more long-term effects. In addition, there are five thematic groups that collect knowledge, as well as make analyses to ensure that projects and programmes will be able to learn from experiences gained earlier. Learning through ongoing evaluation at the project level, which exists in both funds, is another important condition for increasing quality in projects and thus their sustainability. The aim of learning evaluation is to critically examine results and rapidly give feedback to participants in order to continuously and quickly make improvements.

In the Regional Fund the ongoing programme evaluators have been responsible for generating experiences and evaluating the progress of the eight programmes. Three ongoing programme evaluation teams – one for the two northerly programmes, one for the three programmes in mid Sweden and one for the three southern programmes – have continuously evaluated programme implementation. The task has been to capture progress in the programmes, evaluate them to determine if they have contributed to development plans in the 21 counties throughout the country, and determine if regional coordinating bodies have come closer to goal attainment. In addition, the task has involved synthesizing experiences and knowledge from ongoing project evaluation in order to provide feedback to both regional structural fund partnerships and regional development actors, as well as contribute to long-term learning.

A vital question is whether ongoing evaluation initiatives and support functions achieve their intended effects, that is, whether they have contributed to raising quality in projects and improving the efficiency of programme implementation. Have the projects become better and have they created greater usefulness through short-term results and long-term effects? Will the Regional and Social Funds contribute to changing, improving and strengthening regional growth? We will return to these questions in Chapters 6 and 7. But first, what does it mean to use a project to stimulate a change process and how can such a change process be sustainable?

The Project Form is Short-sighted

Project logic may be a crucial obstacle to sustainable development work and learning that provides multiplier effects. What is it about projects as a 'form' that leads to such limited logic, with a focus on planning, implementation and outcome of activities, rather than on long-term effects? This question is important, since more and more development work is run in the form of projects. We live in an era of projects. Everything is transformed into a project – including life itself. Projects are similar to a *draft outline*, that is, they represent a need for future change and testing new ideas. Projects, renewal and innovation have become the characteristics of a society seeking ever more rapid change. At the same time, different investigations and research reports have questioned the value of programme initiatives based on a large number of projects (Pressman and Wildavsky 1984, Andersen 2008, Lerner 2009, Cavanagh 2012, Brulin and Svensson 2011). These studies have shown increasing project 'fatigue' amongst employees and those responsible in companies and administrative bodies. Questions have been raised about the aim of a project and who it is intended for. Are there hidden motives? Isn't the real purpose just to get rid of project funds, create work opportunities for project managers, and enable management to demonstrate drive or an organization to profile itself as innovative?

Despite all the major initiatives in programmes to improve growth, the climate for innovation and conditions in working life, in terms of working environment, influence, gender equality, growth, and so on, experiences gained from project-based development work have not been systematized from a sustainability perspective. These large programmes and their related projects are hardly ever exposed to any in-depth analysis of their long-term effects (Brulin and Svensson 2011). For this reason a wide measure of uncertainty has arisen concerning some fundamental questions – such as the organization of large programmes in projects and their long-term effects – and this poses a problem for politicians and civil servants making decisions on new initiatives.

What is it about the project as a form that can make sustainability of a result difficult? There are a number of explanations. A project has a specific goal, is time limited, often builds on external financing, has its own project management, is often run parallel to both regular activities and management, and too often is implemented with an internal focus. Communication of results, dissemination of experiences and knowledge formation takes place at too late a stage. Overall this working method makes the attainment of long-term sustainability more difficult. Projects are based on rational thinking, where goals are set up, funds chosen, activities implemented and results attained. The starting point is consensus thinking where opposition and conflicts are conspicuous by their absence. There is an underlying thought that the best solution and goals are unambiguous, not full of conflict or contradictions. Surroundings are regarded as stable and the future as predictable. Results are assumed to be capable of being transferred irrespective of situation, and processes are not regarded as important for results. This way of looking at development can function in a project which is limited in time and scope, has clear goals and operates in a stable environment with defined conditions, but not in a complex system (Lerner 2009, Taleb 2010, Engwall 2002).

The question then is: why is a project needed to solve a problem or carry out a task? Our definition of projects is that they should be a solution to something unique, that is, something that requires innovation, learning, process thinking, where there is an openness regarding goals and instruments, as well as a focus on transferability and long-term aspects. In the same way that a dynamic economy is based on development processes in terms of venture capital which succeed to varying degrees, a dynamic society involves high-risk renewal processes in the form of different development programmes and projects. Sustainable development work presupposes above all an ability to manage uncertainty, dilemmas, contradictions and conflicts. Sustainability can be said to consist essentially of how well these dilemmas and contradictions are managed (cf. Van de Ven and Poole 1995).

How to Manage Contradictions

> *As happens so often in discovery, those looking for evidence did not find it; those not looking for it found it and were hailed as discoverers.*
>
> Nassim Taleb (2010: 168)

A complex project is characterized by uncertainties, contradictions, conflicts and paradoxes. But what is a complex project? It is carried out in a domain with a high degree of interdependence between its elements – both temporal (value of a variable depends on its past changes), horizontal (variables depend on each other) and diagonal (variable A depends on the past history of variable B). A complex system is characterized by high interdependence between its parts, and mechanisms are subject to reinforcing, positive feedback loops. A complex system is difficult to estimate and calculate because outcomes are open-ended or, at least, variable (Taleb 2010: 358). A best practice approach that tries to universalize and centralize knowledge will not function in such a complex situation (Fenwick 2011). Instead, a more open and learning-based strategy for change must be used in order to deal with the uncertainties and risks in complex projects. Innovation and exploration cannot be steered from above but only come about through an open approach in which networks and partnerships are used as a sustainable form of collaboration in order to support and strengthen creative actors.

We discuss the dilemmas that sustainable development work must be able to manage in a complex situation (cf. Collins 1998). There are different dilemmas that cannot be solved, but on the other hand can be handled with varying degrees of insight and success based on prevailing conditions. These dilemmas concern different ways of steering development work – innovativeness versus daily problem-solving, action versus reflection, changing individuals or changing organizations.

STEERING WHAT CANNOT BE STEERED

It is difficult to steer development work, especially if it is to be innovative, as the final result is not known in advance. The question is how creative innovation should be steered. There are different ways of steering development work. This can be through goals or with the help of rules, specifying what and how things should be done. Research has shown that both these ways of steering have major limitations. Goals are often unclear, understood in different ways, conflict with each other, easily become static, and so on. Rules easily become limiting, discourage creativity and involvement, which are necessary conditions for innovative development work (Weick and Quinn 1999).

The difficulties of goal steering in EU Structural Fund programmes have been apparent in a number of evaluations. These show that goal formulations have been regarded as excessively imprecise. This also applies to indicators and synthesizing reporting (European Commission, 2006a) that exaggerate goal achievement (Tarschy 2011). The horizontal criteria (in the Regional Fund) and the programme criteria on gender equality and accessibility (in the Social Fund) are considered to be particularly problematic. They are often badly integrated with other goals in projects. Formulations expressed in different criteria are not sufficient for steering a project towards politically determined goals. Is this related to how clearly the goals are formulated, or that there are too many goals to strive towards?

When programmes are formulated, those responsible often have the notion that having more and clearer goals facilitates the management of programmes and ultimately their projects. In reality, each new clearly defined goal and criteria reduces exponentially the value of earlier formulated goals and criteria: a single goal provides 100 per cent clarity; two goals in reality leads to 25 per cent clarity, three goals to 10 per cent clarity, and so on. When the number of goals becomes excessive, as is the case in Structural Fund programmes, perhaps it is time to start talking about steering by intentions rather than goals. Programme goals lie in the domain of broader intentions, namely the overarching aim of contributing to structural transformation and cohesion through initiatives in the form of projects to increase the capacity for innovation, creation of jobs and ultimately growth.

In other words, goals can be formulated in different ways and at different levels: 1) as visions; 2) as aims or overarching intentions; or 3) as concrete goals. Visions cannot normally be attained in a project, but they serve to provide inspiration and a belief in the future. Overarching intentions or aims set out the course to be followed and can, as a result, be evaluated. Concrete goals specify what should be achieved and are measurable. Sustainable development involves striking a balance between different levels and learning to live with a situation where goals are formulated in different contexts. Visions entail the risk of being too general and abstract if they are not linked to overarching intentions and aims that set out the direction for development work. The overarching intentions and aims must be broken down into concrete and specific goals to be regarded as meaningful by participants and capable of being followed up and evaluated. But goals are seldom shared or understood.

There is in fact another and opposite risk in formulating goals in development work, and this is that they become too concrete, too numerous, too unrealistic and too dominant, with the result that the original aims and visions fade into the background. The wood cannot be seen for the trees. Prioritization then involves implementing as many activities as possible in order to achieve short-term, measurable changes. The activities and short-term results become more important than the very idea of development work itself.

In this case, the dilemma often relates to how to combine structure and clarity in goal formulations with openness and flexibility in implementation. A structure (in terms of goals, rules and plans) provides context and clarity. It shows what is permitted and feasible within the framework of a programme. At the same time, the tendency to strong and excessively detailed steering should be resisted, and this makes local adaptation and necessary change during the programming period more difficult.

CREATING SOMETHING NEW AND MAKING A DIFFERENCE

The dilemma of steering is reinforced if the aim is also that programmes and projects should be innovative and make a difference. Structural Fund financing should not go to regular activities, but should be innovative – contribute to new thinking, add value and be experimental. This is referred to as 'additionality' in EU programmes. Given these explicit ambitions, there are also local requirements that necessitate solving emergency problems that may have arisen. The financial crisis which broke out in 2008 meant that many companies risked going bankrupt, with many employees becoming redundant. This gave rise to a situation which illustrates the dilemma between emergency problem-solving and strategic development. The risk of excessive focus on practical problem-solving, which many companies demanded in the crisis, was that long-term development could be undermined. If training is given to employees in an occupational area where they have been working, there is a risk that employability will be weakened in a rapidly changing and increasingly knowledge-based economy. The basic question was whether the crisis in 2008 represented a serious downturn in the economy, a structural crisis or both at the same time. Interaction between the expert competence of the managing authorities and the local knowledge and support of Structural Fund partnerships in order to reconcile this dilemma between immediate needs and long-term strategic development is crucial.

FOCUSING ON ACTION OR REFLECTION

Without concrete practices, principles are sterile; but without principles, practices have no life, no character, no heart.

Highsmith (2010: 368)

Projects in the Social and Regional Funds should, of course, provide 'value for money'. But what does this mean? Yes, they should lead to results that are visible changes. It is important for participants, for those responsible and other financiers, that concrete results can be demonstrated. Given this starting point, the focus is then on action and achieving results rapidly – planning, initiating and carrying out a whole range of activities becomes the central focus. The view held by the majority is that action and not just talk is important. The evaluations for the Regional Fund (Brulin, Hammarström and Nilsson 2009) emphasize the importance of projects transforming ideas into products, and that commercialization and market orientation are vital for success. Projects should not be artificial, where there is no demand for results and no market for the product or service. By using modelling, prototyping and simulations, you can base the learning on action and speed up the innovation processes.

However, focusing on action does entail risks. Research shows that the requirement for rapid results can be taken too far (Andersen 2008). Action orientation runs the risk of focusing on quantity of activities, where activities become an end in themselves, and results are merely to satisfy the financier. Long-term sustainability and multiplier effects in other areas of ongoing development work will, as a result, not be the primary focus (Miettinen 2002).

In building up the Regional Fund and the Social Fund, there has been an awareness of the risk of excessive focus on actions. The requirement for pre-project studies, learning through ongoing evaluation where projects should be continuously monitored, represents a correction to the action orientation existing in the indicator system and ongoing status reports to the managing authorities. In the project evaluations carried out, emphasis has been put on the importance of the pre-project phase, and that this should be strengthened to ensure that projects are well-designed and supported. At the same time we have seen a number of examples where action orientation has become excessively determining – for instance, where redundancies have been announced. This necessitated rapid actions to fulfil strong local requirements from companies and trade union organizations. In these situations, Structural Fund partnerships, which should allocate priorities between projects, have not always imposed the same requirements on preparation, pre-project analysis and long-term thinking.

Action must always be combined and blended with reflection – the ability to 'walk on two legs' – to solve the dilemma between short-term results and long-term sustainability. This is the conclusion reached by different evaluations of the Social and Regional Funds. However, we know that reflection does not occur spontaneously. Some type of 'disturbance' is needed to achieve innovation and new thinking, both in terms of ideas and working forms. By disturbance, we are referring to ongoing questioning and problematizing of what and how things are to be done. One way of creating reflection and new thinking is to use learning through ongoing evaluation as a means of carrying out a dialogue about planned and completed activities and measures. Another way is to organize learning networks or some form of peer review.

A critical and independent ongoing evaluation and interactive research can be regarded as tools for assuring the quality of development work. Ongoing evaluation can initially make an ex ante evaluation to determine if the project idea is innovative, realistic, well supported and integrated with other development work. Critical examination and constructive proposals in the initial phases provide the best conditions for identifying possible paths for the development of the project, since participants have not yet become 'locked into' different activities and processes. The idea is that if evaluation is to have the preconditions to impact programmes and projects, it should take place at an early stage. This is an approach which is diametrically opposed to traditional evaluation which almost always deals with ex post evaluation, that is, when impact on the programme is at best marginal.

If evaluation is to have any practical significance, it should increasingly be done in real-time, that is, at the same time as changes and development activities take place in the project setting. If interactive learning is to take place, the evaluators must be engaged in the processes they are evaluating and studying. They cannot simply stand by as passive observers. Learning processes occur when the evaluators are involved – this is one of the key benefits of ongoing evaluation. Evaluators should test their communicative ability to convince programme and project management on what the problems and opportunities are. Ongoing evaluation and interactive research are not aimed at providing ready-made answers based on general theories. The intention is rather to improve action strategies in cooperation with the practitioners involved. Ongoing evaluators should provide knowledge that is relevant, in the sense that it can be used for gradual, as well as more strategic, change during the course of a project or programme. Proximity to 'reality' is vital, therefore, as is continuity and a long-term or sustainable approach.

Methods are to be chosen according to the task in hand. Ongoing evaluation can continuously show the progress of a project and whether changes need to be made. It should be evident from the evaluation what results have been achieved and what the project has contributed. Evaluation aimed at learning, and which has elements of ongoing evaluation, should be able to determine if the results are sustainable in the long term, and whether knowledge from the project could lead to multiplier effects.

CHANGING INDIVIDUALS OR CHANGING ORGANIZATIONS

The question is: what should be changed to ensure sustainability? Is it the individuals themselves or organizations? Research shows that change which only originates from individuals seldom provides lasting effects (Weick and Quinn 1999). Long-term sustainability in development work presupposes that change takes place at the same time in the individual's surroundings. We also know that it is not sufficient to change organizations or structures to achieve deeper change in individuals. The risk in this case is that change then becomes only superficial, only formal, not real. Sustainable development thus deals with reconciling this dilemma between individual and organizational change so that interaction takes place between them. Conscious and knowledgeable individuals can take the initiative to change rules and routines so that results achieved in projects lead to lasting and long-term effects, even after project completion.

Here we can see how the Regional and Social Funds, with their different goals, have different ways of reconciling this dilemma between the individual and the organization. The Regional Fund aims to bring about change at the regional level in industry and among companies in the first instance, whilst the Social Fund focuses on individuals and their employability. Dissimilarities in starting points and orientation can be regarded as a problem, but also viewed as an opportunity to manage this dilemma. If projects are coordinated, the results are improved and the effects more enduring. The question is: who is responsible for reconciling the dilemmas presented above. Is it the task of project management? No, we do not think that it is. It requires that a number of actors are involved to find 'solutions' that lead to long-term effects. Not least it requires efforts on the part of the regional development actors, regional Structural Fund partnerships and development actors in regional cooperation bodies, the county administrative boards and the municipalities which are responsible for connecting together different development projects and programmes, so that together they form a well-balanced strategic pattern which leads to increased innovation, employment and growth.

From Project Management to Project Organization

When it comes to working on change, project management is often given a more crucial role. There is a substantial body of literature on the subject and courses are given on the 'art' of managing projects. The role of the project manager is important, but creating long-term effects from development work requires more than just efficient project management. It requires a project *organization*, and what this entails we will discuss in this section.

Figure 1.1 can be used to analyse a project organization with respect to different functions, tasks and areas of responsibility in development work. The functions affect *ownership*, *steering* and *management*. Financiers are also included in the model, a function which, in our view, has a major impact on the sustainability of development work. An active financier can have an impact,

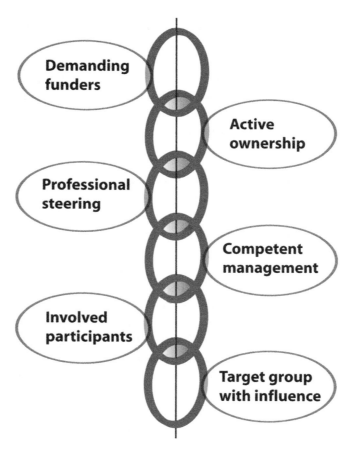

Figure 1.1   A project organization with different functions and responsibilities

both through their requirements and the support measures they provide, as well as through contributing to prioritizing follow-up, evaluation and learning. Participants and target groups are important in development work, that is, customers and users, and they are often forgotten and have no role in the project organization. However, we will concentrate here on the importance of ownership and steering for a project to contribute to sustainable development work.

How a project is initiated is important for its subsequent development and continuation. Often projects are initiated externally (by a consultant, education provider or researcher) or from an intermediate level within an organization. The consequence is a lack of active owners with responsibility for development work, and owners who do not take part in organizing the management of the project.

Active ownership, in our view, requires strong actors able to create conditions for driving a project forward, and who take responsibility for using the results and transforming these into long-term sustainable effects. The owners appoint the steering group which takes strategic decisions and provides feedback on the project's development to the owners. The owners and the steering group are responsible for strategic issues, whilst the task of project managers is the operational work.

The model in Figure 1.1 is intended as an aid in analysing the sustainability of a project. The hypothesis is that a project organization that has correctly balanced and combined the different functions of ownership, steering and management leads to sustainable development work. No link in a chain should be too weak, nor should it be too strong. Often project management is the strongest link as a consequence of the resources (in terms of time and competence) invested in this function. This mobilization of resources to a certain level in the project organization may, in our view, be counter-productive since project management that takes excessive responsibility can easily make the management group and owners of the project passive.

Our hypothesis is that effective project organization is fundamental to sustainable development work. This assumption is backed up by research. The lack of active ownership and professional steering of development work is a common (possibly the most common) explanation for the lack of sustainability. Steering groups often function more as reference groups and lack a mandate to take necessary decisions. Studies carried out show the importance of active owners who support and impose requirements on the steering group, and also the importance of the professionalism of the steering group, and that it has a close dialogue with project management (Andersen 2008, Svensson et al. 2009). If the interactions between actors on different levels in the project organization function, conditions for learning are created and a more effective action will be the outcome. The overlapping circles in Figure 1.1 illustrate how the different functions of a project organization link together and depend on each other.

How can transparency be created in a project organization where a several different activities are ongoing and a large number of persons are involved? In Figure 1.1 there is a line linking together the different functions. This symbolizes the learning which ongoing evaluation should contribute between different levels in the project organization. The owners need to know if the project essentially follows a charted path, what difficulties occur, whether additional resources are required, and how linkages to other development work can be achieved. The same applies to the steering group which needs to know what activities have been completed, their outcome, progress in the project, participation and results achieved. In this way ongoing evaluation fulfils a strategic function and is necessary in order to create learning and make the project organization transparent.

In our theory about project organization, it is possible at the same time to handle a classic dilemma inherent in all development work. The question as to whether development work should be driven from the top down or bottom up is a genuine dilemma, as there is no simple or best solution applicable in all contexts. Creating a balance between tasks and functions in the project organization (see Figure 1.1) is an attempt to resolve this dilemma. It also involves combining top-down and bottom-up development in a way that allows steering with a high degree of participation, and learning.

About Methods and Research Perspectives

Research and theory can function in different ways – as prescriptive instructions for action or as an orientation guide. In the first case, the research has a strong impact on praxis with definitive views on how development should be run; in the latter case, theory and research provide support and orientation on how to act, but more as a basis for reflection and analysis linked to participants' own experiences. We support this latter perspective on how theory can be used to support development work, and we emphasize joint knowledge formation between researchers and participants. In this book we refer to research in the area, but we do it relatively liberally without numerous references and conceptual explanations. Our hope is that our reasoning can provide a basis for such a joint learning process together with participants and those responsible for different programmes and projects.

A large part of the book is the result of joint knowledge formation with project case handlers, those responsible for programmes, regional development actors, project managers, evaluators and representatives of partnerships. The aim of this joint learning has not been to find off-the-shelf solutions to a number of problems. On the contrary, we are critical of the effort to find simple solutions and best practice, something which is often aimed for in different EU programmes. This represents one way of driving development, but it can only be done under special conditions – in predictable situations where standardized solutions are at hand. It may also involve developing tools for reporting, administration and financial management in different projects. The Structural Funds – which deal with innovative projects that are 'additional' in relation to mainstream activity – require other approaches for effective implementation, feedback from experience and learning.

Instead, we take as our point of departure a more complex, and at the same time more realistic, model of how long-term sustainable development work can be carried out. Development, especially where there is a focus on innovation, is something that takes place in open and dynamic systems. Sustainable development, aiming at achieving long-term effects, builds on learning and reflection from past experiences that give an understanding of the broader contexts of which a project is a part. An open learning approach is necessary to be able to manage different dilemmas and problems, so that these can be assessed and analysed based on local contexts and conditions for sustainable development. In a specific situation, a dilemma involves being able to strike a balance between different interests, weighing up the advantages and disadvantages of different methods in relation to each other, looking at how individual and organizational changes can counteract or reinforce each other, and combining focus on short-term results while striving for long-term sustainability and multiplier effects. There is a risk or a downside in choosing this superficially contradictory perspective on development, as it may appear to be unclear and complex, without providing concrete guidance for those involved. We will try to avoid these pitfalls in the elaboration of our own thinking, but essentially the question should not be determined by the content of the text per se, but on how these ideas are applied. The aim is that the book be used in a dialogue with those involved in and responsible for different development programmes and projects, and it should provide them with support, enabling them to manage their own dilemmas and difficulties.

OUR EMPIRICAL BASIS

We will briefly look at the methods which we have used and the material on which we build our conclusions. The methods are based on a large number of evaluations, interactive research and 100 ongoing project evaluation reports, 20 ongoing programme evaluations, interviews with responsible persons, extensive questionnaires, group dialogues, reviews of existing material, and so on. The empirical basis is presented and thoroughly discussed in a book in Swedish, *Att äga, styra and utvärdera stora project* ('To own, steer and manage comprehensive projects', Brulin and Svensson 2011).

Conclusions and Starting Points

The introductory chapter provides starting points, problem formulations, definitions of key concepts and important assumptions. Later on, we will delve more deeply into these. Here we will briefly summarize the introductory discussions. The focus of the book is on sustainable development work. More specifically, the book deals with programmes and projects that aim to contribute to innovation, employment and growth in a way that favours companies, employees, customers and society in a broader sense. Our interest lies in examining the relationship between activities, results and long-term effects. We obtain the most important empirical evidence from the implementation of the EU Structural Funds – the Regional and Social Funds. These should provide an innovative and additional contribution to regional development. Activities, processes and results in projects should demonstrate long-term sustainable development work which leads to multiplier effects in other development activity and programmes. Research shows that most of the development work carried out in these areas is seldom sustainable in this sense. We have tested different explanations, which can be regarded as tentative in the sense that we will continue our testing of these on studies which we have already done on the Social and Regional Funds.

One explanation concerns financially and administratively conditioned project logic, where too much emphasis has been put on activities and their outcomes. The risk is particularly high in EU programmes where the overriding aim has often been to 'bring back' the money. In addition, many of the programmes are run in project forms which, by their very nature (external financing, especially project management, limitations in time, and so on), make sustainability more difficult.

Another explanation is that steering of innovative activities is somewhat problematic. The risk is that goals either become too visionary or too concrete and detailed. Thinking that is rational in terms of goals and steered by planning runs the risk of taking over, and development is regarded as self-evident and free of conflict, not full of dilemmas and contradictions. We present an alternative perspective which is illustrated by a number of contradictions and dilemmas identified in the evaluations carried out of the Regional and Social Funds.

An additional explanation deals with the view of project management as crucial for success in development work. As an alternative, we present an analytical model for a project organization with different functions and tasks, where ownership and steering are regarded as vital for sustainability. Essentially it is the interaction between different functions and tasks which guarantees both short-term results and long-term effects. The following chapter examines in greater detail these prerequisites for sustainability.

2

Models of Change
and Evaluation

The discussion on how long-term sustainability in development can be achieved by programme and project initiatives has intensified in recent years. Not very much empirical research exists on how public programmes and their related projects can lead to sustainable development in terms of growth, innovation, employment and competence enhancement. One explanation is the difficulty of studying long-term effects, as well as the lack of interest among financiers and politicians in these questions. Perhaps it is because the latter are satisfied with the prestige from different programme initiatives, and do not always wish to have a critical examination of whether results and effects are lasting and long term? Another problem is the lack of sustainability in project initiatives. The question can be put as to whether it is possible to secure long-term sustainable effects in projects with a very limited time frame, for example, two or three years?

Our belief is the opposite, namely that long-term sustainability, extending beyond the formal programme and project period, should be very much more interesting than the more immediate yet transitory results. Particularly when this involves programmes with the goal of contributing to innovative projects which should be 'additional' in relation to regular activities, long-term sustainability should be the focal point in such cases. An analysis of company and regional development based on the sustainability concept is also important for other reasons, such as the adoption of a holistic perspective that provides knowledge which will have an impact on other development activity.

An analysis of sustainability in development work is difficult to implement, and requires a combination of theories and new thinking on concepts and analytical models. In this chapter we provide an overview of research that looks at the questions we examined in the previous chapter, but from slightly different entry points and perspectives. The aim of our review is to show how research has tried to create a deeper understanding of programme and project initiatives, as well as how these lead to knowledge formation that provides the foundation for sustainable development. Research should provide assistance in reconciling the dilemmas and difficulties inherent in such knowledge formation. Learning through evaluation and an interactive research approach becomes particularly important when the ambition is to create sustainable development. This is the reason that evaluation is given such great scope in the book. Evaluation becomes a foundation for reflection, adaptation and further development of a project which is difficult to steer and plan in advance.

In the previous chapter, we presented a number of dilemmas and difficulties that must be managed in complex programmes and projects. The sustainability perspective means that we must question a number of assumptions made in the research, and look to new theories and approaches where growth is combined with good working conditions, an inclusive working life, quality for users, and takes account of environmental concerns.

Traditional planning-steered developmental models are not in themselves sufficient to ensure sustainable development, but must be supplemented with other approaches, theories and concepts. We will try to refine the follow-up, evaluation and knowledge formation models that should ensure long-term sustainability in development by sketching two ideal types – the planning-steered and the development-supportive evaluation models.

The ideal types are a methodological tool in the sense that the sociologist Max Weber used ideal types to refine and clarify different theoretical conceptual constructions and models. Examples of ideal types originating from Weber are 'bureaucracy' and neoclassical economic theory based on the 'economic man'. The ideal type is not confirmation of the value or existence of a phenomenon, but rather an aid for analysing empirical phenomena using conceptual constructions or models based on theory. The theoretical approach means that different models can be compared and analysed, and their practical implications can be investigated. This enables certain elements in a project to be made clearer and more understandable when they are put into a clear theoretical context. In this chapter we will also discuss the potential and the limitations of both ideal types in relation to sustainable development work.

The Planning-Steered Developmental Model

The roots of the planning-steered developmental model can be traced far back in time. Since the sixteenth century, Western thinking has tried to replace *reasonable* uncertainty and doubt with new forms of *rational certainty and evidence* that can be measured and evaluated. René Descartes's (1637) philosophical thinking 'swept away' such practical-based knowledge with elements of 'reasonable' uncertainty and doubt, in favour of knowledge based on mathematical formulae and evidence expected to provide 'rational' certainty and action. Reducing the value of the verbal, the individual, the local, the time related and the concrete, in the view of Stephen Toulmin (Toulmin and Gustavsen 1996), has been thought necessary for smoothing over tensions and conflicting interests with theories based on abstract, universal and timeless concepts. During the first half of the nineteenth century, abstract thinking made great strides forwards with the advent of Auguste Comte's positivism. Inspired by progress in the natural sciences, he developed a sociology that built on social facts that could be studied objectively and treated statistically. The tasks which positivism set itself were to identify the 'objective' laws governing human actions and behaviour. Based on this view of knowledge, during the 1950s and 1960s great expectations were connected with the idea of social engineering, of which Popper (2002), amongst others, was an advocate.

An important tool of social engineering was the large programmes which the state and society launched to fight just about everything from poverty to sickness. The US President, Lyndon B. Johnson, spoke about building 'the Great Society'. In Sweden the Million housing programme was launched. The planning-steered developmental model received a real boost as a result of the requirement to follow up large programmes. The knowledge gained about human organization, social processes and actions aimed at in the planning-steered developmental model have their foundations in the Cartesian ideal and the positivism of Comte.

It is believed that Descartes, when one morning he lay in his bedroom at Stockholm Castle, had a sudden insight while observing a fly walking across the tiled ceiling. As he watched the fly's walk, he wondered how it would be possible to describe its exact path. At that moment he came up with the idea of coordinate geometry, or *Cartesian geometry*. This approach (Descartes 1637) would later be used to describe scientific phenomena, both in social and traditional science.

A classic study of some of the major American welfare programmes was carried out by Pressman and Wildavsky (1984). The overall aim of these programmes was the creation of jobs for persons from different minority groups. Despite a number of organizations and authorities supporting the goal, in practice it was difficult to realize. The original ideas were diluted, conflicts and delays occurred in a complex system where there were a number of different actors and organizations that should have been cooperating. One conclusion which the researchers drew was that implementation should not be detached from policy and handed over to experts. It is meaningless to formulate good ideas in the absence of a credible political strategy and an ongoing critical discussion (in our words, evaluation) of how this can be implemented.

In recent decades, the planning-steered development model has received a new lease of life. It has been re-launched in a number of different variants, such as result-based management and evidence-based decision-making. Evidence-based approaches have their origins in the medical world. It was there that attempts were made to find evidence to support the efficacy of an intervention, through experimental studies that compared one intervention with a placebo, that is, with an expected effect. Those responsible wanted answers to the question of what an intervention would lead to under ceteris paribus assumptions. Often, this is not easy to achieve, whereas an evidence-based approach has come to mean that you aggregate different scientific studies.

The planning-steered developmental model takes as its point of departure that politicians formulate the overall goals of the programme. These goals are then operationalized into derived goals which can then be evaluated. The fact that they can be evaluated, in the view of advocates of the planning-steered developmental model, is often regarded as crucial for the programme's success. A commonly used form for goal formulation is based on the SMART criteria, that is, goals should be *specific, measurable, attainable, relevant* and *time-bound*. Counter-factual studies, experiments and ceteris paribus assumptions (other things being equal) are the foundation for choosing evaluation methods. The criteria of measurability means that each derived goal is given a numerical value to enable the quantitative follow-up of results (other things supposedly being equal, of course!)

The strong focus on measurability in the planning-steered developmental model means that one can question whether it really functions for evaluation, or whether it is more a model for follow-up. However, advocates consider that trying to operationalize outcomes in terms of measurable results facilitates insight and control of programme implementation. By measuring and compiling outcomes in projects under a given programme, material to support politicians and administrative authorities in their decision-making can be created. Advocates of the planning-steered developmental model argue that measuring results and outcomes leads to enhancement of the quality of the programme, its productivity and efficiency, at the same time as insight, control and steering are facilitated.

Planning-steered developmental models are based on a linear, mechanical and controlled approach to development. From this perspective it becomes natural to use evaluation for measuring, controlling and steering. Evaluators communicate mainly with those responsible for programmes and projects, and communication usually takes place through reports. It then becomes one-way communication and deals with providing information, that is, making the results about measured outcomes and short-term results known. Information is presented mainly in written form and based on a distanced attitude to those affected, who are regarded as 'outsiders'. Conditions are given in advance, and views of how development work should be organized are predetermined (see Table 2.1).

The knowledge produced builds on investigating adaptive learning, in terms of how things are done, and if they have been done in the right way as set out in the plan. This means that learning processes are about reproducing existing knowledge (Ellström 2001). Evaluators look for answers to the following types of questions: Was the result what was expected? Have the goals been realized, or has the project solved the problems on which the project was based? This is more like a revision or follow-up than an evaluation. The planning-steered developmental model is not only about analysing, that is, assessing the value of a project in a larger and more long-term context. The main task of evaluation is to check that programmes and projects really do what they were aimed to do. This provides an answer to questions on whether results have been attained, and whether resources have been used in line with the plan.

There are a number of objections that can be made against planning-steered developmental models. The first concerns their focus on measurement and control of goal attainment. The paradox is that this focus appears to risk missing the real goals of the programme. The second applies to how the planning-steered developmental model tends to steer programmes and projects in the direction of what can be evaluated. A third objection concerns the lack of transparency in programmes and projects, arising as a consequence of 'remote controlled steering', an element inherent in the planning-steered developmental model. This type of evaluation (and this applies particularly to programmes that should be innovative) does not provide relevant insight and a basis for disseminating knowledge, quality assurance and decision-making. The conditions for sustainable development appear to be at risk.

Pfeffer and Sutton (2000) came to similar conclusions in terms of how evaluation in companies in the USA operates. The focus is on short-term financial results, that is, those that are easily measured. The tactical aim becomes more important than the strategic. An excessive number of measures are used in an excessive number of areas and in a number of dimensions, where precision is more important than relevance and understanding. This type of evaluation often leads to frustration and stress, and not to learning and development. The authors try to explain why this type of evaluation continues, despite its obvious failures and difficulties. As an explanation, we refer to the simplifying assumptions about how people function, the needs of the stock market for short-term reports, as well as the habits and traditions that have been established and institutionalized. The alternative model of evaluation which they present is based on the following: more focus on the organization than on individuals; processes are central, where information should provide support for learning about operations; adaptation to the company's situation and specific needs; ongoing attempts to improve evaluation to highlight what is most important, both in the short- and long-term; focus on important and critical factors, rather than giving an overall picture of the activity. Evaluation should, above all, ensure that 'the knowing–doing gap' is reduced, that is, ensure that the company uses existing knowledge and does what has been decided.

CONTROL

The planning-steered developmental model's fixation on goals and verifiability risks overlooking the overall goals. These are determined in a political process, and they should be in line with the SMART criteria and broken down into measurable sub-goals in order to make possible ongoing quantitative follow-up. The correlation of measurable sub-goals with overall goals is seldom particularly high, since it is their very measurability that leads to their disaggregation into sub-goals. Often the overall goals are not sufficiently clear to enable their validity to be preserved when broken down into sub-goals. The contrary is often true, as the overall goals represent compromises. This is not because politicians are bad at formulating goals, but rather that the reality which the programme should impact on is multifaceted, complex and ever-changing.

When the overall goals in line with the SMART criteria are broken down into sub-goals, there is a risk that the foundation of the original goals will be diluted. Measurable and controllable sub-goals thus give a completely different view of the goals compared with the original formulation. In a number of meta-evaluations of large programmes and projects, auditing bodies (such as the Swedish National Audit Office and the Swedish Agency for Public Management) were surprised by the lack of focus on overall goals. This is especially surprising given that the planning-steered developmental model often promises measurements of results and outcomes (using SMART criteria) which measure real goal attainment, but the question is which goal attainment is measured: is it the overall goals or the operationalized sub-goals? Distance steering in a number of stages dilutes the aim and point of the overall goals.

The fixation of the planning-steered developmental model on simple goals that can be followed up and verified also leads to a situation where applicants for project funds are compelled to spend considerable time and energy in formulating measurable goals to satisfy programme administrators. This lays a foundation for a culture of 'pseudo-faked' results which are often based on less well-defined indicators of goal attainment. Unfortunately what is measurable and verifiable usually involves short-term perspectives. In addition, these criteria lead to sub-goals which are hardly valid; they also run the risk that energy will be put into formulating sub-goals that focus on short-term verifiability.

The criticism directed at the planning-steered developmental model, however, should not be interpreted as support for any type of general criticism of project planning or quantitative methods. Good planning is per se very important, but evaluation using SMART criteria that focuses on following up outcomes and results in terms of measurable and verifiable goals often takes us in the wrong direction, thereby making sustainable development more difficult. Such follow-up is also needed, but then it should serve the purpose of control and reporting. This is an important function in publicly financed projects, but it should not be allowed to obscure and take over the idea and aims of a development programme.

To understand what measures lead to long-term effects, it is important to analyse the different stages of a project's development. A prerequisite for success is goals that are as clear as possible, as well as processes based on review points, stages and milestones. However, it is also important to bear in mind that processes should lead to results that produce long-term effects and sustainable development. Questions about what brought about change, causality and mechanisms, are difficult to simply and clearly calculate and plan for: strategies like sub-goals must be reviewed all the time in an ongoing 'experiment' of how overall goals can be reached. A number of factors can be interlinked and their effects may be delayed, indirect or non-intended, which makes causal relationships difficult to simply determine. The question about what would have happened in the absence of a specific intervention, that is, counterfactual reasoning, is an important ingredient in understanding the results and effects which a project has created.

Despite these difficulties of determining causal relationships, especially in the field of behavioural and social sciences, it is nonetheless an important part of learning evaluation. There is substantial knowledge to be obtained within the framework of a retroactive evaluation, which has the ambition of explaining relationships and building on the evaluator's experience of handling such complex issues, with the help of both theoretical perspectives and awareness of conditions in the surrounding world (see Delander and Månsson 2009). In other words, evaluators of programmes and projects aiming at growth and employment should recognize that counter-factual reasoning may be needed, but it should be clear that this is largely based on the good judgement of evaluators and their skill in assessing mechanisms and causal relationships, as well as their theoretical preferences and knowledge of the surrounding world.

We have expanded the question in this section on planning and control to also deal with explaining what a project initiative leads to. In our view, this is a prerequisite for being able to steer a project in the right direction.

STEERING

Apart from the fact that the planning-steered developmental model runs the risk of measuring the wrong things, it can also lead to doing the wrong things, and this of course leads to the risk of steering projects and programmes wrongly. In two respects, the model risks steering projects and programmes wrongly: 1) the measurability criteria lead to steering a project towards what is measurable; 2) it risks (through the demand for planning-steered evaluations) that projects are steered by the extent to which they can be evaluated, instead of the problems they aim to solve. The requirement of being able to evaluate the planning-steered model creates a fear of whether the project really is being steered towards the overall intentions and visions. To avoid this uncertainty, the model encourages those responsible for projects to make a choice, and to steer the project in the direction of what can be evaluated. They must be able to show that they have used the right methods, and not that they have done the right things. On the other hand, there is a risk that projects will be structured on the basis of criteria that will facilitate evaluation. A narrow focus on evaluation has a tendency to result in limiting projects – or, as Dahlberg et al. put it with regard to schooling: 'The tail of the evaluation waves the pedagogical dog' (Dahlberg, Moss and Pence 2003: 175).

Lindgren (2011) argues that measuring quality and results is based on problematic preconditions – having an unfamiliar discussion, lack of clarity over goals and the sheer number of goals. Evaluation is difficult to implement and results are seldom applied, or are often used for tactical or manipulative purposes. Both measurement and explanation of causal relationships are uncertain, and interpretations vary between different groups. Measurements, which are political constructions, have a tendency to become goals in themselves. Measurement leads to secondary effects in terms of exaggerated focus on simple activities that can be followed up, at the same time as uncertain processes that can lead to innovation and new ways of thinking are obscured or undermined. The professionals are relieved of making their own quality assessments, and ongoing checking puts stress on staff, so that they end up continuously measuring themselves and each other.

Steering towards goals is a necessity in all types of projects, but evaluation of goal attainment can take place in a number of different ways. We believe that goals can be formulated and re-formulated within the framework of an open, learning and formative evaluation that determines the direction in which a project is to be developed. The starting point is that goals are often contradictory, subject to change, and sometimes difficult to separate from instruments. Steering towards concrete goals may be needed to create the driving force to show results, but these goals must be related to the overall goals and aims which show the direction of progress and its long-term nature. A vision is also required to show what is unique and innovative, to motivate participants and to give them a feeling of working with something special. Steering towards a combination of concrete goals, overall aims and a long-term vision provides a coherent direction. An evaluation should take into account what is unique in a programme, where the local, concrete and situational settings provide the foundation for steering towards the overall goals in a programme. In the context of Structural Fund projects, it might perhaps be better to talk about ERDF/ESF criteria, rather than SMART criteria – that is, lasting results and long-term effects through development-supportive evaluation.

STEERING BY GOALS

An important reason for the strong position occupied by the planning steered-development model is that a model which promises insight and transparency in publicly financed programmes and projects is attractive. There are few who object to politicians, decision-makers and citizens having better insight into public programmes and projects. There is a great need amongst authorities and decision-makers to better understand and analyse which programmes and projects lead to sustainable development effects and which do not. Based on such knowledge, it is possible to make decisions on better grounds as to what should be given priority and thus send signals about the type of projects that should be initiated.

The problem, however, is that the planning-steered developmental model does not mobilize the experiences that have been gained from different projects and extend knowledge based on these. There is a great need for better knowledge material, in the initiation, prioritization and implementation phases, and also for creating lasting results and long-term effects. The planning-steered developmental model offers insight but does not deliver. The SMART criteria give an illusory feeling of control and steering towards clear goals. In reality these criteria mean steering towards goals which, on very weak grounds, originate from the overall aims of programmes and projects. The planning-steered developmental model is based on the expectation of being able to remotely manage programmes and projects without getting involved in the details, what the premises are for implementation and how initiatives can contribute to sustainable development.

Strict requirements on goals and result steering mean that authorities and decision-makers do not dare to recognize that 'the emperor is actually naked', that is, programmes and projects are based on weak foundations. The requirement for short-term goal and result attainment forces those responsible to use evaluation models that make learning and long-term development work more difficult. In public bureaucracies, those who make mistakes are not convicted. The main asset of the planning-steered evaluation model is that it provides the illusion that we know what we are doing, and that we can also present it in figures. In a slimmed-down implementation organization, it is refreshing not to have to confess that the actions taken are based on a high degree of uncertainty and doubt. Recognizing a reasonable degree of uncertainty and lack of evidence for measures undermines the foundation for 'production orientation' which is expected to guide operations. Instead, investing evaluation resources in knowledge formation that combines qualitative and quantitative methods, which take as their starting point that reality is complicated and leads to the requirement for ongoing learning and evaluation, appears to be more difficult and uncertain than relying on models which provide simple and clear measurability and verifiability. The whole of our book could be regarded as an argument for taking the difficult route rather than the easy one.

The Development-Supportive Evaluation Model

Every year, billions of Swedish crowns are invested in Sweden and hundreds of billions of Euros in the EU in different programmes and their related projects, in order to create a more innovative Europe that should grow faster, and where the competence of the labour force should be raised, and more people get jobs. Substantial resources are used, but they are not used for ongoing activities in terms of education, research and development that are discussed here. This book focuses on all the billions allocated to programmes and projects which are innovative and 'additional' in relation to regular activities that aim at changing, improving and renewing regional growth policy and the capacity for innovation. The question, in other words, is: how can sustainable development be created through public programmes and projects in terms of jobs and growth, or – as it is put in the EU strategy for Europe 2020 – how can it create 'a more innovative, smarter and more inclusive Europe'? This does not just involve resources coming from the EU, but also the investment of a large amount of national funds into making labour market and regional policy more creative and innovative.

There is substantial research, often of a political science nature, which has studied sustainability in programme and project-based development initiatives. Essentially this research shows the complexity and sluggishness in implementation of political goals through such programmes and projects (Svensson and Nilsson 2008, Ekman et al. 2010). Ellström and Kock (2009) show the difficulties of carrying out changes that have an impact on mainstream operations. They point out the risks of technocratic and centralized solutions, especially in terms of steering entrepreneurs and professional groups to collaborate over sustainable development. Often additional resources are required, among other things, in the form of EU funding, in order to create interest in such collaboration, but there is a high risk that projects will not be supported in organizations. The consequence is that no real development of mainstream operations will take place.

Sustainable development involves one thing above all, and that is knowledge formation – getting people to work and collaborate in a better way.

The review of the planning-steered developmental model above shows that it does not produce knowledge that will ensure sustainable development through programmes and projects. Sustainable development means that programmes and projects leave a permanent legacy in the form of better structures and processes that will lead to innovation, growth and the creation of jobs. Leaving such traces involves making an impact by providing feedback on experiences and knowledge formation that will continuously improve ongoing processes, and which will recreate structures so that they better promote growth and job creation. Here we will try to show that the conditions for such knowledge formation can be found in the development-supportive evaluation model. In Table 2.1, a comparison is made between the planning-steered developmental model and the development-supportive evaluation model in terms of different ideal types.

Table 2.1   Ideal types for evaluation (cf. Svensson et al. 2009: 25)

| | EVALUATION MODEL: | |
	Planning-steered	Development-supportive
Orientation	Result (summative)	Process (formative)
Goals	Measurement/control	Learning/understanding
Effects	Identification of deviations	Multiplier effects
Reporting	Written	Oral and written
Perspective	From above	Integrated – from below and from above
Communication	One-way	Two-way
Approach	Distanced	Proximity
Prerequisites	Closed, predictable	Open, unpredictable
Learning	Adaptive-oriented	Development-oriented

In the planning-steered developmental model, the evaluator is outside the process. The development-supportive evaluation model, on the other hand, means that the relationship between the evaluator and the project is redefined. In the development-supportive evaluation model, the evaluator is present and drives ongoing critical monitoring of the project. This means that the evaluator takes part in ongoing reconstruction of the project to see how it can be continuously reorganized and clarified, in terms of both goals and possible instruments in order to reach the goals. However, this requires that the evaluation be carried out in direct and immediate connection with the project and that it results in knowledge and learning products which evaluate the project in relation to the overarching programme goals. As in the planning-steered developmental model, waiting for evidence-based results from randomized and controlled studies that produce verification of progress towards desired results is just not possible, given that the normal situation is that most projects require ongoing action.

Underlying the planning-steered developmental model is the supposition that you cannot or even should not go into the 'black box' of the programme, but simply look at the effects, not the interaction between initiatives and effects. It is a major problem that such evaluations take as their starting point that programmes and projects are optimally designed and that they 'live their own lives' in a static unchanging world (Greene and Storey 2007). Programme and project initiators are assumed to be clear about what they want to achieve and that they have designed the programme or project in a logical and relevant way in relation to the goals that have been set up.

A lack of any close link to reality in the evaluations – either they deal with simple measurements of the number of participants or more advanced matching studies – does, however, result in difficulties. A common feature of many evaluations is that they are not able to describe programme participants accurately (Svensson et al. 2009, Patton 2010). In addition, Greene and Storey (2007) argue that it is often impossible to find control groups that have not been affected by large programmes, either negatively (perhaps not included) or positively (not included, but positively affected) – and this affects evaluations based on ceteris paribus assumptions. This means that the effects of programmes and projects become very difficult to assess. In addition, the authors argue that the goals of many large programmes are often so divergent, and sometimes simply contradictory, that in reality it is virtually impossible to retroactively reconstruct the development effect that they have given rise to.

The development-supportive evaluation model, on the other hand, takes as its starting point that the interactive researcher or ongoing evaluator is involved in project and programme implementation right from the very start. It is based on creating knowledge through ongoing reflection and feedback from the results achieved. Knowledge of outcomes and results provides the foundations for future actions, that is, choice of new development routes for the project. Action and learning are blended together in ongoing interaction.

The main objective of the planning-steered evaluation is to study whether the plan for the programme and project has been followed, where deviations by definition are undesired and bad. But the very idea of programmes and projects being innovative and 'additional' is that they should generate knowledge which breaks existing arrangements and patterns, and can continuously adapt to new situations.

Mapping, understanding and explaining new thinking and possibly surprising development routes is the main task of the development-supportive evaluation model. What is required in an evaluation in this model is that methods and tools be combined in different perspectives and approaches, at the same time as it results in knowledge of how innovative projects can lead to sustainable development. As in the evaluation model, it becomes necessary to be able to manage complex issues containing dilemmas and contradictions. Knowledge formation and learning occupy centre stage. Learning processes can with advantage be organized in interaction with regional actors – amongst others, the labour market partners, regional associations, higher education and R&D centres.

Evaluation is included as a requirement in many projects, most often because financiers require this, but evaluation can, however, mean very different things and be used for different purposes, as we have seen. In the development-supportive evaluation model, learning is regarded as an integral part of project implementation. The organization of evaluation takes this as its starting point. The need for evaluation of this type – that is, evaluation taking place in an ongoing, shifting process that aims at learning, and builds on reflection and the reprocessing of knowledge – is an approach that programme and project management shares with, for example, venture capitalists and entrepreneurs. For the latter, evaluation is not something that is done retroactively using a standardized checklist. On the contrary, evaluation is something that takes place on an ongoing basis in order to provide a better understanding of both goals and instruments. A venture capitalist or entrepreneur must be continuously prepared to reorient focus when new opportunities for creating value appear, and often these could not have been predicted in advance – this does not entail working without goals, plans and methods, but rather working on the basis of ongoing knowledge formation, so that goals and plans are being continuously revised. The intention of the development-supportive model is that evaluation should be useful in both the programme itself and in its implementation. But if venture capitalists or entrepreneurs continuously form knowledge for their own purposes, the objectives in programme and project implementation are that both those involved and also outsiders should have access to that knowledge.

The perspective and ways of working in development-supportive evaluation models are based on the needs of the activity and the interests of participants, but they should also result in knowledge of value that is worth transferring onwards to other programmes and projects, and other development work.

The exposition of the two evaluation models refines certain elements in the respective models, where the aim is to clarify the models to support the analysis of different projects and programmes. In principle, this does not mean that we take a position that one specific model is more valuable or better than another. Both models can be used since they fulfil different functions, where usefulness is connected with the aim of development work, how the evaluation will be used and its context. Both models should thus be regarded as valuable and complementary. In a number of places we refer to output evaluations which have been carried out in accordance with the planning-steered developmental model. Openness applies to an even higher degree to the methods that can be used in evaluation. Planning-steered methods of working can function well in a specific context, where quantitative methods and experimental design are used. In development-supportive models, both qualitative and quantitative methods are used, and the fifth generation of evaluation is typified by this combination of approaches and methods (Svensson et al. 2009). In the book we highlight the development-supportive model for evaluation since our focus is on how sustainable development can be organized where learning from innovative and 'additionality' projects is fundamental. Our criticism of how different result indicators have often become over-determining and limiting is not directed towards the evaluators, but more to the kind of project logic that has been permitted to dominate large development programmes. An important area for future development is thus to try to identify and conceptualize relevant and usable indicators of processes, results and effects to enable learning that will facilitate the implementation of complex projects and programmes, where the aim is the achievement of multiplier effects.

In favour of the latter model is the turbulence at societal level that occurred in connection with the establishment of the present Structural Fund programming period – in the form of a crisis in the US mortgage market which rapidly became a flashpoint for spreading financial and economic crisis to large parts of the world. The conditions for the operational programmes in the Regional Fund and the regional plans in the Social Fund were completely changed as a result. In the Social Fund, a number of redundancy projects were organized so that companies would not have to lay off staff. Views on whether these have been justified and successful vary between different groups (Brulin and Svensson 2011). However, it is interesting that the Social Fund programme quickly succeeded in satisfying these new needs on the part of companies when conditions changed rapidly and when traditional planning no longer functioned. The example of the redundancy projects shows two things: 1) it is difficult to plan for development in a rapidly changing and unpredictable future; 2) in order to provide a basis for decision-making, learning evaluation that is flexibly organized and based on a high degree of interaction is required. The operational programmes of the Regional Fund demonstrated that they could provide the foundations for flexible implementation despite changing conditions.

Mechanisms for Sustainable Development Work

We have restricted ourselves to learning evaluation as a precondition for sustainable development work to be implemented in a complex and rapidly changing activity, where traditional project planning or goal steering are in themselves insufficient. In the following sections in this chapter, we will go into greater detail regarding a number of important conditions for sustainable development work run in the form of programmes and projects. We believe that the three most important conditions can be summarized in a number of mechanisms – namely driving forces or explanations of causal relationships. The mechanisms for sustainable development work which we will focus on are the following: active ownership, collaboration and developmental learning. The key element is ongoing feedback from experience and knowledge formation, which are the fundamental assumptions underpinning the development-supportive evaluation model.

ACTIVE OWNERSHIP

Project theory is often identified with the theory of project management. Literature on project management, however, very seldom discusses issues of ownership and steering. There are some exceptions. In *Rethinking Project Management: An Organisational Perspective*, Andersen (2008: 101) briefly mentions the role of the project owner. This role is seen as important in order to connect the project organization with the base organization, namely the temporary with the permanent. Who is the active owner of a project? Moore (2010) points to the need for involving the executives in large organizations in strategic goal-setting in order to make the outcome of projects more sustainable (cf. Maylor 2010). We think it is important to include more owners in a large project in order to support the implementation of results.

Ownership is just one function in the project organization; steering is another (see Figure 1.1). Andersen (2008) deals with the role of the steering committee, a function which is more common in projects in the Nordic countries. Such a committee is especially important in a situation where many stakeholders are involved, when an organization lacks experience of project work or when change issues are of low priority. There is a risk with such a strong function, especially if it tries to take over responsibilities from project management and if it gets involved in technical decisions.

Research findings emphasize that top management should be represented in the initial phase of a project when objectives are established, responsibilities are decided, and budgets and schedules are defined (Meredith and Mantel 2010: 272). But often a more passive and temporary involvement is asked for in the project literature. Different methods for portfolio management and management of programmes are presented to CEOs to help them select among projects (Jenner 2010, Turner 2008). The role of executives in a project is also stressed in order to ensure the outcome of a project and to guarantee its sustainability.

The point of departure is the project management literature, namely the project organization with its tasks and distribution of responsibility. We also include financiers as a part of the project organization (see Figure 1.1). A strong project manager is usually regarded as vital for the success of a project. However, there are obvious dangers in over-emphasizing the importance of the project manager or project management as crucial for success. Certainly, if the focus is on activity and short-term results, then project management plays a crucial role. If the focus is on sustainable development instead, there is a danger in exaggerating the importance of the project manager and project management as vital for success. One project manager hardly has the capacity or mandate to exercise strategic impact, particularly as regards what happens to project results after project completion.

In what follows, we will highlight the risks inherent in a project manager who expands his/her mission and area of responsibility too much in order to achieve success in a project. Our experience is that this often takes place at the cost of, or as a consequence of, project owners and steering groups being too passive, leading to total responsibility for the project ending up 'in the hands' of project management. Project managers are seldom interested in involving the steering group in decision-making and communication about the development of a project (Thomsett 2002: 292).

Research shows that project management plays an important role in the success of a project, but if the aim is that a project should contribute to sustainable development, project owners must be involved in implementation, learning processes and knowledge formation. Andersen (2008) analyses project organizations and how their work and responsibilities are distributed, their decisions and powers, and discusses how management and coordination can take place. He emphasizes the value of viewing the project as a whole in interaction with its settings, as well as the capacity of the project organization for learning and flexibility. The author emphasizes that the steering group should have overall responsibility, ensure that there are sufficient resources, disseminate information, as well as actively support the project and link it to the organization's core operations.

Research has studied project organizations with these different roles, and the distribution of responsibility and work. Svensson et al. (2009) present a large national development programme in the public sector, with some 80 million Swedish crowns of government funding, where the aim was better health and a reduction in sickness absenteeism. The research aimed at identifying and analysing the factors that favour sustainable development in the area of the working environment. A number of results were achieved, covering education, healthcare activities, annual healthcare reports, and so on, but the research showed that few of the results would survive after completion of the project.

There are a number of explanations for the lack of sustainability in the programme initiative, despite soundly implemented activities and positive results in individual projects. Above all, there was a noticeable lack of active ownership on the part of management and politicians in the municipalities and county councils. These actors had not appreciated that they needed to involve themselves in the project, but had in fact transferred all responsibility, including dissemination of the results, to the project management. How the programme and the individual projects were initiated was an important explanation for the lack of sustainability. The decision on financing was taken rapidly within the Ministry of Industry, since there was a surplus in the budget and funds had to be used before year-end. There was also little time to provide information locally on the aim of the initiative, and the application period was short. The consequence was that a number of projects were 'sold' by consultants or researchers to municipal management, and politicians did not make the time to familiarize themselves, but accepted project funding. Passive ownership was an important explanation as to why the project did not become a strategic part of the development work run in the organizations. Instead it was something temporary and sidelined.

Ownership is connected to steering, but steering can take place in different ways. A project is associated with planned and goal-steered initiatives to solve a known problem, or to develop an area, something that should take place within a given time frame, with its own budget and project management (Turner 2008). Standardized methods are used most often for planning and goal steering. Research reveals a number of weaknesses in projects using these planning-, goal- and method-steered approaches, based on stable internal and external conditions, and with consensus thinking between actors who are assumed to have common interests. The research shows that the methods should not be excessively steering and become an end in themselves, but should rather function to support learning blended with action. The methods, apart from a number of definite techniques for budget steering and follow-up, must also contain a unifying idea, incorporating the different intentions of interest groups, covering their aims and visions.

Modern performance management deals with combining hard and soft steering methods, that is, both figures but also assessments of how norms, values and motivation changes in the course of development work. Steering should aim at facilitating learning and participation amongst the different interest groups. The data produced is intended to facilitate coordination and comparability, be easy to review, provide context, create transparency and, above all, be useful. Measurement and assessment should also show the value which an activity creates for customers, as a consequence of value-oriented steering becoming increasingly important in relation to cost orientation. Instead of a reactive and retrospective approach, a proactive approach, oriented to the surrounding world and future-oriented, is needed. 'You can't drive a car just by looking in the back mirror' is not inapposite in this context. The theoretical basis for steering is not just formal decision theory, but rather a combination of theories and strategies on how development can be steered, organized and managed. Activity steering is linked together with the company's own strategies and is intended to function as a support for operational work. This requires that line management takes responsibility for development and ensures that it does not end up in the background (Andersen 2008).

In summary, we can state that research deals with the question of ownership in different ways, usually connected to steering assisted by plans, methods or goals. Project research and modern performance management show the value of an open, learning approach that provides better conditions for active ownership. Our analysis of ownership originates in the project organization, with its distribution of decision-making, responsibility and work.

COLLABORATION

Research into business economics and industrial policy increasingly emphasizes cooperation and collaboration as prerequisites for sustainable development. Collaboration can take place in the form of networks, clusters and innovation systems, Triple Helix, strategic alliances or partnerships. Often the collaboration is organized between companies and in certain cases also with authorities and the research community. Such collaboration takes place within the framework of a systems view of development and innovation, which also applies to initiatives financed by different funding organizations. The mission which the government has given the authorities covers supporting different forms of collaboration and joint knowledge formation such as clusters and innovation systems. The intention is to make regional and industrial policy more coherent and strategic (Svensson and Nilsson 2008).

Is this policy well founded, or is it the result of a theoretically steered and transitory trend? Earlier generations of innovation policy have focused on technology. The term innovation policy did not include cultural or social policy at that time, nor such areas as entrepreneurship, marketing or customer relations. The starting point was to contribute to innovations on the basis of science and technological research. The approach in innovation research and policy has been static rather than supporting processes. Dynamic learning processes and joint knowledge formation were conspicuous by their absence. An innovation system should normally entail interaction and coordination between a large number of actors and organizations in an open, dynamic, decentralized and process-oriented system.

The open nature and uncertain conditions in the system, however, can create problems for policy (Lundvall 1992). How can innovations be steered by policy in a complex and virtually chaotic environment, and how can the results of initiatives be measured? Even though the goal of innovation processes – a commercial venture or a dynamic development initiative – cannot be defined in advance, innovation processes must be steered towards expected goals. Steering involves the use of policy instruments, such as procurement, and creates so-called development blocks (Dahmén 1950). Special R&D initiatives are another tool for creating development blocks. In other words, this involves accepting that goals cannot be defined in advance, but rather that the preconditions for success are inherent in the processes and joint knowledge formation which are created in development blocks. Collaboration through joint knowledge formation is, in other words, a criterion for sustainable development in terms of development blocks or in other forms of collaboration.

In the last decade, attempts have been made to organize collaboration between companies, public actors and research along the lines of the Triple Helix model. This is based on and emphasizes the concept of regional cluster formations between companies and it should support entrepreneurship in networks, through mentorship and in other ways. A study shows a number of difficulties in innovation systems where industry, the state and higher education cooperate (Laestadius, Nuur and Ylinenpää 2007). It has proved difficult to transform theories on innovation systems into reality. Programmes and projects aiming at innovation systems and clusters run the risk of being over-focused on concepts. The right partners must be involved from the very beginning (Bourne 2009). Most often, a partnership is dominated by public officials, while entrepreneurs, youth and women are missing. The homogeneity of the group is an obstacle to innovation and developmental learning (Svensson and Nilsson 2008).

Problems in the programme were above all connected with weaknesses in steering, such as planning and selection of projects. Competition over development funds contributed to streamlining application processes that were adapted to the formulations used in calls for tenders, as opposed to being driven by regional needs and the visions of companies. The expectation of creating leading-edge regional innovation systems has seldom proved to be realistic. Instead of allowing joint knowledge formation to emerge organically, different types of organizational rules have been set up where constellations define themselves as regional innovation systems or clusters. Practical examples show that organizing member companies into industrial concentrations geographically, with marketing perspectives and global links – such as in the Paper Providence programme – are successful (Sölvell 2009).

Research shows that networks, clusters and innovation systems can be important in creating competitive companies and regions, but programme initiatives should then be part of an innovation policy that is consciously and consistently run at different levels, based on an idea that is realistic and implementable, and which can be developed organically. In most contexts, learning processes supporting programme initiatives in innovation systems are regarded as a vital factor for success (Lundvall 1992). There are, however, few descriptions of how this learning works in practice, and what it means for growth, innovation and business development. Miettinen (2002) asks whether innovation systems should be regarded as a scientific or political concept. The answer is that innovation systems should not be regarded as either, but more as a metaphor for conceptualizing joint knowledge formation that is vital for successful programme and project initiatives. The conditions for success in such initiatives are that they are operated in such a way that the different spheres in Triple Helix or the actors in an innovation system begin to understand each other, and this understanding leads to joint action.

Partnership is another concept with a fairly similar purpose. It is increasingly used as a description of a new and stronger form of collaboration between public and private spheres. The public sector resembles more closely the company sector at the same time as companies are expected to accept greater social responsibility. The vision is to be able to steer without hierarchies and compulsion. This involves a transition from *government* to *governance*, that is, from a state to a joint steering process through shared knowledge formation. The view of those supporting partnership thinking is that complicated and intractable problems (such as the labour market, social issues, the environment, and so on) and large initiatives require joint action from strategic public and private actors.

EQUAL was a comprehensive EU programme aimed at counteracting exclusion and discrimination in the labour market. A precondition for receiving project funds in this programme was participating in a development partnership. The partnership included the Public Employment Service, the Swedish Social Insurance Agency, employers, the social economy, and so on. Wistus (2008) shows that there are advantages to this type of collaboration, including joint and united actions, decision-making capacity, strategic competence, and so on. There are also weaknesses in development partnerships in terms of organizational and working forms, especially because of their cumbersomeness and the difficulty of involving participants in decision-making processes. The special link between strategic and operational work is another problem, as is the lack of innovative solutions. A democratic problem in the EQUAL programme was 'homogenous' representation consisting mainly of well-educated, middle-aged, publicly employed Swedes, whilst young people, immigrants and business owners have seldom been involved in partnerships. One overall conclusion is that partnerships are not a universal solution for creating joint knowledge formation, or effectively managing the dilemma between top-down and bottom–up steering.

Hedlund (2008), who has studied Structural Funds at a regional level, criticizes networks and partnerships from a gender perspective. She shows that the ideals of efficiency, flexibility and participation do not correspond with reality. Elitist male regional power structures are strengthened as a result of male officials, financiers, experts and politicians taking decisions without insight and in forums that are not accessible to women. When women started to establish a stronger position in political life, increasingly issues ended up in closed circles where it became difficult for citizens to ensure accountability. Attempts to enlarge regions strengthen this tendency towards large-scale and non-transparent decision-making. The motive is to create efficiency, flexibility and growth, whilst other values (such as fairness, gender equality, inclusion, environmental concern, and so on) are given lower priority and become invisible.

The result is that questions concerning growth and innovation are distorted and limited to certain areas of application, whilst questions concerning tourism, culture, experiences, design, and so on, do not receive the same attention. Representative democracy is replaced by a deliberative form, a democracy based on dialogue, consensus thinking and agreements between different groups, but within the framework of gender neutral thinking. In this way, new forms of collaboration make it more difficult for women to act as an interest group and drive their own issues. Evaluation of regional growth programmes shows similar patterns, namely the weak influence of women in and over their work (Hedlund 2008).

Networks are another form of cooperation and joint knowledge formation between companies in voluntary and informal forms. The aim may be learning, production and personnel collaboration, strengthening the value chain, improving quality, and so on. In the first programming period of the Social Funds in Sweden, networks rapidly became popular and were powered by companies' interest in participating. Close to 2,000 networks were established.

There was no overall evaluation carried out into how these networks functioned in practice, but one research project showed that some of the networks strengthened company development. However, special conditions and support systems were required for networks to function in terms of learning and development orientation – that is, resources, time, confidence, joint problems or goals, access to external support. Different studies have shown that networks often become introspective and socially supportive, and not action-oriented or critically questioning (Brulin and Svensson 2011).

An overall conclusion from this and other studies shows the importance of joint knowledge formation in networks also leading to action. Action blended with critical and peer examination of programme and project results has a better chance of leading to sustainable development. When the research community participates in networks, the conditions for multiplier effects in other activities are increased. Research shows that complex forms of collaboration, such as innovation systems and partnerships, require the existence of unifying and organizing forces (Wistus 2008). Theories such as those on intermediaries start from this need for collaboration, support and professional steering of innovative development work.

Current and growing research shows that experienced intermediaries are an important prerequisite for programme and project initiatives leading to sustainable development, for example, within the framework of different cluster organizations (Sölvell 2009). The role of intermediaries is to ensure that joint knowledge formation in innovation systems, networks and partnerships comes into existence and is transformed into activities and actions. Programme initiatives and larger projects should thus identify intermediaries from the very beginning and clarify their role in the coordination of development work, where the aim is to organize learning processes and create multiplier effects. Which organizations can function as intermediaries for regional development, innovation and growth? The research shows that this may vary in relation to content and context, and may also be dependent on contacts, competence and the strategic position of intermediaries. Research institutes have an explicit role in linking research between universities and companies. One study of a national initiative on excellent research institutes showed that companies and higher education benefited greatly from the mediating and driving function which the institutions adopted (Brulin and Svensson 2011). Different institutes had different roles, but often functions were combined to create meeting forums, to operate as intermediaries and to act as driving forces. In total there are around 100 research institutes in the country, specializing in different R&D areas and industries, but they have no specific regional mission. What other organizations are there that can take on this coordinating role in development and innovation? Industrial development centres, municipal learning centres, higher education and regional R&D units are examples of organizations that can function as intermediaries in different regional development systems.

In summary, we can state that the research on regional development and growth is probably in agreement on the value of collaboration in different forms between different actors from different areas. Learning is regarded as crucial in these collaborative systems, but we know less about how it occurs, and what it contains, given the paucity of research in this area.

DEVELOPMENTAL LEARNING

It is difficult to know what will remain in the long term from large programmes and projects. The absence of a well-thought-out strategy on how results can be leveraged, and how those responsible learn from the project for future initiatives, means that the lasting effects are probably small. At the same time, we cannot ignore the fact that even without planning, learning which provides effects on other activities takes place purely by the transfer of personnel and their knowledge. Learning does not occur by chance, particularly not developmental learning. By developmental learning, we refer to learning that is not just an integral part of development work ('walking on two legs') but as something that also drives development forward. The dynamic element is the driving forces that can occur as a result of specific project outcomes. Developmental learning can take many forms and these are partly unpredictable. How project results are disseminated and have a strategic impact on other areas and in other environments cannot simply be planned, but by looking at the complex problem, communicating and discussing project results, a number of surprising learning effects in other activities, both locally and regionally, can occur. Competence development at the workplace can lead to the commercialization of innovations, and thus growth and new jobs.

In this way we can refer to the generation of multiplier effects from project results. This way of working can inspire others. The new method of working is disseminated, contributes to strategic impact, speed can be changed, and long-term effects created. These multiplier effects require interaction between changes at individual, organizational and societal levels. In different places, we return to this definition and its connection with closely related concepts and current research results. Our way of looking at learning as an integral and dynamic component differs, on the other hand, from how it is viewed in a planning-steered project approach. In this, learning is reduced to one-way information, something that comes at the end of a project, and which neither plays a strategic role in implementation nor provides a foundation for sustainable development. Developmental learning can help whole regions to grow, lead to the dissemination of productivity improvements, contribute to improvements in work organizations, and to the commercial exploitation of innovations.

Stjernberg (1993) shows, in a study of a number of projects run by the labour market partners where the aim was to make working life more effective and human – among other things, through group work, higher skill content and a better personnel policy – that surprising learning processes were achieved after project completion. What is unique about Stjernberg's study is that it was done ten years after the programme was completed. At first glance, the project appeared to be a failure since the results achieved were not lasting. Closer examination, however, showed that it was possible to identify long-term effects from the initiatives, but not those that were initially intended, and not always at the workplaces involved. Instead quite unpredictable effects occurred which had not been planned, and sometimes at different workplaces. It turned out that a number of individuals had been strongly influenced by participating in the project. When they later applied or moved to other workplaces, they took with them their knowledge and ideas, and could use this in their new conditions and from a stronger position in the organization. This applies particularly to some of the managers who became carriers of ideas about the renewal of working life where employee influence was a major element.

Large programmes, however, cannot rely on such types of unplanned and unpredictable learning processes if the ambition is to create multiplier effects. There are strong arguments that the third mechanism, namely developmental learning, could have the greatest effect in creating sustainable development work. The question is: how can this be achieved? What role can research play in creating developmental learning? In the knowledge society, new knowledge is increasingly produced in a context where a large number of different actors take part in the process.

According to Nowotny, Scott and Gibbons (2001), we are in a radically new situation concerning knowledge formation. The boundaries between research and practice are becoming more blurred. Usable knowledge is increasingly created in an application context. The one-way monologue from university to its surroundings does not work in a knowledge society which is typified by genuine uncertainty as to what can be regarded as lasting knowledge and science. Disciplinary boundaries are shifting rapidly. New disciplines are emerging as a consequence of knowledge formation in cooperation with 'practitioners'. Legitimate knowledge is created in a dialogue, where surrounding voices can make themselves heard, 'in which society can "speak back" to science'. Interacting with and making use of researchers, teachers, students, and so on, in different aspects of programme and project implementation provides an entry point to an arena – the research community, regionally and internationally – which has the task of creating critical reflection and knowledge of development processes.

The local and regional surroundings of higher education are beginning to play a growing role in their success as research and educational environments. Traditional knowledge formation at a rate that does not synchronize with surrounding society, and which is only quality evaluated by purely scientific criteria, runs the risk of making universities obsolete as producers of knowledge. Usable knowledge is increasingly produced in application contexts, which compels a contextualization of research and teaching. The impact from authorities, political organizations, interest groups, environmental organizations and others is of growing importance in innovative scientific production. Universities and university colleges have a growing need for cooperation and interaction with practitioners. Traditional academic approaches are being challenged by increasing requirements for entrepreneurial expertise and network building with companies. Holding companies, venture capitalists and science parks in the borderland between the university and its surroundings are changing the academic world's view of itself and how knowledge is formed. Researchers, teachers and students are expected to create contacts with and also link up to working and industrial life outside higher education. Possibly the best opportunity for creating developmental learning and multiplier effects from programmes and projects lies in closer cooperation with the scientific community. Evaluations linked to research and the surrounding world provide new dimensions and perspectives on programme and project implementation which also add input to knowledge formation in the research world.

Individual projects and short-term programmes often achieve only limited impact unless they are supported by an appropriate environment. Lasting innovation and learning processes require ongoing exchange between a number of actors who understand each other and share each other's daily concerns. We have already touched on such joint knowledge formation in the sustainability criteria, namely collaboration. The prerequisite for such knowledge formation is long-term cooperation based on deep familiarity with each other, something that can be achieved in specific geographical spaces. Gustavsen, Finne and Oscarsson (2001) maintain that the starting point for development programmes should always be local, workplace-related and specific company problems. The places, the geographical territories, are important since they enable closeness to and provide critical density between separate workplaces sharing daily experiences. Proximity creates a long-term view and continuity in learning, and opportunities to share each other's tacit knowledge.

Ultimately, this starting point is insufficient, however, and the strategy highly vulnerable. Local and regional dynamics cannot be exclusively based on internal development processes. Such dynamics also presuppose the ability to 'build bridges' to external actors. A 'critical mass' of other involved actors is required to achieve the necessary dynamism in projects and development processes. Different types of learning conferences, if they are organized in the right way, can 'release' developmental learning with the help of external actors. Innovations, new goods and services, changes in processes and organizations often originate from surprising combinations of already existing knowledge. As a result, strategies for promoting innovation deal with creating conditions for different ways of 'pooling' resources. The conditions for pooling can come about through the creation of unexpected relationships. A number of pioneering innovations have been developed through pooling relatively simple knowledge from different industries and areas in more or less unusual combinations. The foundation for such pooling lies in meetings and the creation of relationships between actors with different knowledge and competencies.

Stjernberg (1993), however, makes a telling point when he highlights the importance of specific individuals as bearers of insights and knowledge from projects and programmes. Ultimately, though, it is always individuals who learn, not structures and processes. The knowledge acquired by project management and project participants, regional development actors, politicians and participants in Structural Fund partnerships is invaluable. The question is whether programmes and projects can make better use of these carriers of experience and knowledge. In the discussion on local and regional development dynamics, the importance of social 'enthusiasts' was highlighted. Often it is 'social or civic entrepreneurs' who decide to push forward regional development dynamics, and who contribute to the generation of multiplier effects when they transfer knowledge and insights from other development processes. Programme and project participants should probably consider themselves to a greater degree as social entrepreneurs:

> *Social entrepreneurs help society develop and organise its economic assets by building strong, elastic networks between public, private and civic sectors ... They enjoy taking risks. They are not afraid of failure. They have the strength that comes from strong convictions. They have visions. They are passionate and energetic. (Henton, Melville and Walesh 1997: 33)*

Social entrepreneurs driving development and growth could thus function as the 'spiders in a web' between programmes and projects, industry and civil society.

Developmental learning can be illustrated by a couple of examples which we develop later on in the book. The first concerns the 'Production Boost', which is a national initiative for strengthening competitiveness in smaller companies. Here there was active ownership, where people with strong support among the labour market partners ensured that backing for ownership and professional steering existed to leverage the results from learning evaluation. From the beginning there was a 'future' group which worked actively to strengthen sustainability in the programme.

The most interesting aspect, however, was the multiplier effects which occurred in the public sector, where a similar programme ('Activity Boost') was initiated, drawing on the inspiration of, and the model used in, the Production Boost. The research group functioned as a mediating actor and collaboration partner in the learning process, and provided the foundation for establishing the new programme. The new programme applied for funding from the Social Fund, but received none. The programme was then restructured so that the participating municipalities and county councils were responsible for the costs and paid for the training and support measures organized. Today there are some 60 municipalities and around ten county councils involved in the Activity Boost.

Lack of external funding meant that the ownership requirement became clearer and the conditions for developmental learning were improved. The participants were able to avoid project bureaucracy and could focus on their own development work, in interaction with a large and growing number of actors. The Social Security Fund was an active intermediary in organizing collaboration, and in creating meetings and mediating contacts. Ongoing evaluation was given a strategic role in the learning processes and in the analysis of sustainability.

Another interesting example of developmental learning is the Metal Union's five projects for competence development of employees in small companies in the north of Sweden – totalling some 1,200 people. One project quickly multiplied into five. Contacts with the central organization were strengthened within the framework of the national structure established for working with the Social and Regional Funds. New projects were established at national and regional levels. Learning evaluation was linked to the new projects and given an important role. In addition, the trade union was involved and organized different higher education programmes in sustainable development. Our view is that this involves a learning and development process which is merely beginning and which will have long-term effects in several regions and at a number of workplaces.

Conclusions

Based on research into sustainable development through public programmes and projects, we have tried to synthesize what has been achieved in two ideal types, the planning-steered developmental model and the development-supportive evaluation model. We have tried to show that sustainable development through programmes and projects that should be innovative and additional in relation to regular activities presupposes knowledge formation measures in line with the development-supportive evaluation model. The review of relevant research provides the basis for our conclusions of how vital this type of evaluation is for achieving sustainable development. Later on in the book, we will illustrate our theoretical starting points and central concepts empirically with data obtained primarily from the implementation of Structural Funds during the programming period 2007–2013.

The research review provides a discouraging picture of sustainability in large programmes and projects. It is obvious that the question of knowledge formation is crucial if development work is to be organized so that long-term effects can be achieved. Ongoing development measures in line with the development-supportive evaluation model may be vitally important in determining long-term impact and the contribution to sustainable development of programmes and projects. Such strategic knowledge formation, however, is often the exception, where the norm is one-dimensional orientation to measurement and control in line with the planning-steered developmental model. The question can also be put as to whether the regulatory framework of the programme's rules constitute a barrier, with their short project frames of two to three years, as this creates some irregularity and uncertainty over the long term for project implementation. This risk is that project owners do not dare to think in terms of the long term, for example, in recruitment of leading competence for the project.

Our ambition has been, by using the ideal types of constellations, to synthesize different perspectives of knowledge formation and approaches to evaluation. Programme and project activities implemented in a complex and largely unpredictable environment presuppose an ability to manage dilemmas and contradictions, and continuously search for new development routes. An important starting point for our analysis is that traditional planning and method-steered project thinking must be supplemented, and to some extent replaced, by an alternative view of knowledge formation where processes, learning, innovation and coordination are central elements. This view can be summarized in the development-supportive evaluation model – that is, interactive learning and development logic, where action and reflection are blended together. The ideal type which we have presented is the theoretical construct which provides the starting point for the analysis in our book. The basic idea of a learning approach is that ongoing critical examination of programmes and projects will lead to greater focus on goals, results and long-term effects. Feedback from experience and knowledge formation based on the development-supportive evaluation model leads, in our view, to better conditions for sustainable development. Insight and knowledge that can be used in different types of regional development are created within the framework of learning processes, and can be expected to lead to further 'ripples on the pond', that is, multiplier effects.

Instead of focusing on the role of project management, we believe the starting point should be the project organization itself, where active ownership is the vital criterion for sustainability. A project organization clarifies tasks, responsibilities and decisions, and thereby creates clarity over who is to manage the project results and ensure that multiplier effects are generated. Active ownership and professional project management, which in a dialogue during evaluation are able to make alternative choices and see new opportunities for knowledge formation, provide the preconditions to implement projects so that they lead to sustainable development. The role of project management becomes different and more demanding in a project organization where there are different groupings and clear requirements for development-supportive evaluation.

It is also important to ensure that there is a clear picture of who the project users are and how they are to be involved. The development-supportive evaluation model provides the foundation for a project organization that is transparent, and where ownership aims at long-term impact, joint knowledge formation – together with other actors – and feedback into the public domain. Joint knowledge formation and collaboration in different forms between different actors is one part of a strategy for solving complex problems in an innovative way, influencing the system and mobilizing resources. Complex system solutions run the risk of making participation more difficult and giving priority to bureaucratic, male-dominated types of collaboration, which in themselves can lead to what we might refer to as 'system-blocked learning'. A combination of less informal networks, together with more formalized collaboration in innovation systems, networks and partnerships, can be one means of resolving the dilemma between participation and influence over the system. The importance of intermediaries provides another opportunity for organizing joint knowledge formation between different actors.

Sustainable development in the form of innovative, smarter and inclusive growth should apply to all groups in society, as formulated in the EU 2020 strategy, both as regards content and implementation. The research results showing exclusion of large groups must thus be taken with the greatest seriousness, as this represents a threat to the whole ethos of the strategy. The new organizational forms, such as partnerships, networks and innovation systems, must be critically examined from gender and integration perspectives. The benefits are twofold. First, they involve not only promoting gender equality, inclusion and democracy, in contrast to adherence to homogenous and traditional power structures that are neither innovative nor development-oriented. Second, the development-supportive evaluation model provides programme and project implementation with coherent powerful knowledge that can provide the foundation stone for sustainable development.

3

Key Research Findings

In Chapters 1 and 2 we presented starting points, perspectives and an overview of research. In this chapter, we will examine important research findings of relevance to our analysis. This covers research within a specialized field where the findings can be related to our empirical and theoretical perspectives. The research we look at deals with the following:

- strategies for development;

- learning as support for development work;

- the project organization from the perspective of owners and steering;

- project work and project management from, amongst others, a gender perspective;

- the importance of horizontal criteria – such as gender equality and diversity – in politically steered development processes.

Research into development work has often been non-theoretical and based on a static view. It has been context-dependent and taken a closed system approach with a lack of empirical base (Pettigrew 1985). Our approach instead aims to build up a clear theoretical foundation by combining process and structural perspectives. It should take as its starting point context and an open systems approach, and also have clear theoretical foundations. In this chapter, we will clarify the research-linked starting points for our analysis.

Strategies for Development

Development strategies can be roughly divided into 'top-down' and 'bottom-up' approaches. In the former case, this involved those responsible determining the aim and strategies for implementation. In the latter case, development is driven through high participation and a multiplicity of ideas. The first approach is predetermined and closed, whilst the latter is more open and exploratory. Research shows that both these strategies have their limitations, but also some advantages (Svensson and Nilsson 2008). A top-down-steered development means that the project becomes 'square' and participants' involvement and creativity is not stimulated. No developmental learning is created when goals and instruments are drawn up in advance, making their dissemination and strategic impact more difficult. For this reason no multiplier effects occur in other areas or in other contexts. The project 'walks on one leg, not on two'. Action is not blended with reflection, and as a result development work cannot be improved from the experiences gained.

In the two introductory chapters, we have discussed how dominant project logic is based on thinking that is administrative, planning-steered and financial. Reports on how project funds have been used become the most important issue, whilst the aim and long-term effects fade into the background. Often different methods are used (for example, project calculations, investment assessment, key figures, project audits) to assess, plan, steer and manage a project. These methods have been developed within the framework of a theory of economic steering and reporting which has its own tradition of education, practice and research, and which has later extended into the area of project economics (Collins 2010, Turner 2008). We will not go into these models here, but merely state that development can be viewed over time from a narrow economic steering viewpoint to performance management that encompasses a multiplicity of goals, perspectives and interests. We will highlight a number of important elements from research and literature on performance management which could be useful in complex projects for creating sustainable development work (see, for example, Harrison and Lock 2004, Kerzner 2009, Jaques and Clement 2009, Thomas and Mullaly 2008, Thomsett 2002, Gustavsen 2010).

Research shows that long-term effects are seldom achieved through planning and that results seldom fulfil the original intentions of a project. A Swedish study, *What Happened Next?* (Sundin and Göransson 2006), which followed up different gender equality initiatives ten years later, clearly showed the unpredictability of projects aimed at breaking patterns and resistance in an organization. Very few of the results remain ten years later, for instance, in the 'gender pattern-breaking projects', where the aim was to facilitate the entry of women into male-dominated areas. After a time most of the women had left their jobs, mainly as a consequence of opposition from men. The results were thus not sustainable in any lasting sense. Neither was there any obvious impact on the system in terms of changing gender labelling of work or vertical gender hierarchies. However, one interesting development took place in many projects which was valuable for the women, as they obtained new work tasks, enhanced self-confidence and greater interest in trying something new.

The development strategy driven from below, which is based on broad participation, many ideas, an open approach and energetic 'enthusiasts', also has its shortcomings, particularly from a sustainability perspective. It is a strategy which can function when solving well-defined problems over a short period. However, it is difficult to maintain involvement over a longer period and enthusiasm can fade. Management in an organization often feels a degree of uncertainty prior to this approach, and thus finds it difficult to let it have an impact on rules and systems in an organization.

What alternatives are there to either a top-down or bottom-up approach? One alternative could be a development strategy building on horizontal collaboration between actors and organizations. Collaboration can take place in the form of networks, innovation systems, partnerships, clusters or Triple Helix, where the aim is to achieve something that participants cannot do individually. This approach also has its weaknesses and risks. Cooperation risks becoming inward-looking, bureaucratic and dialogue–based, rather than action-oriented. It is often both focused on individuals rather than being organization-wide and is uncritical instead of being questioning and innovative (Wistus 2008).

How do we view the perspectives presented above? In Chapter 2, we presented a mechanism for sustainable development work that builds on collaboration and joint knowledge formation, that is, development closely aligned with the third strategy above. Essentially we want to combine the three mechanisms for sustainable development work or overcome the limitations of the three-part strategies presented above. Sustainable development requires elements of a top-down-driven strategy in the form of active ownership and professional steering. In this way, resources can be generated, demands imposed, strategic impact exercised, changes disseminated and contributions made to the public debate. Innovation and entrepreneurship presuppose input from a bottom-up strategy, that is, a form that creates energy, motivation and new ideas. At the same time, the collaboration strategy is a precondition for large projects that need to create critical mass. The three development strategies are closely linked with the three mechanisms for sustainable development work which we touched on in an earlier chapter, that is, ownership, collaboration and developmental learning. Ownership involves support from below. Collaboration builds on horizontal contacts within and between organizations. Learning presupposes participation from below.

There are many different ways of categorizing development work. Weick and Quinn (1999) make a theoretical distinction between episodic and continuous changes. The first category is based on short-term adaptation and problem-solving in accordance with linear and goal-steered thinking. The latter takes as its point of departure that change is a natural condition, driven forward by instability in organizations, and something that takes place in permanent ongoing interaction with its surroundings. The central concepts are interaction, adaptation, growth patterns, chance factors, improvisation, transformation and learning. In this case, change involves reorienting what is already happening and ongoing by 'freezing', interpreting and rebalancing, and in this way establishing conditions for improvisation and learning based on creating new meaning contexts (unfreeze). In order to succeed with change, inert structures must be unlocked so that more powerful and coordinated changes can be implemented. Change is regarded as a long-term process, not as a number of disconnected planned events. The later, open view of development lies close to our own perspective, but we believe that continuous and lasting change must be coordinated with structural aspects for multiplier effects to be achieved.

The development strategies which we have touched on above can be compared with the methods used by companies to create efficiency and competitiveness. The similarities are striking, as is development over time. Earlier strategies for business development built on long-term planning and rational decision-making, but more recently they have increasingly come to focus on change and innovation in interaction with changes in the surrounding world. Traditional company strategies have been criticized on different grounds. They have been regarded as being too top-down-steered and driven by experts, building on narrow technical and financial thinking, based on instrumental and short-term rationality, and claiming validity from general reasoning and the fact that the focus is on large companies. The later, more developed strategies try to overcome these limitations by including a number of perspectives and goals, such as involving different interest groups – customers and employees, as well as regional and environmental interests.

Learning as a Driving Force for Development

> *One reason is that too many managers want to learn "how" in terms of detailed practices and behaviours and techniques, rather than "why" in terms of philosophy and general guidance for actions.*
> *Pfeffer and Sutton (2000: 246)*

In this section, we will try to answer the question of why learning is so important in sustainable development work, but also what characterizes such learning, who learns and how it is carried out. A strategy for sustainable development can and should be based on a theory of an action-driven learning process (Ellström and Kock 2009, Ellström 2010). The focus is on action, but it is blended with critical reflection over what the action has led to, and at the same time it shows the scope for further action for development. Learning can thus be regarded as a unifying force, providing dynamics and direction in development work. Projects offer a unique learning platform. They create space for variation and an opportunity to pursue exploration. A project is a temporary organization that generates new knowledge, but the base organization often fails to absorb it. Few organizations have a system in place to learn from projects. This is an answer to the question of *why* learning is so important in sustainable development work. Another answer to the why question is based on participants' learning. Projects provide good opportunities for individual learning by confronting participants with challenges and troubleshooting that go beyond the demands of daily work. The problem is that routines for taking advantage of these learning opportunities are weakly developed (Ellström 2009).

We also view learning as an integral and collaborative part of development work, but the question is: what is meant by learning? What is being learnt? Who is doing the learning? How does the learning take place? What does it mean to think in new and different ways in innovative development work, which should also be sustainable? What does competence for change and development on the part of participants actually cover? What typifies an organization or project that aims to support a combined individual and activity-based learning process? One thing we do know is that it is not based on simple one-way information, measurement or methodological approaches, which confirms the quotation above. Excessive information makes it difficult to focus on what is necessary for learning to contribute to reflection and analyse changes carried out.

The question about *who* is learning can be related to the model for the project organization (see Figure 1.1). Learning covers all levels in the project organization – from the financier to participants and users/customers. Project owners must get to know what resources are required to implement a project, how change takes place over time and what results are achieved. The steering group must have the information to take strategic decisions about direction, allocation of resources, reallocation of priorities and strategic impact. Project management must carry out ongoing follow-up of activities to be able to manage operational work. Participants and customers/users should be given an overview and a context so that they are able to see how they can have an impact and be involved. In this way, learning becomes a vital factor for dialogue and decision-making between different levels in the project organization and thus a prerequisite for determining priorities and steering activities. By means of learning evaluation, the project organization can be made transparent, and communication to all involved is easy, which is represented by the vertical line in Figure 1.1. We can thus think of project-organized learning as comparable to organizational learning, that is, there are systems and routines that support learning (cf. Argyris 1999, Ellström 2010).

We do not have an unequivocal answer to the question of *how* learning in development work should be organized. One way is to use analysis seminars where participants from different levels take part within the framework of joint knowledge formation with ongoing evaluators. This means that researchers organize joint learning opportunities for the whole project organization several times a year, where they present their data and the questions which have been analysed by participants. A report is written at each event covering the joint analysis. The aim of involving participants in joint knowledge formation is to raise the quality of the analysis, and also to make use of the results of the evaluation. The underlying idea is that the knowledge produced by participants is assimilated and used.

The question about learning in development work must be developed, extended and the concept clarified. An important distinction to make is between learning that is development-oriented and that which is adaptive-oriented (Ellström 2001). Developmental learning originates from problematic situations, the need for change or unexpected events. It may also occur as a result of personal questioning and review. More generally, it relates to some form of 'disturbance' occurring, where habitual thought and action patterns are disrupted and a search is initiated for 'solutions' in the form of new ways of dealing with the problematic situation. The focus is on searching for new knowledge or new alternative thought and action patterns. It is a type of learning that leads to increased competence development, and which, under favourable conditions, can be a driving force for innovation.

At the same time, this type of development process can be seen as a movement from the familiar and well known – and thus safe – to something new and at least partly unfamiliar. It is something that in the beginning we try to resist. This then leads to habitual action patterns becoming stronger and consolidated. It is thus important to balance in different ways the uncertainty and anxiety that often occurs after seemingly minor 'disruptions' to habitual ways of working in an activity or project. Here project management has an important role to play, but it may also be important to have some form of external consultancy support. This is one way of creating the necessary security and confidence in a development phase, but also with pedagogical input, such as the type of analytical seminars mentioned above, for supporting and creating understanding and motivation for the development that has been initiated.

So gradually we can learn to gain mastery of new thinking and approaches. This takes place through processes which we refer to as adaptive learning. Adaptive learning is crucial if we are to manage routine, recurring actions in everyday real life, and without excessive effort be able to manage recurring problems, situations or tasks. In this way learning becomes a type of pendulum movement between *development*, in the sense of looking for something new, and *adaptation*, in the sense of mastering and consolidating what is new.

We also wish to reiterate that this distinction between developmental and adaptive learning does *not* imply that there are two specifically distinct forms of learning. This should instead be viewed as a distinction between two complementary aspects of learning, in which one or the other aspect can dominate or be less prominent, depending on the specific situation or phase in a development process.

If we transfer this reasoning about learning to working in a project, it means that, over the project period, there will be a need for both developmental and adaptive learning. For a development project to be genuinely developmental and innovative, management should have scope for and support critical questioning and review, as well as new ways of thinking and acting – in essence, developmental learning. At the same time, the project's results must at a later stage be transformed and applied to practical actions, that is, project results should be implemented and disseminated. This imposes demands on adaptive learning focusing on individual, group and organizational levels. Once again the need was demonstrated for the support of learning, and for the ability of project management, and any consultants involved, to strike a good balance during the project period between development, adaptation and implementation. Learning fulfils important functions both in the development phase of a project and in the dissemination and further use of project results. The difficulties experienced in many projects over combining development and implementation of results originating from the project have sometimes been regarded as a type of project paradox. Based on the view we put forward here, this is not an insurmountable setback, but rather a question of leading and organizing different types of learning in different phases of a project (Ellström 2009).

The project literature seldom deals with the closure and aftermath of a project, but there are exceptions (O'Callaghan 2008). Projects are embedded within specific systems and organizations (Cassin 2012). Sustainability of a change process is related to the implementation of the outcomes in the permanent organization. A project can help the base organization to be more learning-oriented. In this way, the organization can become revitalized and more effective, but this is often difficult to accomplish. Andersen (2008: 227) discusses the role of learning in projects in relation to the base organization. The relationship between project managers and line managers is therefore of the utmost importance (Andersen 2008).

The project managers could promote learning among individuals and teams. The steering group and the project owners are responsible for promoting learning at an organizational and inter-organizational level. When project management is too dependent on pre-determined routines and manuals, learning is restricted to adaptive learning. Learning is often synonymous with adjustment, not radically new ways of doing project work (Andersen 2008: 227).

There is yet another level of learning which is important for sustainability in development work. This involves *inter*-organizational learning, that is, learning between different organizations and actors collaborating on development work. Such learning is facilitated by confidence, openness, external support and resources for coordination, clarity about aims and conditions, as well as action- and result-oriented methods of working. Different types of intermediaries can facilitate and support learning between different organizations and actors (Brulin and Svensson 2011).

Project Organization

To understand how a company functions, theories about work organization are, in the view of most researchers, critical. In terms of understanding how projects function, there is not the same appreciation of the value of an organizational perspective, as often the focus is on project management. Research – both theoretical and empirical – on how a project organization can be structured in order to support sustainable development work is very limited.

This picture of how a project can be organized and managed corresponds closely to the research we have been involved in. One example of an effective project organization is the Production Boost, which is a substantial nationally financed initiative on introducing lean thinking into small and medium-size companies (see Chapter 2). The former chairman of the Metal Union, a person from the Electrolux management group, two female company leaders from smaller companies, together with a couple of experts and researchers, are members of the steering group. The steering group works strategically and proactively in a close dialogue with the programme director, who is responsible for the operational work. Both the chairman and the vice-chairman of the board have allocated time, and their work is financed, which has meant that they have been more actively involved in the development of the programme and in the work of creating strategic impact. The steering group's members were appointed on a personal mandate, but there is still a clear link to the project owners, that is, the labour market partners. The financiers have played an active role in the initiation, development and implementation of the programme.

In a project organization, decision-making processes run concurrently and parallel, and this puts major demands on coordination, transparency and dialogue. A project organization has to be able to deal with ambiguities and uncertainties, and to balance structure with flexibility. This entails finding a balance between rigid and detailed planning, and openness to adaptation and learning from changing outcomes and conditions. It is also about finding a balance between project leaders and individual team members – a balance between self-organization and self-discipline. The project teams should be flexible but not completely ad hoc (Highsmith 2010: 366). A restrictive organizational framework reduces a team's ability to deal with uncertainties and ambiguities, whereas too little framework causes chaos and confusion (Highsmith 2010, Remington and Pollack 2008, Cassin 2012). To undertake impossible projects is usually exciting, because of the high risks in combination with high rewards (Highsmith 2010: 365).

A long-term effect of the programme, which we can already see now, is that a number of university colleges and universities have been involved in working with lean thinking. In this way, the programme has had a strategic impact, and results from the programme have been disseminated. The researchers' explanation for the success of the programme is largely based on the strength of the project organization, with close and ongoing interaction between the steering group, project owners, programme director and representatives of the financiers. Ongoing evaluation has had the task of supporting learning between different levels in the project organization.

PROJECT MANAGEMENT

To understand the role of project management, it is important to differentiate between different kinds of projects, such as engineering and business (Thomsett 2002: 18). The former are production-oriented projects based on fixed expectations, minimal variation, established methods, physical deliverables, clear specifications and performance indicators, standard procedures and formal legal contracts. The latter, on the other hand, are exploratory and innovative projects, characterized by flexible specifications, uncertainties, conflicting methodologies, abstract deliverables, poor performance indicators and a large number of objectives. These mature projects are large scale, complicated with a high level of interaction between different stakeholders, carried out in an uncertain context (Hopkinson 2010). The goals are often indeterminate and conflicting. A system perspective is used in order to accomplish strategic goals (Maylor 2010: 38, Meredith and Mantel 2010). The project organization should stimulate cooperation, interaction, participatory decision-making, conflict resolution, fierce debate and collegial respect (Highsmith 2010: 367).

The literature on project management is abundant, but it seldom makes a distinction between different kinds of projects. Much of this literature is very descriptive (see, for example, Kerzner 2009, Barker and Cole 2009, Collins 2010, Moore 2010, Maylor 2010), and focuses on practical advice about:

- defining objectives and tasks;

- identifying phases in the process;

- methods for detailed planning;

- developing schedules, activity maps, toolboxes and models (Gantt charts, network techniques, and so on);

- reporting, monitoring and visualizing;

- delivering measurable outcomes;

- risk assessment;

- supporting teams.

The literature and research on project management – the science of project management – can also be characterized as follows:

- normative – that is, prescriptive – with volumes of advice and tips about how a project manager should act;

- the data which conclusions are based on is often poorly documented and analysed;

- the theoretical foundation has usually been based on an individual perspective, where strong driving project managers are in the centre, whilst conditions and obstacles to implementation and sustainability are in the background;

- questions about ownership and steering are not treated accurately;

- the planning and method-steered project strategy is the starting point;

- focus is on activities and results, not long-term effects;

- the importance of involving co-workers and creating functioning project teams is emphasized;[1]

- learning is not given a strategic role in the development of quality and sustainability;

- the importance of external and structural factors is unclearly developed;

- the gender perspective is virtually non-existent.

There is also a body of critical literature on project management which states that projects are often characterized by spiralling costs and missed deadlines. Other literature criticizes the practices and theories of project management for being static, inward-looking and based on anecdotal data. Instead they argue for a more open and flexible approach, with relevant stakeholders, in order to deal with the ambiguities, dilemmas and contradictions in a complex and politicized environment (Thomsett 2002, Andersen 2008, Jenner 2010, Harrison and Lock 2004, Hopkinson 2010, Fuller and Unwin 2011). But still the focus on methods, tools and schedules is dominant. There are numerous 'how to'

---

1   US project managers were asked to characterize an effective project manager in their own words. Leadership abilities were ranked highest, especially the capacity to lead project team members. Professional qualifications came third (Andersson 2008: 105). These answers can be seen as a reflection of a limited perception of the role of project manager, based on an experience from a first-order project.

books, but very few critically analyse the conditions for the long-term effects of projects (Thomas and Mullaly 2008).

Despite the abundance of literature, it is difficult to draw definitive conclusions of what works in a project. There are very few comprehensive studies of the effects of project management. A notable exception is the study carried out by the Project Management Institute (Thomas and Mullaly 2008). This study involved 48 researchers from different parts of the world, 60 case studies were carried out and 440 interviews were collected. The findings point to the complexity of implementing projects. The general conclusion is that good (consistent and coherent) project management makes a difference. But the factors which, in some cases, had the highest impact on project performance also had the lowest impact in other cases. It is also interesting to note that none of the traditional elements of project management (planning and control tools and techniques, complex management software, contractual strategies, and so on) top the list of what has the greatest impact on project management implementation. Instead, the most significant factors in project management are strategic and behavioural (Thomas and Mullaly 2008: 154).

There is, of course, important knowledge in this literature and research which may be useful for ideas on initiating, planning and carrying out activities leading to short-term project results. Project management plays an important role in the success of a project, but the tasks and competence needed are different in a complex project with a number of collaborating actors in a changing environment, where the aim is to create long-term effects (cf. Jaques and Clement 2009). The roles, functions and responsibility of project management are different in this type of project. It usually deals with large programmes where there is a programme head or programme director with overall responsibility, but who acts within the framework of a clear project organization. Our ambition is to treat project management holistically rather than as a collection of separate techniques (see Lock 2007). Compared to a functional manager, a project manager is a generalist rather than a specialist, a synthesizer rather than an analyst, and a facilitator rather than a supervisor (Meredith and Mantel 2010: 144).

We will summarize some results from the research we and others have done into the new role of project managers and their responsibilities in a large number of projects (Brulin and Svensson 2011). The results can be summarized in a number of conclusions that reflect new requirements and competencies on the part of project management in a new context with different preconditions:

- The importance of understanding one's own role in a complex organizational setting (Hersey and Blanchard 1972) where project owners are regarded as crucial for sustainability. It is important that the project manager requires clarification of the information and responsibility for his/her task, and the same applies to clarifying the distinction between strategic and operational work.

- The competence of coordinating and communicating with different levels in the project organization (Kerzner 2009, Engwall 2002, Harrison and Lock 2004). It has proved to be particularly important that project managers have ongoing contacts with the chairman of the board of the steering group. Here learning evaluation can be very helpful in providing a reliable basis for the dialogue. Project managers must continuously update the steering group on what is happening in the project, over such questions as possible risks and deviations from plans and goals.

- The capacity to be able to contribute to inter-organizational collaboration and joint knowledge formation, which mainly involves understanding the different preconditions for policy, industry and research. This involves the ability to function in different situations and to understand power processes and cultural differences, as well as traditions and the scope for decision-making in organizations of different kinds. In this way it becomes possible for project managers to determine what the scope is for change, and how far collaboration can be extended (cf. de Herbemont and César 1998).

- The capacity to contribute to developmental learning that will lead to multiplier effects. This requires the ability to interact with ongoing evaluators and to deal with criticism that arises.

- Working in a project management team (Lewis 1998, Briner, Geddes and Hastings 1998). Large, complicated projects often require shared leadership, but with the ability to act rapidly and independently.

- Contributing to public debate (Svensson et al. 2009). Providing information about a project and its results is in itself not sufficient, that is, making it known, as what is required involves the ability to use results to generate multiplier effects. This requires more proactive and strategic work where key actors who can have an impact are chosen at an early stage, in consultation with the steering group.

Perhaps the difference between the old and new project management roles can be illustrated by a comparison between how a small company owner and the managing director of a large company work. A small company owner works informally, does not make decisions on the basis of precise financial calculations, takes decisions himself/herself, has a feeling of what will work, possesses good personal knowledge and the ability to act rapidly and flexibly in response to customer demands. This method of working (applied to a project manager) can function in a small project, where the aim is to carry out activities and achieve short-term results in a relatively predictable and stable environment. This is an action-oriented way of working, where actions are performed in time.

However, this informal way of working does not function in a large programme, where there are complex issues, different interests, a number of dilemmas and contradictions, actors with different ambitions, and where development work takes place in a rapidly changing and partially unpredictable environment. In a development programme of this type, a project manager must instead be able to function as a managing director of a large company, where interaction with the board is crucial and where decisions must be based on more secure grounds. In an open and complex situation, where results and effects are more difficult to assess, project managers must be able to get help from learning evaluation to support the ongoing adaptation of goals and methods based on experiences gained. Such a project manager must learn to 'walk on two legs', that is, be able to switch between action and reflection.

The situation of a project manager, however, differs from the preconditions which an external managing director has in an owner-led company. Here there is stability in ownership and active owners who do not distinguish between strategic and operational work, and in this respect the situation is the opposite of the one we describe for project managers in large and complex projects. However, there are in fact similarities in the situation which a project manager and an external managing director confront in owner-managed companies, in the following respects: lack of documented owner strategy; lack of a professional board; importance of a clear distribution of roles with confidence between owners, board representatives and management; importance of being able to understand cultures and values in order to collaborate; importance of management with access to external dialogue partners. An important conclusion from the comparison above is that the interaction between owners, steering groups and management should be regarded as a significant source of development potential in both owner-led companies and projects.

There are risks and downsides in project organizations – in the form of bureaucratization of contacts and decision paths, increased costs, greater time expenditure, increased information needs, and so on. For this reason, it is important not to over-organize smaller implementation projects that are not complex, which do not involve a number of actors and do not aim to achieve long-term effects. The reluctance of many project managers to become part of a rigidly steered project organization is thus fully understandable.

In summary, our book tries to balance a critical attitude with a constructive perspective. We focus on the complexity of project management and on the emergent and evolutionary aspects of a project. This necessitates open and rolling planning. The role of the stakeholders becomes important, combined with an organization that stimulates interaction and learning. The focus is on the creation of values, the uncertainties, a dynamic and unsure environment, and a continuous holistic project evaluation to promote learning. The ambition of this approach is to make projects more flexible, adaptive, responsive and agile in a situation of speed and constant change.

PROJECT ORGANIZATION FROM A GENDER PERSPECTIVE

Project organizations (see Figure 1.1) are seldom gender neutral. The owners and steering groups usually consist of men, whilst project management is often carried out by women. However, gender distribution depends on the type of project involved. In projects directed to areas such as personnel, welfare questions, exclusion from the labour market, and so on, female project managers clearly dominate. Usually men manage projects involving technology, growth and innovation, and they are often responsible for large, systems-wide and complex programmes involving a number of actors and organizations.

There is very little research on project management from a gender perspective, especially comparative research on leadership in companies and state administration. This may seem strange since project management is becoming an increasingly large and important field in today's rapidly changing society. We will highlight some research which showed surprising results with regard to conditions for men and women, and the exposure of women in the project organization. The study was about a national initiative to counteract ill-health and reduce sickness absenteeism (Brulin and Svensson 2011).

It is a well-known fact that project management is a solitary pursuit, mainly because the project manager often has a different organizational connection, and may experience difficulties in influencing the organization and establishing consensus for development work. Many project managers have an individualized approach that corresponds to the picture given by traditional project management theory of a dynamic and ambitious project manager. It is a way of working which can function in more defined and result-oriented projects, but in order to attain long-term effects, close interaction with steering groups and project owners is required (Andersen 2008).

Project managers who take on too much responsibility are vulnerable and can be affected by reprisals and even mobbing. Conflicts may originate from project management with evident shortcomings in organization and weak involvement in externally financed development work. Project managers run the risk, in such situations, of coming into conflict with leaders in both staff and line organizations, and also with politicians, especially when a project fails to achieve its goals. Projects are time-limited and a project manager often lacks a formal mandate in the organization. A project manager recruited internally, who is driving a development process strongly in project form and who will remain in the organization, risks being a source of discomfort for leaders and management. Externally recruited project managers do not face the same risk since they leave the organization at the end of the project.

The study we referred to above showed that female project managers are more exposed in these respects. Why? It does not appear to be directly dependent on individual differences between the genders, for example, different leadership styles. Possibly women were more ambitious and defended a bottom-up perspective, and they were more often open to participants' interests and requirements. In an organization subject to stress, these requirements can create irritation and come into conflict with priorities in the operational organization. The explanations for gender differences were connected with how recruitment was carried out, education level, different experiences and structural conditions. The women were much more often internally recruited, whilst men were externally recruited, with a higher level of education and a stronger position on the labour market. Men were less dependent on the organization where the project was being run, and thus less exposed in the event of a conflict.

Another explanation was that the project was gender-labelled. Women often worked with competence development, the working environment and health issues, that is, projects based on the participation and involvement of those affected and their leaders, but which were seldom regarded as strategic by management and thus not given high priority. On the other hand, men worked more often with large projects, including new forms of collaboration and health audits, which were not as demanding or threatening for management, but which could be perceived as strategically more important. Male project managers thus had better opportunities to interact with the steering group and project owners, whilst female project managers risked working in greater isolation, without support from the project organization.

Many of the women then chose to try and take responsibility for steering and ownership themselves, which further increased their exposure. When projects failed, they were often made responsible for tasks and functions that were not theirs. Thus the women in a sense 'pawned' their careers. Project management did not become a springboard for career development; in fact the opposite occurred in the form of worsened relationships and weakened involvement. The example of female project managers shows that the rational and consensus-dominating project theory is not sufficient. Instead a new perspective must be brought in for development work to be effective and sustainable.

Contradictions, Interests and Conflicts

There are different ways of viewing and analysing development work. The rationalist approach is just one perspective, even though it may be dominant. An alternative approach is to understand that different actors and groups have different interests, driving forces and goals. This applies particularly in politically steered organizations with external project financing, such as in EU programmes.

In the Lisbon Agenda, it is stated that Structural Funds play an important role in the EU's strategic policy of structural transformation and cohesion. This should contribute to sustainable social and economic development throughout the Union. Based on this overall strategy, Sweden developed a national strategy for the Structural Funds over the period 2007–2013. This states that the Structural Funds should incorporate the three dimensions of social sustainability, environmental sustainability and economic sustainability in all programme implementation phases. Special focus should be placed on equality between women and men, integration and diversity, as well as a better and sustainable environment.

The evaluations carried out show that these political goals were difficult to realize and to create interest in. The process support existing for these questions is seldom used actively and strategically to challenge existing ideas and ways of working. The same can be said about the use of learning through ongoing evaluation. It is difficult to transform programme texts and ambitious goals on gender equality, accessibility and integration into concrete actions.

In the following sections, we will discuss the importance of such political requirements in development work. The intention is not to go into details or formulations, but more to show how political requirements can be combined with driving forces for profitability and regional development. A consequence of these complex projects is that ownership becomes less clear and steering more difficult. Sustainability in these projects can be analysed in terms of the three mechanisms (ownership, collaboration and learning) which we take as our starting points.

How, in a large programme, can impact on horizontal goals be achieved? Will business goals and returns always be superordinate to the horizontal goals? Should work be based on support or steering? Is it knowledge that is poor, or are there counteracting structures where knowledge has no impact?

Integration and Diversity

Three reasons were given for the importance of integration and diversity perspectives in EU programmes: growth, fairness and democracy. Industrial policy in Sweden has, over the course of many years, been interested in entrepreneurship and different kinds of stimulation measures for starting new companies. Companies run by those with foreign-born parents have often found it more difficult to survive and develop. This is because many companies were started by immigrants, but also because they received less support.

The proportion of inhabitants with a foreign background is so large that total growth is strongly affected by this group not receiving the same opportunities as others when it comes to innovation and new business enterprise. Nevertheless, integration and diversity thinking have not had a real impact in different programmes. This applies particularly to the Regional Fund which works to promote entrepreneurship. Using programmes to stimulate and support entrepreneurship is part of a general problem. Some even consider that such programmes may have a negative impact (Storey 2000). Generally the labour market is typified by structural exclusion which programmes and projects can only marginally affect. Programmes seldom succeed in describing participants in a realistic way, and those responsible for projects also experience difficulties in accessing specific target groups due to shortcomings in register data. This is why support measures of different kinds cannot be provided to promote their companies. A number of researchers believe that a new approach is required, one which does not focus on methods and projects, but is more oriented to creating conditions for entrepreneurship by means of powerful political measures (Brulin and Svensson 2011).

Projects and programmes aiming to contribute to integration and diversity have experienced difficulties in achieving this and also in focusing on these issues. The questions become marginalized and neglected in competition with other 'more important' criteria. Evaluation is seldom used to steer projects correctly along these lines, one reason being that integration and diversity are difficult to identify by means of different types of indicators. Often, reliable statistics which allow comparisons between different groups are not available.

If the structure is the problem, why then should one have projects? Projects can still fulfil a function, but more indirectly, and have an impact on ideas and attitudes over time – for example, the view of immigrant women as active, business-oriented and enterprising (Hedlund 2008). Projects can better reach their intended target groups in the following ways: through access to venture capital at a lower level; by taking into account regional differences in the programme; by creating networks; by using existing ethnic networks and outreach activities; by emphasizing integration goals in calls for tenders and in a dialogue with applicants; by evaluators taking the question of integration and diversity seriously.

Gender Equality

The dominant strategies for company development are based on rational goal thinking, where consensus is assumed to exist over goals and instruments, and where differences between groups are overlooked. There are other perspectives on development, where differences in approaches, perspectives, resources, power and interests are clarified (Pettigrew 1985, Collins 1998). The limitations of using a rational perspective and consensus thinking reveal themselves, for instance, when a change has an impact on the distribution of work between men and women in a company. Suddenly change becomes much more difficult to implement, even though it may be effective and contribute to greater profitability. Successful changes are actively worked against, and after a time the original situation is re-established. In order to understand shortcomings in sustainability in development work, more theories are required that deal with power, conflicts of interest, opposition to change, as well as the importance of norms, values and traditions.

Evaluations carried out so far show that gender equality is often something which is added to a project in the final rounds of an application. It is seldom an integral and strategic component in development. The evaluation of implementation in the Social and Regional Funds shows that the question of gender equality is considered difficult, and often viewed as irrelevant for projects. Nor has gender equality had an impact on content or ways of working with development and innovation, despite the fact that evaluators consider that this should have been the case. For this reason, there is a great risk that gender equality becomes a symbolic political issue in the Social and Regional Funds (Brulin and Svensson 2011).

What are the reasons for these difficulties in living up to gender equality requirements? Is it a lack of knowledge or is it due to power and opposition from a male-dominated order? The research referred to above favours the latter explanation. The starting perspective has major consequences on where a solution to the problem can be found. Is factual information sufficient, or is some element of compulsion necessary to bring about more comprehensive changes in gender equality? A study of prioritization patterns in Sweden's innovation policy shows that close to 80 per cent of the innovation systems and clusters given prominence, and which received funds in national and regional policy programmes, mainly involve male-dominated industries. There are two groups of industries that principally dominate: basic and manufacturing industry, and new technology, both of which are mainly male-dominated industries. A lower priority was given to services and 'adventure' tourism, which employ many women. Research from a gender perspective shows a clear pattern. In a number of the studies carried out into innovation systems, the following issues were apparent: 1) women are overlooked and given a lower priority as initiative-takers in innovation and innovation systems; 2) business areas employing many women as company owners or employees are disregarded and given lower priority. The point is that women in general – irrespective of whether they are active in male-dominated, female-dominated or gender-balanced industries – are seldom regarded as a driving force (Brulin and Svensson 2011).

Different researchers have pointed out a number of weaknesses in the support for innovation and entrepreneurship initiatives targeting women. This means that support can have the opposite effect if there is too much gender-'labelling'. Typical of these programmes is what we could refer to as 'gender blindness' concerning delimitation of the area, the view of entrepreneurship, the presentation of the programme and how support is made available. Women are not attracted by the support and they do not feel that they are there for their company. The researchers consider that a deeper understanding of these relationships is required and new support forms and methods must be designed from a gender-theory perspective. They also wish to shift the focus from the individual entrepreneur to factors at the system level which make the participation of women more difficult.

An important question is what theories govern work on gender equality, and what importance is gender equality given in the dominant theories on development work. In theories about business and performance management, the gender dimension is weakly developed. The same applies to theories about strategic development, projects and project management, which we touched on above. These theories need to be supplemented by results from gender research to be useful in work on sustainable development.

Here there are a large number of theories to choose between, but they have different perspectives and points of departure. Gender budgeting involves analysing how public funds are used from a gender perspective, that is, distribution of funds between men and women. One problem with formalizing gender equality in this way and its measurement in purely economic terms is that contradictions and conflicts are not easily visible. An even distribution of funds is no guarantee of gender equality. This is a political goal and it is not certain that it would be accepted in circles where narrow business values and consensus-oriented management thinking dominate. Questions about gender equality must be made transparent and a deeper analysis carried out if fundamental power structures are to be changed. Different evaluations of large programmes show this shortcoming in the analysis.

A dominant trend is gender equality integration, which means that gender equality should be mainstreamed. The aim is to develop an activity by increasing efficiency and quality, but this should take place through taking into account the needs and preconditions of both genders. Women should not receive worse healthcare or services because men have been made the norm in research and decision-making processes. Experience shows that this perspective on gender equality makes it easier to get acceptance from professional groups, managers and politicians. At the same time there is a risk that attempts to promote gender equality policy will fade into the background and that mobilization against unfairness will be made more difficult if the perspective of 'usefulness' becomes too narrow and dominant (Hedlund 2008).

Practical Guidelines in the Form of Three Ps

If we transform the theoretical discussion in this chapter into practical reasoning, what will the conclusions then be? No simple templates or instructions on how to organize projects and run ongoing evaluation exist, but it would be useful to summarize the task of ongoing evaluation in terms of the three Ps – *project logic, processes* and *public debate.*

Ongoing evaluation should critically examine project logic and state how a project can work in line with the goals set up and the results aimed for. Evaluation must critically examine the following: whether research activities can contribute to innovations which lead to results that can be commercialized; whether education can be expected to lead to greater employability and business development; whether the project is based on an analysis of conditions and earlier experiences from development work. If there are shortcomings in project logic in these respects, there is a low probability that the project will lead to sustainable development.

The importance of understanding processes is fundamental to learning evaluation. Running projects successfully involves managing processes that are interwoven with other development processes in the region and in the organizations where projects are run. Process indicators – reflecting learning, participation, ownership and steering – are supplemented by different result indicators, which also deal with the impact on the local environment where the project is run.

Ongoing evaluators also have the task of contributing to public debate and learning about the Structural Fund programmes. Public debate not only involves providing information about results, but above all creating a public debate about conditions, results and effects. The task of ongoing evaluation is to ensure that knowledge of learning examples is disseminated and becomes generally accessible, that is, knowledge of how goals are reached on innovations, commercialization, new jobs and companies, as well as on inclusion in the labour market. Evaluators also have a great responsibility for ensuring that knowledge and results are reported and communicated in different networks to promote the exchange of that knowledge and experience. The focus of learning and evaluation should be on the innovative and pioneering phases of a project.

4

Evaluation for Sustainable Development

Managers and decision-makers need to continuously evaluate and learn in order to be able to steer development work appropriately. Steering requires knowledge about goals, requirements, processes, outcomes, results and effects. The difficulties of steering complex development projects, despite clear goals and a predetermined plan, are well-known. The alternative, however, is not to do away with steering, but make it more flexible and relate it to learning from continuously generated experience (Engwall 2002). Participants and those responsible need to learn from past experiences and mistakes to be able to subsequently make corrections and know that they are on the right path. This provides motivation, data for further work and knowledge about what different activities and measures might lead to. Financiers need to continuously learn from projects and programmes, both during and between programming periods, so that new calls and decisions can be based on experience gained from earlier projects. The focus in this chapter is on learning through ongoing evaluation, where the aim is to make development work sustainable, that is, generate long-term effects.

The aim of evaluation is to establish what difference a specific measure makes. Evaluation is done systematically in order to assess an activity, measure, programme or product. It is a critical and investigative process, where established methods are used in a professional way (Svensson et al. 2009). Often critical checking is confused with disapproval. In this interpretation, being critical is being negative, being sceptical and rejecting. However, the main point of a critical examination process is the precise opposite – to be constructive. If we follow in the footsteps of Immanuel Kant's *Critique of Pure Reason*, the critical checking process deals with in-depth scrutiny of a phenomenon in order to investigate its properties and limitations. In this sense, learning evaluation can be compared to a process of critical examination.

How this is done can vary, but it presupposes proximity, continuity and involvement between participants and evaluators. Continuity in examination makes ongoing feedback of data and experiences possible, as well as joint analysis and discussion of conclusions, which together can lay the foundations for future development work. (Of course, we are fully aware of the extreme scenario where, due to mismanagement, the continuation of a project becomes impossible if it does not receive the approval of the evaluators.)

One means of taking critical examination processes forward is that the evaluator invites participants to analysis seminars where participants jointly interpret and discuss preliminary results. On such occasions, the whole organization should be represented including the financiers. The methods used in the critical examination process can vary but do not differ much from those which are normally used in traditional evaluation, except for the involvement, continuity in feedback and learning processes that supplement it. In learning through ongoing evaluation, emphasis is put on joint and ongoing learning between evaluators and participants.

Evaluation can be carried out internally or externally, that is, by independent researchers or consultants. An internal evaluation is mainly concerned with following up different activities or measures, whilst external evaluations are often more overarching and focus on the quality, results and effects of different programmes. At the same time the value of self-evaluation should not be underestimated. There are examples of both project owners and project managers who have been able to critically examine their own input by taking on the role of self-evaluators, synthesizing experiences of what has functioned better and worse, and have thus formed knowledge through such self-reflection. The question of why an external evaluation is needed is primarily related to credibility and critical distance.

An evaluation should 'stir up' the status quo, that is, question, problematize and criticize. This is essential if outsiders are to rely on the results that emerge. But critical distance also helps participants to view things in a new way. Critical distance is attained by linking evaluation to theory, to the surrounding world, and opening it up to public discussion. In this book we discuss the evaluation of large, publicly funded programmes and projects. The ambition when evaluating these is that they are examined in some type of public context. The Structural Funds are intended to lead to structural transformation. Public debate about different programmes and projects creates a multiplier effect in itself since the very act of making it public creates interest among a well-informed populace about the tasks and problems that programmes and projects aim to solve.

Different Generations of Evaluation

How is learning through ongoing evaluation related to other forms of evaluation? From an historical perspective of evaluation, different patterns can be identified that have either developed over time or have been undertaken in parallel. Guba and Lincoln (1989) discuss from an American perspective four generations of evaluation which can be viewed in relation to aims such as measurement, description, values and dialogue. The first generation, developed during the early decades of the twentieth century, was dominated by measurement, and was initially developed through tests on students. The starting point was a non-problematized, technical, limited and neutral view of evaluation. The aim was to measure a specific phenomenon, not to explain or problematize it.

The second generation of evaluation was descriptive. It involved studying or mapping goal achievement, often in large programmes and policy reforms relating to improvements in society and standards of living. The results were described in relation to the initiatives. In this generation of evaluation, the perspective was also delimited and not problematized, as if evaluation was value-neutral. Although the prerequisites and goals of the reform were not challenged, there was a desire to develop better tools and methods in order to implement new programmes and reforms. With knowledge and facts, the world could be improved. The perspective was future-oriented, and not, as in the first generation, retrospective. This kind of evaluation, which was very popular during the 1960s, was typified by strong elements of social engineering.

In the third generation, evaluation has been given a more independent, autonomous and critical checking function. This involves determining the relative merits of different initiatives, that is, making assessments of goals, aims and visions. The evaluator now becomes a judge, an independent examiner. Assessment in this generation can be made on the basis of a greater range of independent criteria and perspectives, and not, as earlier, just from the perspective of an authority. Research becomes important and is viewed as a guarantee of independence. Theories become significant in order to understand context, analyse effects and generalize the results. The linkage to research gives status and legitimacy, although there are substantial risks in expert thinking and a top-down perspective. The point of departure was to arrive at the best possible solution and a single truth.

Fourth-generation evaluation, discussed by Guba and Lincoln (1989), questions this unequivocal one-sidedness. Instead the complexity of a situation is emphasized, together with how it can be understood from different perspectives and where different interests are represented. The focus is on dialogue, participants' understanding and individual meaning-making (a responsive constructivist evaluation). The importance of identifying different interests and the dialogue between them is emphasized. Research-based evaluation is advocated, as is a pluralistic approach, where the answers are less definitive, results more context-related and the links more complex. Different methods are used and combined freely. Analysis is based on a holistic, partnership and process perspective that takes participants' experiences and perceptions into account within the framework of a joint and equal learning process. Overall, a clear development can be identified with regard to the models and ideas about evaluation, from a more limited, technical and non-problematic view to an approach that is more complex, questioning, theory-based, interactive and related to the surrounding world. The ambitions of evaluation have increased with the four successive generations. In summary, it can be stated that evaluation has become more pluralistic with regard to who takes part and the methods and assessment criteria used.

The view of evaluation expressed in this book is in line with the developments described above. Evaluation is regarded as a support for learning, critical examination and reflection. However, we emphasize the interactive (research) approach – both for its benefits and usability, but above all to increase quality and support for analysis. We consider that none of the first four generations of evaluation are appropriate for learning through ongoing evaluation that should be practically useful in terms of critical assessment and should also contribute to long-term effects and the development of theory. Our approach to evaluation is based on dialogue, interaction and participatory inquiry as central elements. This interactive approach to evaluation is also consistent with how we view the relation between researchers and participants in interactive research (Aagaard Nielsen and Svensson 2006). It is worth noting how interactive research is blended together with learning through ongoing evaluation by emphasizing joint knowledge formation processes, continuity and involvement in the phenomena that knowledge is formed from, and expectations over contributing to public transparency and debate.

For evaluation to contribute to long-term sustainability in development and the generation of multiplier effects for learning, we have tried to formulate an alternative approach, namely fifth-generation evaluation.[1] This alternative

---

1   Patton (2010) talks about *developmental evaluation* in a similar way. It includes the following elements: an ongoing and learning approach; a system perspective with dynamic relationships;

should be regarded as no more than a tentative idea, an approach that is under development. This fifth generation of evaluation combines elements of the earlier generations where critical examination and constructive dialogue were primary elements. In addition, the fifth generation supplements the earlier generation of evaluation models with requirements for links to theory, surrounding world monitoring and contributions to long-term learning. Fifth-generation evaluation should result in a learning product attracting the interest of the public sphere. The learning product synthesizes different experiences and knowledge. Feedback from experience and knowledge formation enables the generation of multiplier effects in other activities.

Fifth-generation evaluation requires methodological competence for constructive criticism covering both individuals and organizations. In the fifth generation, the main task of the evaluator is to organize reflective learning processes to enable ongoing critical and constructive evaluation of large projects and programmes to achieve ongoing improvements. But critical examination in the form of evaluation is carried out not just to determine the value of an initiative, but also to evaluate it in relation to the overarching goals. The evaluation approach is rational as regards goals and instruments, at the same time as there is a clear requirement to contribute to further learning. Our view is that it is possible to study and assess cause and effect within the framework of a learning evaluation without necessarily needing controlled and randomized studies. On the contrary, such attempts at simple 'evidence-based realism' are doomed to failure in broad social programme and project initiatives. The focus on these should be on long-term effects rather than direct outcomes and short-term results, that is, analysing which measures contribute to sustainable development. The analysis of cause and effect thus becomes more complicated, although it is possible to develop indicators of what is required for results to lead to long-term effects. The analysis can be facilitated by joint knowledge formation between participants and evaluators where contextual conditions are clear (Aagaard Nielsen and Svensson 2006).

The learning perspective is crucial in fifth-generation evaluation and should take place both in and between projects, and cover both the individual and organizations. The evaluations should also lead to the incorporation of results and knowledge in future projects and programmes, and they should contribute to strategic impact. The strategic role of evaluation is perhaps what most

---

a rapid response to changes made; working with emerging ideas; trying to find general principles and adapting them to new contexts.

clearly distinguishes the fifth generation from earlier generations of evaluation. The goal of fifth-generation evaluation, in other words, is joint knowledge formation for long-term sustainable development. The hope is that evaluation will generate multiplier effects at local, regional, national and supranational levels. Learning through ongoing evaluation is thus a logical approach to evaluating programmes and projects for growth driven by knowledge and sustainable development.

Learning and Reflection

The role of learning is essential in a complex system. The learning used cannot be too precise. It must give an observant participant a practical sense of how complicated things are and how they are related. There are both psychological (hubris and biases) and philosophical (mathematical) limits to learning, especially when it comes to rare events. Rare events cannot be predicted by reliance on the past or on theories of probability. It is better to have no maps rather than bad maps. The simplified and academified notion of evidence is useless in a complicated world. Sustainable change must be based on a careful analysis of data and an assessment of the unknown uncertainties and the risks of failure (Taleb 2010: 128).

Learning and reflection are increasingly emphasized as crucial to the survival and autonomous development of projects, particularly in theories about innovation systems and regional development. Traditional planning-controlled, linear and mechanistic development models are criticized for their lack of reflection and developmental learning when applied to new and complex problems (Adler, Shani and Styhre 2004). Development work based on feedback and 'learning loops' is considered to be more effective in contexts where peoples' involvement and participation create the prerequisites for the success and impact of development work. It appears that theories about organizational leaning have affected views on project development, but it is mainly innovative and developmental learning that is emphasized (Ellström 2001, Elkjaer 2001, Engeström 1996, March 1991). Emphasis on openness and learning in development does not mean that planning itself is unimportant, but rather that evaluation which provides too much focus on following up direct outcomes and short-term results in terms of measurable goals can be misconceived, and thereby make sustainable development more difficult. Then there is a risk that the outcome from activities and short-term results becomes the focal point, rather than the long-term effects.

It is important to clarify what is meant by process evaluation, and how it is differentiated from learning through ongoing evaluation. Process-oriented or formative evaluation takes place at an early stage and recurs (Tessmer 1993), involves feedback (above all to the project managers) in order to improve what is being studied (George and Cowan 1999), but does not cover the developmental responsibility of the evaluator (Cronbach 1982, Scriven 1998); it is also flexible, in that a number of different methods are used (Chen 2004). Process evaluation, or so-called formative evaluation, however, differs from learning through ongoing evaluation in certain respects. Development work can be evaluated continuously without any organized learning process and definitively without any learning process for public debate. Learning can also take place without being process-oriented. Ex-post evaluation is definitively aimed at learning, namely in relation to other development work and future programmes, but not for improving the project or programme that have been evaluated.

Learning through ongoing evaluation takes place in the form of an organized learning process that takes place continuously and as a part of development work. The aim is to improve development work, both with regard to short-term results and long-term effects. The learning involves participants, project managers, project owners, financiers, and so on, which means that learning takes place at both an individual and organizational level (see also Ellström 2009). This can be conducted through learning and analysis seminars, where representatives of the whole project organization are supposed to discuss a report which the ongoing evaluator has produced and analyse further steps to be taken to develop the project at hand. Learning through ongoing evaluation can also be used in more strategic, long-term and systematic considerations to analyse and critically reflect on both goals and instruments.

In summary, the value of a project can be assessed in different ways – in terms of satisfaction, alignment, process outcomes, business outcomes and return on investment. A comprehensive study of projects in different countries shows that such a measurement of project implementation was never made in the 65 case-study organizations (Thomas and Mullaly 2008: 246). Despite this, more than half of the organizations could demonstrate that both tangible and intangible values had been realized from the implementation of the projects. But many of these organizations had no assurance of sustaining this value. In some organizations, values were declining, in fact being destroyed (Thomas and Mullaly 2008: 357). A sustainable change process must allow for the continuous creation of value. The refinement and renewal of implementation is needed in order to enable continued sustainment of the implementation. The same study points to the necessity of analysing the value of projects in relation to their implementation and context.

Interactive Research and Learning through Ongoing Evaluation

Learning through ongoing evaluation is closely related to and overlaps with interactive research. It does not mean that there must be a researcher who carries out the ongoing evaluation, but that an approach that resembles interactive research is used. Learning through ongoing evaluation involves the systematic use of theoretically derived concepts and hypotheses. Problems and challenges that projects and programmes face should be analysed in the light of the theoretical state of the art and discussions in the surrounding community, and be presented in public debate. Ongoing evaluation means taking a critical approach, using well-established methods and linking with research findings. Above all, the research aspect entails an attempt to obtain greater transparency and public debate through the evaluation approach chosen.

However, ongoing evaluation also differs from traditional academic research. The aim of learning through ongoing evaluation is primarily to continuously contribute to steering projects and programmes towards their stated goals. A further aim is to feed the results and experiences gained from the project and programme back into the public debate. There is also an ambition to contribute to systematic learning about how, for example, general challenges such as regional growth and labour market policies can be carried out in better forms. In this respect, knowledge formation in collaboration with the research community plays an important role.

Our view is that in a research approach to evaluation, the research and consultancy roles can to some extent be merged. Many consultancy firms employ researchers or collaborate with them. Some researchers carry out evaluations parallel with their regular work. In addition, there is also considerable experience of evaluation in the consultancy world, where well-established knowledge of how it can work in different contexts exists with a high guarantee of delivery. At the same time, the research community has a completely different tradition of reporting back in a wider and public context.

A New Evaluation Approach

We have discussed above what learning through ongoing evaluation can cover and what it entails. In the following sections, we will relate this evaluation approach to an illustrative case of programme implementation and its related project catalogue in the EU Structural Fund. Since Sweden became a member of the EU, more than 100,000 small and large projects have received EU

Structural Fund financing. In the first two programming periods, 1995–1999 and 2000–2006, Sweden received around 30 billion Swedish crowns. In the third programming period, 2007–2013, Sweden will receive more than 17.7 billion Swedish crowns from the Structural Funds, of which more than 9 billion will go to the eight Regional Fund programmes, and more than 7 billion to the national Social Programme. The requirement of at least 50 per cent national co-funding in all projects completed with co-funding from the business sector means that the Structural Funds will have about 40 billion Swedish crowns available during the programming period.

How can and should such large programmes be evaluated? Evaluation in previous programming periods has been very conventional, ex ante, mid-term and ex post. Evaluation has been regarded as just for its own sake. Evaluations carried out have been ritual and symbolic activities rather than processes for critical and constructive knowledge formation. There has been a lack of processes for feedback of experiences and an absence of approaches for learning from generated knowledge. The evaluations in the programmes have either come too early (mid-term evaluations) or too late (update of the mid-term evaluation and ex-post evaluation). Mid-term evaluations have often given a somewhat split and fuzzy view of what has been achieved, at the same time as they have often been fairly general. The initial costs of mid-term evaluations have been high, a fact that has been criticized by the managing authorities responsible for implementing the programmes, whereas knowledge feedback has often been regarded as marginal. The critique of previous evaluations indicates the difficulty and complexity of making accurate evaluations that create sustainable impact on regional growth, structural change and job creation. Since Structural Funds are part of a political area which itself is part of a significantly broader context, this becomes an even worse, more costly problem.

Neither those responsible for implementation of programmes and projects, nor those regional development actors that have co-funded, have felt that they have received knowledge from evaluation at the right time and in the right form to be able to have an impact on implementation. Nor does the general understanding and legitimacy of the Structural Funds appear to have been affected positively by the evaluation done in earlier programming periods. The ritual element in evaluation appears to have been significant. Too often evaluators have come up with a conclusion such as: this has been good, this worse, but overall it is a well-run set-up. It has been evaluation without any learning potential whatsoever in respect of the overarching goals and development which the programmes and projects are supposed to boost.

As a result of criticism of the evaluation undertaken in previous programming periods, the EU Commission has recommended that a new approach to evaluation be used for the current programming period, namely ongoing evaluation. In Sweden, an approach that was labelled 'learning through ongoing evaluation' has been used by the Social Fund and the Regional Fund programmes. The ambition is to promote learning with a clear focus on regional growth and job creation.

As a consequence of this criticism of the evaluation, the huge amount of small projects has been lowered. During this programming period, the overgrown 'flora' of projects that characterized the previous period has been turned in to less, but larger, strategic projects. The idea is that large projects can have more professional project management, active ownership and ongoing evaluation. However, we know that large strategic projects do not necessarily tend to be more efficient (Svensson et al. 2009). For instance, there are clear indications that large projects often have long start-up phases, where ownership is at times unclear, as are goals, distribution of tasks and responsibility, especially where a project consists of a number of sub-projects. Not least, the transition to large projects has made it urgent to invest in learning through ongoing evaluation.

Another area that needs to be given more attention, and which is also part of the strategy above, is the validation of project results, both in comparison with other similar projects and by means of scientific methods. Involving relevant actors in learning through ongoing evaluation, especially those which can contribute to multiplier effects – universities, university colleges, learning centres, R&D centres, business associations, and so on, is regarded as essential. It is also important that individual projects are encouraged to work in different thematic project clusters in order to enhance learning from each other. Furthermore, learning based on ongoing evaluation should be stimulated in and between regions in Sweden, as well as transnationally between member states of the EU.

What Has Been Done?

The Regional and Social Funds in Sweden have taken substantial steps to realize the idea of learning through ongoing evaluation. The Swedish government (Government Communication 2009/10: 221) states that it has set aside significant resources for learning and evaluation in the programming period 2007–2013, in order to ensure both long-term effects and continuing improvements in projects and programmes:

Evaluation approaches have been designed in such a way that learning and exchange of experiences between the Structural Fund programmes should be ensured. The government monitors this work in order to initiate proposals for necessary adjustments to the programmes. Ongoing evaluation is carried out at three levels: project, programme and implementing organisational level. All in all, evaluation initiatives will provide opportunities for lasting ongoing learning and improvement. It is essential that all actors involved in work on regional growth participate in evaluation and that learning between both projects and different administrative levels is stimulated. The lessons learned from follow-up and evaluation implemented within the framework of the Structural Fund programme should also be leveraged for the implementation of other measures in regional growth policy.

Learning systems in both the Regional and Social Funds also have the aim of generating knowledge for the implementation organization, as well as contributing to development and quality assurance. The ambition of learning can be summarized in the following aims linked to different phases in a project:

- ensuring that regional development actors have sufficient knowledge of results from ongoing and completed projects to develop and improve future decisions – the *project initiation* phase;

- ensuring that the decision-making organization (the Structural Fund partnerships) has sufficient knowledge of potential projects in order to decide which projects should be supported – the *project prioritization* phase;

- ensuring that prospective projects have sufficient knowledge about the aims and overarching goals of the programme, and also ensuring that ongoing projects have opportunities to learn by their own ongoing evaluation and others' implementation – the *project implementation* phase.

The idea of learning through ongoing evaluation, as stated in EU guidelines and in the interpretation by the Regional and Social Funds in Sweden, could be summarized in the following way: learning through ongoing evaluation is not regarded as a method that can be determined once and for all, but should rather be seen as an approach and a perspective which aim to continuously improve programmes and projects. However, the methods used will vary according to the situation, the task and the conditions. Learning through ongoing evaluation is characterized by the following:

1.   formative, that is, process-based and ongoing;

2.   critically examining;

3.   initiated in the early stages of a programme or project;

4.   requires proximity to the participants and their involvement;

5.   should be of direct use to those concerned;

6.   presupposes ongoing feedback with various levels of ambition, from one-way feedback to dialogue and joint knowledge formation;

7.   creates cooperation and joint knowledge formation between different actors;

8.   researches project goal achievement in respect of overarching programme goals, but with an awareness that goals can be changed over time;

9.   gives rise to multiplier effects, leading to developmental learning in other development activities and in public debate.

There is reason to emphasize that this type of summary is preliminary. Additional points will be added to the list above. It is possible to reinterpret, depending on the needs which learning through ongoing evaluation should measure up to. No expert can provide ready answers or clear-cut definitions, since ongoing evaluation is expected to provide feedback and learning in a changing world and be used in politically steered contexts.

What Can We See So Far?

What lessons can be drawn from the implementation of learning through ongoing evaluation so far, that is, in the middle of the programming period. A study (see Brulin and Svensson 2011) shows consistently positive results:

•   a high level of awareness that a new approach, that is, learning through ongoing evaluation, was introduced (93–100 per cent), but lower amongst evaluators themselves (67 per cent);

•   considered important (82–89 per cent);

- importance of getting started early in the project (about 75 per cent make this assessment);

- 90 per cent responded that feedback reporting takes place, often in both written and spoken forms;

- two thirds considered that the new approach to evaluation led to practical changes in projects and programmes;

- two thirds considered that processes, results and indicated long-term effects should be evaluated;

- the vast majority considered that a good balance was struck between proximity and distance.

However, many argued that it was still too small a proportion of resources set aside for ongoing evaluation (with substantial variation between regions). There were different interpretations of what learning means in practice (according to 40–50 per cent in the response groups). Furthermore there were different views about who had the greatest influence on content and implementation of the evaluation, as well as to whom the evaluator is accountable – project manager, steering group, owner of the project or the managing authority. Overall, we make the assessment that we have sufficient material to draw certain conclusions from the learning through ongoing evaluation carried out so far. Our conclusions can be summarized in terms of the following critical points:

- There is a risk of the ongoing evaluator becoming a 'deputy project manager'.

- There are shortcomings in purchasing competence for procurement.

- An evaluation plan with clear expectations for learning through ongoing evaluation is often lacking in funding applications.

- Too few resources are set aside for interactive research and ongoing evaluation.

- There is too often a focus on outcomes and activities, rather than critical examination of results and long-term effects in respect to the overarching goals.

- Lack of access to interactive researchers and skilled ongoing evaluators, experienced in learning through ongoing evaluation, leads to inferior participation in public debate.

We will comment on these conclusions in what follows, particularly by focusing on evaluations of individual projects, since this is where the major weaknesses appear. We will also briefly discuss what can be done to strengthen learning evaluation in projects.

THE RISK THAT THE ONGOING EVALUATOR BECOMES A 'DEPUTY PROJECT MANAGER'

With whom should the interactive researcher and ongoing evaluator cooperate and learn together? In a study of the evaluation system during the previous programming period, it was argued that the task of the managing authorities should be to support the development of methods and feedback of results from projects to a wide group of stakeholders, if the results were to lead to the renewal of the country's regions. Learning through ongoing evaluation close to operational activities – in the project and at the regional level – should provide the foundation for knowledge formation to promote innovation and renewal. Learning within and between projects must become better, as must feedback in the regional discussion, if effective growth, innovation and development strategies are to function. Furthermore it is argued in the study that 'the forms for exchange of experience and learning within and between different levels of the organization, and also within and between regions, should be facilitated so that participants are able to benefit from each other's experiences through feedback'.

The Structural Funds have a huge learning mission. They should, by changing, improving and strengthening regional growth policy and job creation, contribute to the development of competitive regions. The learning mission can also be interpreted as a requirement that the Structural Funds should contribute to a more knowledge-driven regional development strategy. The ambition to achieve learning is thus high and there are many target groups.

How has learning been organized, and who were the target groups of the learning processes? Despite the high ambitions, it is possible to interpret the requirement for learning through ongoing evaluation in a more limited way, where the focus is mainly on organizational learning for more effective implementation of programmes and projects. Our experiences show that it is too often directed at supporting project management. There are a number of explanations as to why this has been the case. Often, it is the project management which has been the actual purchaser of the evaluation, and has had most contact with the evaluators and had time to digest the reports. In this respect, evaluation has been close and process-oriented. On the other hand, steering groups, project owners, coordinators, partnerships and external actors were seldom actively involved in an ongoing and critical dialogue with the evaluator.

Structural Fund partnerships, management authorities and regional development actors do not seem to use evaluation in a systematic way to draw up selection criteria, to initiate projects, in prioritization and in support of project implementation. Those responsible for programme implementation seem to lack systematic information on how projects that have already been decided on are developed with respect to goal attainment, results and effects. A questionnaire which was directed to decision-making organizations shows, however, that the Structural Fund partnerships generally wish to receive more knowledge about the project, and particularly better knowledge of how they should prioritize projects in relation to each other, and in relation to their costs.

A too narrow target group for evaluation, that is, project and process management, is due primarily to a lack of demand from other groups. Most of them are not used to using evaluation; there is a weak culture of evaluation in much programme and project implementation, and there is an even weaker understanding of how to learn through ongoing evaluation. In Chapter 1, we highlighted effective project organization as vital for sustainability in development work. Learning through ongoing evaluation should link together the levels in the project and programme organization and make this more transparent. It can be a means of helping project owners to act more proactively, the steering group to act more strategically and the authorities to learn from ongoing projects as regards fulfilling the overarching goals. Such a coherent and strategic function does not fully match up with how learning through ongoing evaluation has functioned hitherto, although steps have been taken in this direction in the Regional and Social Funds in Sweden. Major ongoing evaluation initiatives have been taken in programmes and projects. Reports have been submitted to the monitoring committees and Structural Fund partnerships. Regional and national learning conferences have been held. Nevertheless, the goal of a more knowledge-driven regional growth and development policy is still not at hand. A culture of learning through ongoing evaluation is still absent.

SHORTCOMINGS IN PURCHASING COMPETENCE

The ongoing evaluation system presupposes learning as an integral part of all project plans and that its inclusion is a natural part of the project. There are a number of different ways in which projects can satisfy these demands – by integrating different systems for self-evaluation in projects, or linking external evaluation to monitor the project. The idea is that evaluation, in order to be beneficial to projects, should be ongoing and contribute continuously to the further development of projects.

There exists, however, a lack of understanding of learning through ongoing evaluation in a number of areas and at different levels – amongst project management, project owners, managing authorities, regional development actors, state agents, and so on. One explanation may be that project logic dominates interest in development logic, that is, the focus is on the outcome of activities and short-term results, rather than long-term effects. Project logic involves taking decisions, making a rapid start, following the project plan, reporting activities and their outcomes, completing on time and reporting financial status. If this logic, which of course must be included in all publicly funded activities, becomes too strong and dominant, interest in learning and critical reflection will decrease. An offer of ongoing evaluation can, in this perspective, be regarded as a disturbing and demanding phase in the work to set up the project. The question is how a situation where learning through ongoing evaluation is not taken seriously or given priority in the project, or the implementing organization, could be changed. One way so far has been to impose requirements, among other things, on an evaluation plan, and on clear roles and processes for reporting.

EVALUATION PLANS ARE TOO OFTEN NON-EXISTENT

The starting point is that all projects should have a plan for evaluation, either through self-assessment or through an external ongoing evaluator or interactive researcher. Ongoing evaluation should be procured in open competition, and roles and structures on how evaluation results should be continuously fed back must be clarified in advance. With clearer requirements, possibly more elements of learning through ongoing evaluation can be incorporated into projects, such as more professional handling and greater focus on evaluation, but this is not sufficient, particularly if the aim is to create active interest. Instead long-term work is required to demonstrate the benefits of the approach, particularly in order to increase the quality and efficiency of projects. The strategy must be to continue with and intensify training (in the form of courses, networking, seminars, and so on) which has been started by both authorities. Learning examples from ongoing projects can be used to show the value of ongoing evaluation. The requirement for an evaluation plan must thus be combined with time and support for learning throughout the implementation organization (including financiers), if the ambitions are to be fulfilled.

TOO FEW RESOURCES ARE SET ASIDE

The level of scarce resources set aside for evaluation is a problem both in the Regional and Social Funds. The recommendation from the Swedish Agency for Economic and Regional Growth is that about 4 per cent should be set aside for evaluation (in a project with total financing of 20 million Swedish crowns), which would mean about 800,000 Swedish crowns in a project of this size. In the Social Fund, a number of projects did not set aside any resources for external evaluation, and often the amounts were very small (about 100,000–200,000 Swedish crowns). In practice, this means that it is very hard to carry out an evaluation with the ambitions presented in the programme. In projects relating to the competence development of employees, a somewhat higher proportion has been set aside for evaluation and the proportion for national projects is even higher (5.65 per cent). There are also clear variations in how much is invested in evaluation in the different regions, where the amounts range between 2.20 and 3.70 per cent. Paradoxically, it appears to be the case that the larger the project, the greater the amount invested in evaluation. At the same time, the figures and comparisons above show that learning through ongoing evaluation has not been given the priority which was envisaged. Variations between types of calls for tender and regions show, moreover, that there are diverse views on the value of learning through ongoing evaluation within different co-working organizations.

FOCUS ON OUTCOMES AND ACTIVITIES

Learning through ongoing evaluation is something new that many are either not familiar with or are unable to see its value. Evaluations of large programmes – especially for innovation, entrepreneurship and labour market policies – encounter difficulties in demonstrating goal attainment, results and above all long-term effects. During the previous programming period, the Swedish National Audit Office carried out an examination into the internal steering and control. The examination showed that control of the Structural Funds focused excessively on compliance with laws and rules, as did the financial reporting of projects, rather than on their effectiveness in relation to the overarching goals. Follow-up and evaluation, in other words, had focused far too little on the contribution of the project to regional growth and employment.

The lack of analysis, reflection and learning frequently involves excessive confidence in indicators and follow-up systems (Ellström 2009). Systems for follow-up and evaluation have seldom been designed for evaluation during the 'journey' or for a critical analysis of effects attained. Many project managers are good at initiating and implementing projects, but less ambitious when it comes to comparing, analysing and reflecting, as well as communicating experiences from the different projects they have run. Knowledge of successful and less successful components of projects is not generated on a sufficiently wide scale. Instead of encouraging a constructive public discussion, evaluation reports and follow-up often involve documentation and technicalities of administrative procedures.

Ensuring that universities and university colleges – which received the largest amounts of funds from the Regional Fund during the programming period 2007–2013 – become genuinely more innovative, that is, transform knowledge into commercial applications and real development ideas, presupposes a high degree of experimentation and some unusual relationship-building with other partners. These are processes which cannot simply be pre-determined, and are thus difficult to control in advance and evaluate in a pre-planned manner. The task becomes one of ensuring that learning through ongoing evaluation is achieved.

LACK OF ACCESS TO THE RIGHTINTERACTIVE RESEARCHERS AND ONGOING EVALUATORS

Projects in both the Social Fund and the Regional Fund have as a goal the development and testing of new methods within a given area of activity or the development of innovations. If real knowledge is to be attained of which working methods – for instance, policies concerning the labour market policy, innovation and growth – are actually better than others, different projects must be allowed to try different methods where results will differ. In other words the planning-steered developmental model is not suitable for creating knowledge of performance in this type of innovative development project where the definitive outcome cannot be defined in advance. In fact, the very purpose of the Regional and Social Funds is method development. The purpose is to find methods that over time will lead to better ways of working and new knowledge to disseminate. However, one weak link has been finding out how projects obtain knowledge from other projects or from evaluations of other projects.

There are a large number of experienced evaluators and interactive researchers on the market, but few have experience of working with learning through ongoing evaluation. Higher education has produced around a 200 people with qualifications in learning through ongoing evaluation. At least the same number has participated in different networks for evaluators. In this way, the authorities, in collaboration with higher education and process support, have contributed to the rapid development of competence. This group with training and experience is often otherwise involved, and in different parts of the country it may be difficult to obtain tenders from qualified applicants for ongoing evaluation. However, this problem will be transitory, and plans exist for future education and training, as well as the ambition of organizing new networks and conferences.

Proposals for Improvement

What can be done to improve learning through ongoing evaluation? We believe that the idea itself is sound, but that the difficulties are mainly due to shortcomings in implementation. Our conclusions and proposals for improvements can be summarized as follows:

1.   Create conditions for systematic learning from approved projects (ongoing and completed). Such learning has a number of purposes, but two of the most important are disseminating knowledge on success factors, and risks in projects and other regional development, as well as transferring this knowledge to those making decisions on new projects. Both funds have not invested enough in this type of learning. In addition, there is a need for clearer steering and better coordination of learning through ongoing evaluation in projects.

2.   A clearer standard needs to be established to determine what should be included in self-evaluation. Creating an evaluation culture resembling what exists in 'lean' production requires that the project itself organizes and procures evaluation and ongoing evaluation in order to accomplish continuous improvements. At the same time, this poses a dilemma for the independence of evaluators. The dilemma over the independence of evaluators in relation to purchasers could be resolved by clearer demands in the evaluation. This also applies to how results should be fed back to authorities and implementation organizations.

3.   The project's contribution to changing, improving and strengthening regional growth and the creation of jobs is the central issue for

learning through ongoing evaluation. The long-term sustainability of the project should be assessed. Evaluation must thus combine the process approach with a study of outcomes, results and long-term effects with respect to overarching goals for the programme.

4.   None of the funds have in practice succeeded in creating rapid and clear feedback of knowledge from ongoing evaluators to decision-makers at the project level. The main information about project development is collected regularly by the authorities through status reports, requisition of funds and reports from project and ongoing evaluation. This information is not used for steering and developmental purposes. An important part of achieving learning at the authority level involves how evaluation results from projects are received in the organizations. Making full use of the learning potential requires that the implementing organization is able to access the knowledge in an effective way. For this reason, it is important to clarify how recipient processes function.

5.   At a more general level, however, the assessment of evaluators is that decision-making organizations, despite their shortcomings, have reasonable access to knowledge. The main sources for this knowledge are the dialogue which the authorities have with the project and the measures which, in the first instance, the authorities responsible for regional development implement, as well as evaluation measures that have already been implemented.

6.   Furthermore, results should also be reported to the authorities and ongoing evaluation should contribute to the public debate. The thematic groups can play an important role in this work. One problem with the thematic groups, however, has been their relatively weak linkage to the regional level. There has also been a complex set of problems surrounding thematic groups, namely coordination, general efficiency and cost-effectiveness.

7.   And last but not least, organizing for *broader* learning is pivotal for success in a societal context. The Regional Fund does not have the same scope as the Social Fund for enabling programmes to contribute to the learning impact on societal actors outside the responsibility area of the Structural Funds. The key factors in further dissemination of learning in the Regional Fund have mainly been ongoing programme evaluators and public debate. The 'learning conferences' have also been important for further learning. The method of ongoing evaluation does not itself ensure cross-

disciplinary learning between projects. The Regional and Social Funds have as a result invested in these learning conferences, both at regional and national levels. The aim of the learning conferences has been to disseminate experiences and knowledge from project to project. Such learning conferences have been arranged for all regions.

Conclusions

The implementation of the Regional and Social Funds in Sweden is an illustrative example of how to adopt learning through ongoing evaluation in programmes and projects. The aim is to create a more knowledge-driven regional growth and employment policy. The different elements of this strategy – ongoing project, programme and implementation evaluations, and also the thematic groups, support projects, training, networks and conferences – provide the foundation for the learning systems of the Social and Regional Funds. Learning through ongoing evaluation at the project level has introduced a new instrument. It can be really useful for projects, for decision-making organizations and more broadly for learning. However, the full potential has not been fully exploited. For learning evaluation to function as intended, a number of measures of different kinds are required to strengthen those parts that already exist. The importance of effective project organizations with active ownership and professional project steering, as well as demanding financiers, has to be fully understood and made known. This involves consciously working for an evaluation culture that combines action with reflection, that is, development based on 'walking on two legs' learning and evaluation.

Simple evaluation of projects, programmes and implementing organizations is 'walking on one leg'. Without also supporting evaluation – with feedback from experiences and knowledge formation, blended with action – the goal of becoming a learning organization will not be accomplished. Much has been achieved; at the same time it is important to think through how, in the future, implementation organizations can be created that really do 'walk on two legs'. From this perspective, evaluation becomes a *necessary* condition, but it is not per se a *sufficient* condition. Evaluation can only be one piece of the jigsaw puzzle, where a number of other parts must interact under the right conditions. There must be decision-makers in strategic positions from different organizations who require knowledge that they will use to achieve results which can be transformed into long-term effects and will lead to strategic impact. This really deals with being able to 'walk on two legs' – that is, taking action and learning from it – but it also involves synchronizing action and learning so that they take place at the right time and are coordinated. It is this necessary interaction between strategic action and learning which we have not yet found in the two funds, despite all the ambitious attempts.

The real challenge facing the Structural Funds is to realize the strategic goals of Europe 2020 to build a smarter, more innovative and more inclusive Europe. Regional development policy more closely linked to theory and the surrounding world has the potential to increase quality and efficiency in both EU-financed and nationally and regionally financed regional growth policy. Ultimately the learning through ongoing evaluation approach involves creating legitimacy for the EU policy of structural transformation and cohesion. In the concluding chapter, we will present a summary of our reasoning on how sustainable development work that generates multiplier effects in other development activities can be organized on the basis of experiences gained from the Regional and Social Funds. We put the main emphasis on the importance of an effective project organization, with active ownership and professional steering of projects, as well as demanding financiers.

5

Lessons from Earlier Programme Initiatives

In modern growth theories, the geographical place, the region, plays a prominent role. Innovative regional environments can be characterized either as an industrial district or as a high-tech ITC or biotech cluster. In Sweden, there are both world-class clusters, for example, Kista in Stockholm and Mjärdevi in Linköping, and traditional small-scale entrepreneurial industrial districts, such as Gnosjö. In the latter, learning in companies has traditionally taken place at the workplace. The underlying idea of the Structural Fund-financed programme *Learning Company Networks* (Brulin 2002) was that systematic networking between participants with similar work tasks in four large companies in the industrial district should increase developmental learning. Co-workers in the same position from different companies met and exchanged experiences over development work. Little by little they were also introduced to scientific knowledge, which is not usually very highly ranked in such industrial districts. Linkages and networks with the nearby universities and university colleges were established. High-technology clusters, which in Kista and Mjärdevi take different measures for competence transfer and increasing innovation capacity, by such means as incubators for new companies, have become important for cluster dynamics.

This chapter provides the background and context for the following two chapters which deal with knowledge that can be generated from carrying through large programmes such as the Social and Regional Funds. We will examine the conditions for achieving success with different programme initiatives for increasing innovation and competence. We will discuss a number of strategic programme initiatives and critically examine their sustainability. The first part examines a number of innovation programmes. We raise questions about what an innovation is, whether initiatives in innovation are meaningful, how they can be organized and what results have been achieved. The Swedish and not least European paradox – with large R&D initiatives in innovation, but until now very poor outcomes – is discussed. Interestingly, it seems less and less to be a Swedish paradox, whereas it still lingers as a European one. Changes initiated by, for example, the Structural Fund programmes (Brulin 2000) seem to bear fruit in more innovations, a change in export patterns towards high-tech services and more entrepreneurial universities.

The second part takes up a number of programmes and large projects where the focus is on competence development. The idea is that this should lead to a better supply of competence and lower the thresholds for gaining entry to working life. Ambition levels have been high, but the question is: what long-term effects have the programmes led to? In a concluding part, we try to draw some practical conclusions on how a competence initiative can be made successful.

Innovation Programmes

Major initiatives are taken to increase innovation capacity – regionally, nationally and at the EU level. A number of different programmes aim to improve innovation in a number of respects. It may appear slightly strange that these major initiatives are taken, given that there is no clear-cut definition of what an innovation is. There is a traditional view of innovation which states that it deals with the creation of new industrial products. In recent years, however, the concept of innovation has been broadened, to cover products, processes and service, as well as social, innovations. Inclusive growth is one example where the Social Fund works with social innovations which in new ways support the entry into working life of people with functional impairments and different ethnic backgrounds. An innovation does not need to be a radically new creation. The degrees of newness, value and usefulness are three aspects which contribute to what can be regarded as an innovation. One way of handling the degree of newness in an innovation is to position it on a scale from radical to incremental, that is, from a completely new product or service to a step-wise improvement of an existing product or service. At the same time as the concept of innovation has been broadened, it has also been diluted of its original meaning. A large number of new creations are called innovations.

A new creation, however, does not necessarily entail an innovation. To be regarded as an innovation, it should also be used. An innovation should be brought into use either as a commercial business idea or as a tool for change and development. If the new creation, invention or scientific discovery is not used, it can hardly be regarded as contributing to change, development and growth, and thus can hardly be regarded as an innovation.

There is substantial research into innovation processes. Traditional theories about innovation processes emphasize the planning of goal-oriented activities in a linear development chain from research to final product. In this representation, basic research and transfer of technology play a prominent role. The model is based on pioneering ideas and knowledge developed in basic research. Thereafter they are transferred to applied research and industrial research institutes. After this, applicable results are transferred to laboratories and development departments, especially in large companies. From development departments and laboratories, prototypes are handed over to the production departments in the company for mass production. In recent decades, this linear model of innovation has been subjected to severe criticism (Brulin 2004). The dominant view is that currently there is no linear sequence from research to commercial products which are ready for marketing.

Instead of the linear model, discussion in recent decades has been about innovation systems. There are a number of programme initiatives that are based on promoting regional development through support for innovation systems. Innovation systems are characterized by three spheres (Triple Helix) – the academic world, industrial life and authorities – collaborating and exchanging knowledge. Many programme initiatives try to leverage the potential for knowledge-based innovations and business entrepreneurship which universities, university colleges and other knowledge centres provide by cooperating with industry and authorities regionally. One problem is that the concept of an innovation system lacks a physical counterpart and seems unusual in industry (Bjurulf and Vedung 2009). Supporters of innovation systems argue that new products and services are more often the result of an interactively operating system than the consequence of a linear process. The development of new products and processes is typified by cross-feedback and joint shared commitments between companies, authorities and research institutions. In order to increase innovation capacity, feedback and cooperation between these three spheres should be supported and strengthened.

According to Cooke and others, productivity improvements drive growth, but productivity is less and less dependent on efficient production systems per se, and more dependent on the capacity to innovate; and here the regional environment plays a crucial role. These authors' view is that the importance of enhancing innovation capacity has only increased in recent decades. Thus the capacity to innovate becomes vital for national and regional competitiveness (Cooke et al. 2007: 297):

> *In an era when theory and policy are agreed that productivity drives growth while innovation drives productivity, the insights of the leading scholarship on innovation, which are those of the evolutionary or neo-Schumpeterian school [Lundvall 1992] will remain influential. From a spatial perspective rooted in evolutionary economic geography, regional innovation systems (RISs) have played and will continue to play a strategic role in promoting the innovativeness and competitiveness of regions ... Essentially, the RIS approach has strengthened policy by the attention it directs towards the need – perceived by policy makers at OECD, EU-member state and regional levels – for constructing regional advantage. The regional innovation system can be thought of as the knowledge infrastructure supporting innovation in interaction with the production structure. It is necessary to think in post-sectorial or "platform" terms to capture the full flavour of this contribution.*

THE SWEDISH AND THE EUROPEAN PARADOX

What problems are innovation programmes meant to solve? Many would argue that the problem is the Swedish so-called paradox, which is a European paradox. Essentially this is based on the notion that we should extract more from our huge initiatives in research and development – in products and services with high R&D, companies and exports. Even though this conclusion is not indisputable, Sweden and Europe should be able to get a better return from their R&D initiatives. Measured as a percentage of GDP, Sweden is the second largest investor in R&D in the world. Only Israel, the USA and perhaps a few other countries invest more resources. In contrast to these countries, different researchers consider that there have not been particularly many R&D-intensive companies and surprisingly few advanced products and high-tech services (Edquist 2010) innovated in Sweden. The so-called paradox illustrates the fact that research and new knowledge are per se no guarantee of growth. Growth in the economy requires that knowledge is transformed into businesses and development processes, that is, competent personnel exist who can transform new creations into goods and services that can be produced and sold. Initiatives in patents and innovations are prioritized in the Structural Funds 2007–2013 in Sweden, and in different EU framework programmes. Such initiatives are in line with a number of other programme initiatives nationally and in the EU. In Sweden, initiatives have also been taken to establish innovation offices at universities to further support patenting and commercialization of knowledge.

The Swedish paradox is a term used to describe the situation where Sweden as a nation invests substantial resources in R&D, and this leads to scientific publications, but not to patents and ultimately commercialization. The lack of patenting of scientific knowledge and research-based results produced by Swedish universities and university colleges is cited as one of the main reasons for the Swedish paradox.

This relationship in its turn may arise from the fact that in Sweden, as in a number of other countries, researchers themselves own the results of their research – referred to as the 'teacher exception'. The teacher exception gives Swedish researchers great freedom, at the same time as it does not provide solid foundations for supporting patents and commercialization originating from the universities and university colleges where the researchers are active. These institutions do not become, as in the USA, owners or partial owners of the patent, and so they are not able to share in the returns from licensing arrangements. Not all new product development, probably not even the major part, leads to patenting. Large companies have tended to argue against patent applications, and instead put the emphasis on accelerating market introduction of innovations. Lack of respect for patent protection in a number of countries is yet another reason that some companies regard patenting as less important.

Nevertheless, an important part of the knowledge developed by researchers and academics leads to new jobs and companies through patenting of knowledge. One question which has been discussed is whether the lack of patenting could be an explanation for the Swedish, as well as the European, paradox. Through patents, new knowledge and research become commercial innovations. Patents are a means of transferring knowledge for researchers and provide important intellectual property rights to protect inventions. Patenting by the academic world is an important part of the transfer of knowledge between that world and industry. Patents are a key instrument for protecting innovative ideas in a number of different scientific areas, such as chemistry, pharmaceuticals, biotechnology and microelectronics. Patenting means that the researcher or university, depending on who owns the patent, can protect their intellectual property.

Later research, however, shows that Swedish R&D initiatives have resulted in a high proportion of patent applications. After declining somewhat at the beginning of the first decade of the new millennium, patent applications have once again started to rise rapidly. Lissoni et al. (2008) argue that shortcomings in patenting in Sweden, and also in Europe, have in many respects been an optical illusion:

The key piece of evidence produced in this paper can be summarized as follows: universities in France, Italy and Sweden do not contribute much less than their US counterparts to their nations' patenting activity: rather they are less likely to reclaim the prosperity of the patents they produce. (Lissoni et al. 2008: 14)

The paradoxical aspect, however, appears to be that much has been invested in scientific R&D in Sweden and Europe which actually leads not just to scientific publications, but also patents, but nevertheless they have not, until now, resulted in commercial innovations. In all probability it is in the next stage where the problems exist. The lack of strategies and methods for knowledge spillover with actors outside the research world appear to have been strong reasons for the Swedish paradox, according to a number of researchers (Ejermo and Karlsson 2005). The problem appears to be that knowledge spillovers between R&D and business enterprises do not seem to function particularly well in Europe. New patents with defective mechanisms for knowledge spillover, in terms of active ownership of knowledge and joint knowledge formation with other actors, are obstacles to commercialization. Active leadership and a clear regional strategy, supported by company leaders and key actors in the academic world, would create legitimacy for changing attitudes. Greater confidence amongst actors from the academic, political and industrial worlds creates the conditions for joint strategies and increasing collaboration that can serve as a foundation for increased innovation (Bjurulf and Olsson 2009).

Knowledge spillovers do not occur as a result of logical necessity, but presuppose different mechanisms for transfer and learning – such as functioning markets, entrepreneurship, well-functioning labour markets, mutual trust and confidence, venture capital, and so on. Lundström, Almerud and Stevenson (2008) believe that if innovation programmes were run in tandem with programmes for entrepreneurship, the prerequisites would be increased for contributing significantly to knowledge spillovers and the commercialization of new ideas and companies. Based on studies of 11 member states, they argue that if Europe is to reach its growth goals, a much more coherent approach is needed. Member states that integrate entrepreneurship and innovation programmes are more successful than those running fragmented programmes. Interweaving the programmes will make a greater contribution to the global competitiveness of Europe.

Even though there are benefits in running different programmes concurrently, there is still a lack of insight into how knowledge spillovers resulting in innovation occur. Can knowledge spillovers be planned and organized in programme activities? Yes, but more knowledge is required about how this can be achieved:

> *Theories on entrepreneurship need to be able to explain where opportunities come from, how knowledge spillovers occur and how occupational choices arise in existing corporations that lead to new firm formation. Prevailing theories of the firm are not able to answer these questions. Second, more micro-economic studies are required to fully understand the channels and mechanisms through which knowledge spillovers occur from corporate R&D as well as from academic research, and to measure spillovers more directly. (Acs et al. 2005: 24)*

However, little by little the paradox seems to be less of a problem in Sweden. Structures for knowledge spillovers are being formed. The so-called entrepreneurial university is becoming a widespread notion.

ARE PROGRAMMES FOR INNOVATION SYSTEMS THE SOLUTION?

Over the last ten to 15 years, different theories emphasizing the importance of a limited geographical area for knowledge spillovers have become popular. A focus on industrial districts, technology parks, clusters, and so on, applies, not least among politicians and decision-makers. This view is based on theories about innovation systems. These theories focus on the transfer and dissemination of knowledge between companies, as well as showing the importance of mutual confidence in facilitating this. Whilst different theories propagate the view that it is businesses which provide the platform for the emergence of confidence and transfer, increasingly emphasis is being put on place – usually a specific region – as the arena where confidence can emerge, and where knowledge can be disseminated between companies and other organizations. Companies and people working in a limited geographical area will probably meet and interact with each other more often than if they are located at a greater distance from each other. Are there other institutions – such as churches, sports clubs, associations, and so on – where participants can meet and build up mutual confidence? At these places, there are not only companies but also other organizations and institutions such as universities and university colleges. The reason the mechanism is described as important for the development of innovations is that it enables collaborative learning. Knowledge spillovers have a tendency to be greater in places where companies, organizations and individuals have confidence in each other.

After some decades of large public programme initiatives in innovation systems, however, this approach has also started to encounter increasing criticism (Doloreux and Saeed 2004). Innovation systems do not solve the problem of shortcomings in knowledge spillovers. The criticism can be summarized under three points (Laestadius, Nuur and Ylinenpää 2007). First, there is criticism directed at the idea that a mechanically operating system in a region should be able to organize knowledge spillovers where knowledge from the three spheres emerges as innovations. The objection is that, without the creation of applications through value-creating production and business, knowledge is not transformed into innovations. Someone, preferably an entrepreneur, must own the knowledge and have the drive to commercialize it. It is not rare that programmes for innovation systems implicitly have a view that research-based results and scientific knowledge are superior to applied knowledge. Second, there is a tendency for entrepreneurs aiming to transform knowledge into business to be reduced to a footnote in these types of sophisticated policy systems. Third, the importance of closeness to a regional higher education institution in the innovation system is exaggerated.

One reason for the dilution of the concept of innovation is a strong focus on innovation systems and on Triple Helix. The foundation for innovation is argued to be close and confidential cooperation between the academic world, industry and authorities – the three spheres that should function as cogs in mechanic innovation systems. Many ask whether it really is these actors who deliver innovations that are brought into use and create benefits. If anything, these three spheres appear to be involved in developing knowledge that could become innovations, but which perhaps in the best case only lead to patents.

For joint knowledge formation to function, driving actors are required that are willing to take the risk of commercializing knowledge, that is, companies and entrepreneurs. Even though it might appear to be self-evident that innovation systems promote innovation, in practice it has been difficult to really increase innovation capacity through publicly financed programme initiatives. A number of studies, ranging from programmes to support innovation, indicate that these types of initiatives have had a limited effect in relation to commercialization of knowledge and research (European Commission 2007b). For instance, in its evaluations of the framework programmes, Technopolis (2009) shows that far too seldom have 'sharp' innovations been developed. The majority of the projects appear to have led to 'intermediate knowledge outputs', that is, knowledge which could become innovations. And far too often, it is traditional companies, for example, Telia or Volvo in Sweden, which participate in framework projects, rather than innovative gazelles, that is, companies which really aim at commercialization, growth and job creation.

According to its critics, an innovation system provides a framework that is too narrow and adapted to national policy-making. In reality, the development of new products, processes and services with cross-feedback and shared commitments between different companies and actors, consultants and research institutions at a number of different levels, and various geographical places, is evident. Feedback and collaboration cannot be planned in advance, but must be allowed to emerge during the course of the innovation process. Innovation processes are not abstract factors and mechanisms, but people participating in individual and collective meetings and acting in concert. Innovative environments are not created in the system but through relationships. The creation of relationships is often specifically related to location, but is becoming increasingly independent of geography. Unexpected relationships, collaboration and experimental search processes appear to play an increasingly important role in the development of new products and services (Storper 1998). There are many secondary tracks and, instead of working linearly, it is a question of working parallel in numerous simultaneous processes. Not least, this involves linking to many skilled suppliers with high competence in their specialist areas.

The challenge today is that innovation processes are currently being run in so many different forms (von Hippel 2005) – for example, orchestrated innovation or user-led innovation. As a result, there must be a substantially greater degree of openness in how innovation projects should be organized. It is no longer possible to mechanically organize effective innovation systems through projects where actions and activity plans deliver innovations which in their turn result in a certain number of company start-ups and new jobs.

Criticism of programmes for innovation systems has led to more focused public initiatives to increase innovation capacity, amongst other things, in clusters and incubators. In our increasingly global and knowledge-oriented world, companies and organizations tend, in different ways (especially geographically), to come closer to each other to achieve competitive advantages through knowledge spillovers – amongst other things, through exchange of experience and competence. This is usually referred to as collaborating in clusters (Brulin and Svensson 2011). Well-known and oft-studied clusters are those in Silicon Valley and the financial cluster in central London. In Sweden, there are a number of such small clusters. The majority of these are in different public programmes where they receive support to grow and develop. For example, the Paper Province in Värmland (a Swedish county) and the biotechnology cluster in the Malmö and Copenhagen region have aroused international interest. Different studies show that clusters are something positive, in the sense that they add value, both for the actors involved and the economy as a whole – through learning and the build-up of knowledge, synergy effects from collaboration, economies of scale, social relations and networks, information flows and the build-up of infrastructure. Clusters in these studies appear to be more dynamic and flexible than innovation systems. Sölvell (2009) argues that clusters are a very different model for creating knowledge spillovers, and must continuously evolve:

> But there is another model where national, regional and local policy actors, academic actors and business actors play constructive roles. A constant reconstruction of clusters – moving them from a group of co-located companies to dynamic clusters with more innovation, interaction and spillovers – is a central task for all actors on the cluster scene. Cluster initiatives are an important tool to achieve this goal; they help by creating a new type of policy process that involves local and regional public–private–academic constellations and encourage members to open up for dialogue and actions across organisational and regulatory boundaries.

The majority of cluster studies focus on describing the benefits and characteristics of different types of clusters. But do programme initiatives in clusters give more certain and better returns in innovation, compared with initiatives in innovation systems? The truth is that we do not know if either programmes for regional innovation systems or programmes for cluster development give 'value for money'. We are in urgent need of more knowledge and new forms for evaluating and generating insights.

Parallel with programmes for clusters, company incubators, incubators and science/technology parks have become common programme initiatives for contributing to knowledge spillovers in research environments and the development of new knowledge-based companies. A company incubator is designed to support an entrepreneur in developing business expertise in an environment that promotes company development.

Even though incubators vary in the extent to which support is provided, there are some general features which are normally part of an incubator concept. An incubator generally supports start-ups by helping entrepreneurs to prepare and develop their ability to run companies, and also functions as a guide to external financing. Incubators often aim to develop new, strong companies that will generate new ideas and technologies. Support for incubators can contribute to the creation of new jobs and serve as a foundation for companies in industries with high growth, which in the future are expected to generate jobs and raise standards of living.

The Swedish Governmental Agency for Innovation Systems (VINNOVA) launched a special national incubator programme in 2002 and has, in a couple of studies, focused specifically on the development of incubator companies. We have some knowledge in this area, but we know much less about different ways of establishing, developing and maintaining supportive incubators, despite the fact that there are indications of major knowledge gaps in this area. Different studies show that a smaller proportion of technology parks, with their related incubators, are successful, but that many often fail to support innovation, entrepreneurship and regional development (Tamásy 2008).

The fact that incubators have not succeeded in living up to expectations may be due to how they are managed and organized. The problem is that there are few studies focusing on ownership, management and development of incubators. Studies in this area today focus primarily on university-related incubators, incubators for technology-based companies or the development of companies in incubators.

Essentially, there are two different types of incubators in Sweden – university-related incubators, which are more specialized, and non-university-related incubators, which are more general. Consequently different incubators have different target groups, provide different types of support and require different types of competencies and resources to support new companies in their start-up processes. Dissimilarities between incubators also mean that the key success factors differ.

Evaluations of the Regional Fund show that there are a number of general success factors – such as long-term financing, entry criteria for the target group, as well as a high level of involvement and experience of running a business. In addition, there are specific success factors for different types of incubators. University-related incubators, for example, must have personnel competence in the focus area, access to specialist equipment and seed financing (start-up funds), as well as good relations with a university that is positively involved in its commercialization. For non-university-related incubators, a broad network and general business development competence amongst personnel are important factors to be able to support many different types of companies.

ARE INNOVATION PROGRAMMES MEANINGFUL?

The question of whether innovation programmes are meaningful depends on which perspective on the market economy one applies. The market can be viewed in different ways, either as a large number of competing companies or as a bundle of relations between companies and organizations. From the first perspective, companies lack contact with each other and they act with complete autonomy. The strategy is to keep other companies at a distance and compete in the first instance on the basis of price. In such a market, innovations are something which, if they do take place, are developed through internal company processes and can hardly be affected by public programme initiatives.

From the second perspective, the market consists of relationships between companies and organizations. These relationships are usually long-term and, within the framework of these long-term relationships, companies interact. Companies cannot own and have access to all the resources they need, as there is a constant shortage. This applies to both small and large companies. Other companies and organizations which have these resources can, as a result, be important for a company's capacity to innovate. The most important type of knowledge when working on innovation is tacit and experience-based knowledge. This occurs and exists from the relationships emerging between companies and organizations when they act within the framework of the relationships that make up the market. It is on the market where business is done – that is, different types of innovation are sold, bought and used by companies on the market. Business in general, and innovation in particular, are affected by uncertainty. Companies can never be certain that the result they want or have planned will be achieved. For this reason, confidence is so important as it reduces perceived uncertainty, which has a positive impact on the company's willingness to be open and to share information and knowledge. In this latter perspective on the market economy – that is, perceived as a bundle of relationships – better preconditions for knowledge spillovers are created by facilitating relationship building, for example, through programmes for joint knowledge formation.

Innovation programmes enable project structures to be created for joint knowledge formation in the market. These structures facilitate knowledge spillovers. Fundamentally, this is not a planned and systematically implemented activity, but rather something that takes place in an unplanned and spontaneous fashion. Conditions to encourage this, however, can be created and processes facilitated. Different development projects consist of companies, organizations and individuals, and the relationships between them. Within the framework of these relationships, different types of joint knowledge formation are pursued, which can result in innovations. How learning is organized, and the nature of the mix of companies and organizations, are important for their activity, and also in creating the preconditions for knowledge spillovers. Not all projects function in the same way. The strength of the relationships existing between participating companies varies, as do the relationships they might wish to develop.

The number of companies involved in a project determines how many relationships can theoretically be developed. Since relationships are the cornerstone of this type of project, the number of participating companies is an important factor. The more companies involved, the greater the number of relationships that can be developed. But time and resources set their limits: the more relationships, the weaker they are. However, this need not necessarily be a disadvantage. Whether it is a disadvantage or an advantage depends on what the aim of the project is. A large number of companies implies that the cost of activities in the project can be distributed amongst a number of actors, that is, if the aim of the project is costly, a larger number of companies may be an advantage.

Nor is it just the number of companies that is important; the number of relationships can be both an obstacle and an opportunity for the project. Companies, through their relationships with other companies, can receive unexpected information and surprising knowledge. Such relationships provide a platform for working together, and can also give access to other relationships and knowledge networking. This does not mean that more relationships are a clear-cut advantage for participating companies. A few strong relationships can be more effective for a company if the aim is to work intensively together and really learn from each other. Relations with companies that have access to critical resources, of course, are more important when the company specifically needs those resources, as opposed to a large number of relations with companies that do not have the critical resources.

Apart from the relationships between the actors in a project, the relationships that participating companies have with other companies outside the project can also be important for what takes place within it. This can give rise to unexpected knowledge spillovers. Such relationships provide access, information, resources, markets and technologies, and create opportunities for knowledge spillovers. These relationships may be more or less integrated into the project, that is, activities in the project may be more or less related to companies' core business activities. If these relationships can be mobilized, they can serve as a strategic asset for the participating companies and the project.

How the project is put together will influence the opportunities for joint knowledge formation, and thus the conditions for knowledge spillovers and ultimately innovation. Joint knowledge formation can take place at seminars, workshops, training, company associations, and so on. Important factors for knowledge spillover are mobility in labour markets, that is, change of workplace by the labour force, as well as access to entrepreneurs. Entrepreneurs can ensure that knowledge spillovers will lead to completely new companies. With these different types of knowledge spillovers, not only formalized knowledge is transferred, but also critical experience and tacit knowledge, which often provide the keys to innovation.

As a result of the gradual regionalization of industrial and growth policy, regional responsibility for creating meaningful structures from projects within the framework of different innovation programmes is increasing. Not all project initiatives can and will be given priority. At the same time, it is important that it is not just established industry and working life that has the opportunity to influence the project structures that are emerging. Projects can be chosen and discarded on arbitrary grounds. Those with the right channels probably have an advantage. Those that can demonstrate back-up, such as public co-financing, have an advantage over others, despite the fact that they may not be best placed to contribute to regional industrial growth.

One must dare to think along new lines, and to prioritize new areas and actors. Successful programme implementation ideally strikes a balance between support and investments in new and established project structures. Mobilizing resources regionally in decision-making partnerships could be one means of structuring project activities. One example is the cooperation between different regions in the 'System Management of Innovative Environments' project. The collaboration involves a strong focus on learning, but also collaboration at the national level – in the form of learning conferences on regional development with VINNOVA and the Swedish Agency for Economic and Regional Growth.

However, it appears that systematic reflection and feedback from experience is lacking in work on regional growth (Brulin and Svensson 2011). One task which has become more important regionally is fitting together the pieces from different project initiatives so that a dynamic whole can be created from different programme initiatives. One experience from earlier innovation programmes has been allowing 'too many flowers to blossom', that is, the focus has been too weak. A number of smaller projects have been prioritized, without being part of a strategic whole. Even though project initiatives should be chosen because they reflect the priorities of regional growth and development strategies, it is not certain that they really 'mesh' with a greater whole. How often do decision-making partnerships and other regional development actors juggle together different project initiatives so that the structures of the projects formed reach a critical mass and contribute to sustainable development? Do we have knowledge and experience from ongoing projects and from monitoring the surrounding world that enable strategic choices to be made?

One reason why innovation programmes risk failure may be that partnerships often choose to prioritize support to projects with high symbolic value – such as innovation systems in higher education with their roots in the scientific community. The question can be put as to whether the scientific community is the most appropriate for developing commercially viable knowledge and innovations. Power and Malmberg (2008: 14) argue as follows:

> *Policy makers, and to some degree universities themselves, seem eager to recast academia as a part of wider innovation systems. At regional levels the potential of universities to contribute to innovation has meant calls for linking them more strongly to regions' innovation and industrial systems ... The notion that universities can contribute to regional innovation has been built upon two key ideas: that universities increase knowledge production through the provision of new workers and scientific results that can be turned into patents, products and services and that the existence of universities in regions can lead to university-industry knowledge transfer and exchange ... our main point of departure is a questioning of the role of universities in innovation and in regional innovation in particular. We will argue that universities simultaneously play a number of roles at local, regional and even global scales and that the question of how to best harness university research for the purpose of social and economic development might not primarily be a regional problem.*

The international success of Swedish companies comes in both low-technology production and distribution – furniture and clothes, IKEA and Hennes & Mauritz – and also in high technology. It is through production and distribution adapted to global markets, rather than through high technology, where Sweden and the Scandinavian countries have been successful. In a review of the competitiveness of Scandinavian countries, Eskelinen and Maskell (1998) argued more than a decade ago that these countries should avoid the enormous investment costs involved in trying to be in the front line of research in different leading-edge technologies. Success for small countries and peripheral regions involves trying to use their practical knowledge and effective non-bureaucratic production organizations to invest in developing advanced knowledge.

It is more important for smaller countries and regions on the periphery of the world economy to develop regional clusters than to be at the leading edge of technology. These clusters do not need to be oriented to high technology and based on scientific knowledge and research findings; they can just as easily be based on local and regional leverage of practical expertise, modern production technology, organization and marketing. Programmes with the ambition of supporting innovation of this type can be just as successful as those with the ambition of supporting innovation of significantly higher status and symbolic value.

The conclusion is that there are no simple truths, neither scientific nor practical, about how success can be achieved in innovation programmes. Experience from decades of programme implementation shows that projects for joint knowledge formation create conditions for knowledge spillovers, but exactly how these are to be organized is a practical problem of which we have little knowledge. We know that there are no simple solutions to be achieved through innovation systems and increased support for patenting. A whole complex of factors must work together if programme implementation is to be successful. Knowledge spillovers through the mobility of the labour force and entrepreneurship cannot be planned, but can be facilitated. Programmes for creating innovation and entrepreneurship should be run in tandem. Lifelong learning and competence development are other components in programme initiatives for regional growth and job creation. Ensuring quality in the implementation of programmes appears to be less a question of applying the right theory, and more about gradually acquiring knowledge and learning through evaluation and ongoing evaluation during implementation.

Programmes for Competence Development

In innovation programmes, learning and experimentation are fundamental. These aim at learning both at inter-organizational and system levels. In this section, we focus on learning in the workplace, and the strategies applied in different programme initiatives to develop the competence of employees and the unemployed. This section builds more on concrete programmes and projects. Theories and strategies about competence development are not as well developed as those for innovation, growth and regional development. It is interesting that competence development and vocational training have been regarded as instrumental and short-term measures, and not as a strategy for the development of companies and regions. Competence development is often considered to be a task for the HR department and not as a strategic management issue in a company. In regional growth programmes, competence initiatives are not given any strategic role in growth, apart from research and building up expertise in leading-edge competence. However, we begin by looking at labour market training and some national programmes for competence development. After this, we will review a number of larger projects aimed at competence development.

LABOUR MARKET TRAINING AND OTHER NATIONAL PROGRAMMES

Competence development has been an important part of labour market policy where work has been the starting point. Labour market training has been one means of stimulating mobility and structural transformation, where the individual's security is no longer regarded as linked to a specific job, but to the labour market. The unemployed should not be passive and live off allowances, but active and strengthened through education and other measures. Labour market training should be made accessible to everyone and strengthen individuals and their position on the labour market – an idea which originated from popular adult education.

During the 1990s, there was growing criticism of labour market training and volume-oriented programmes aimed at reducing unemployment. At the end of the 1990s, labour market training changed to focus more specifically on vocational training and better adaptation to labour market demand. After the recession of 2008, the Institute for Labour Market Policy Evaluation discussed how active labour market policy works in such a situation. They found it important to rely more heavily on certain kinds of programmes. Their argument was tied to the varying size of the lock-in effects in boom and recession. Their conclusion was that if programmes with relatively large lock-in effects should ever be used, they should be used in a downturn. The reason was that the cost of search time would be lower in a recession. In particular they compared an on-the-job training scheme with (traditional) labour market training and found that labour market training is probably relatively more effective in a recession. The result found is consistent with prior results since labour market training features relatively large lock-in effects.

One conclusion from an overarching review shows that labour market policy – and thus also labour market training – has become increasingly reactive and short-term. The wide-ranging national programmes implemented to compensate for these shortcomings have strengthened participating individuals, but the programmes have lacked mechanisms for sustainable development work – active ownership by the labour market partners, collaboration based on joint knowledge formation, and developmental learning to generate multiplier effects.

An important question is: why has it been so difficult to bring about effective competence development for unemployed persons and job seekers? These difficulties reflect a more general one concerning competence development in companies. This has been difficult to implement, despite large national initiatives undertaken, where different EU programmes have been an important component. The annual reports of the national labour union (LO) indicate both over- and under-education of their members. Nor have employers increased their investment in training employees over the last two decades, and inequality between different groups of employees is large in terms of access to paid in-service training. Well-educated male civil servants get most further education and training, whilst low-educated women in small companies receive the least. Employees with project and hourly employment contracts do not generally receive paid in-service training.

We consider that the answer to this question is connected with the fact that competence measures have not been designed within the framework of a strategy for sustainable development work. Instead they are typified by temporary solutions of an ad hoc nature. The measures have not been integrated with other development work in companies or linked to regional conditions in the labour market. The learning has not been explicit or used to improve ongoing operations, and strategies for dissemination and achieving strategic impact have often been lacking.

A number of major development programmes have been implemented over a long period to increase the competence of individuals and employees. At the end of the 1980s, Working Life Funds were introduced, which was a five-year programme covering 25,000 workplaces. The aim was to remove jobs which had the worst working environments by upgrading employee competence. This would take place through changes in the terms and conditions of employees in the work organization. The Working Life Funds, which in total had more than 30 billion Swedish crowns, did not function as intended when the crisis of the 1990s (around 10 per cent unemployment) hit companies, where there was a lack of time, money and involvement in development (Brulin and Nilsson 1997).

One explanation for the difficulties in competence development may be connected with responsibility and organization for implementation. Responsibility for education and training in Sweden is clearly distributed. The state and the municipalities are responsible for basic education, whilst further education and training in working life generally lies outside the state sphere. Questions about competence development, work organization, retraining, and so on, must be solved by companies themselves, in conjunction with the trade unions, local politicians and authorities.

However, the state has not withdrawn from responsibility for competence development in working life. A number of educational reforms with different aims have been carried out – to strengthen individuals with more education, even-out opportunities, contribute to social fairness, support democratic development, guarantee supply of competence to companies, as well as contribute to growth and efficiency. Ambitions concerning democracy and distribution policy have been prominent and often linked to a vision of lifelong learning. A wide-ranging national initiative at the end of the 1990s was the Adult Education Initiative, which aimed to raise formal competence for groups with low levels of education up to compulsory and upper secondary school level, as a step in halving unemployment. At its peak, the Adult Education Initiative provided close to 150,000 places a year. The major subject areas were computing and IT skills, health and social care, as well as mathematics. The majority of participants were women in the public sector. Evaluation shows good results from implementation and effects at the individual level. These programmes for competence development have not been steered by particular theories or concepts, but based on the assumption that education is good and the formal view of learning has dominated.

An overall assessment shows that the national initiative in adult education has been extensive. Sweden has been successful and also functioned as an international model in terms of adult education provision, including recurring education, study support and the build-up of municipal learning centres. As regards initiatives in vocational education and competence development in companies, there have been a number of difficulties, amongst which are scope, continuity, distribution to different groups and company involvement. More recently, workplace learning and informal competence have been given more attention and are more in demand.

Our focus in this book is not on individually oriented programmes of the type touched on in the different national programmes above. The presentation has, however, provided background for other more workplace-related projects and programmes. In the following sections, we will take up some programmes which have attempted to combine individual and organizational learning, that is, the linkage we discussed in Chapter 1 as a precondition for sustainability. We begin by looking at the earlier programmes of the Social Fund.

PROGRAMMES FOR COMPETENCE DEVELOPMENT TO INCREASE EMPLOYABILITY

Competence development has been funded in part by a number of large programmes. It is natural to begin by examining earlier initiatives in the Social Fund, where competence development and increased employability were the major goals. A research project carried out a number of case studies in this programme (see Ellström and Kock 2009) and pointed to some of the factors for achieving success in competence development in these studies.

The motives of the organizations for taking part in a project proved to be important for the results achieved. The workplaces that cited business-oriented reasons for participating achieved the best results, since their work on competence development was long-term and proactive. Companies that gave more 'opportunistic' reasons, that is, participated because money was available or because they wanted to make a good impression, achieved significantly worse results – both in terms of individual and organizational learning.

The most common form of competence development was courses carried out either in or outside the workplace, where a variety of different methods were used. The evaluators could show three fundamental patterns in the use of methods:

1.   The 'learning on the job' strategy, which is based on courses in the workplace, individual meetings, team-building, cooperation in projects, supervision, and so on. Learning here becomes a part of doing things at work, trying different approaches, discussing and exchanging experiences.

2.   The 'self-learning' strategy, which builds on courses outside the workplace, the purchase of course literature and self-study. The starting point is that knowledge should be transferred from teacher to student. This represents a linear development strategy, where application takes place at a later stage.

3.   The 'learning from others' strategy, which takes place through participation in networks and external study visits. The idea is that participants should learn through seeing how others do things, that is, a form of 'benchmarking' where personal comparisons are made.

The evaluation showed that the 'self-learning' strategy dominated in the project (56 per cent), followed by the 'learning on the job' strategy (38 per cent) and the 'learning from others' strategy (29 per cent). A comparison was made of strategies used in the earlier programming period (Structural Funds Objective 4). It turned out that the more classical competence strategies had gained favour at the cost of the 'learning on the job' strategy. On the other hand, the strategy of 'learning from others' became more common during the later programming period. An interesting question, which we will return to in Chapter 6, is: what scope exists for choosing learning strategies in the Social Fund in the current programming period?

In Chapters 2 and 3, we touched on how financiers can play an important role in raising the quality of projects. The workplaces which received most support and demands from the ESF offices had put most time into analytical work. They had also worked more on methods of linking their activities to competence development. At these workplaces, participation of the employees and the union was higher in the projects. It is interesting to note that project owners did not receive visits, involvement and feedback from the Social Fund, and some even thought that control over how project funds were used should be strengthened. The Social Fund was generally regarded as an administrative organization, not as a learning and competence-disseminating development organization.

The evaluation shows that it was difficult for many companies to take a long-term view as a consequence, amongst other things, of different changes: rapidly increasing demand, downturn in the economy or high staff turnover. Competence development was difficult to plan, and it was hard to make conscious choices of strategies and work forms based on different competencies that could be identified and were demanded. The evaluation shows the value of combining a number of different learning processes and strategies, but the 'learning on the job' strategy has major advantages compared to traditional knowledge transfer, particularly if the aim is to achieve effects at the operations level. The 'learning from others' strategy proved to be particularly useful for stimulating development and creativity (cf. Kock and Ellström 2011).

The competence initiatives led to greater professional competence and increased capacity to change on the part of participants, as well as increased interest in learning, but what did the project mean for operations and the organizations involved? Were participants able to use their newly acquired knowledge? According to the assessment of those responsible, the following were the results achieved by the project: 70 per cent responded that they had taken measures to improve work organization and 58 per cent stated that they had increased delegation of responsibility in the organization. Results at the operating level were connected to how well projects had been prepared, amongst other things, whether an initial analysis had been carried out, how long it had continued and how much time had been set aside. An important prerequisite was the existence of supportive learning environments in the workplace, where management was involved and external pressure for change occured (Ellström and Kock 2009). The Social Fund builds on a joint working approach. How was this handled in the project? The trade unions actively participated in about 30 per cent of the projects, usually at larger workplaces and in the public sector. In cases where the trade union participated, results were more positive and have been used more often in competence development related to core operations.

In summary, we can state that the projects appear to provide results both at an individual and organizational level, but these results are largely dependent on the learning strategies applied, what back-up the project had, management support, trade union participation and external pressure for change.

AN INITIATIVE ON INFORMAL COMPETENCE

A vital welfare question is how competence development for care of the elderly should be solved to provide assistance to 250,000 care providers. In total around 180,000 nursing assistants and care providers work in this area, and they make up the largest occupational group in the country. A very large majority of the employees are women, and most of them lack formal occupational competence. There are no strategies on how to solve the question of competence development for this occupational group, either at national or municipal level. It is evident that traditional formal education approaches cannot keep pace, primarily as a consequence of rapid change in the occupation.

An interesting strategy for working with competence development linked to the workplace has been developed in the Social Fund programme. From the beginning, 'Certified Trainee' was a project developed out of an earlier project, which has now become part of mainstream operations. In the beginning (2005), the project was funded by the Competence Ladder (a comprehensive national programme directed towards care of the elderly, see below) and the Social Fund. The project led to new methods and tools for developing learning in the workplace, where the aim was to improve quality by developing a model for testing, recognizing and assessing professional requirements and the competence of employees.

The methods include making business analyses (through creative learning meetings and validation), as well as training dialogue leaders, vocational assessors (a nursing assistant and a nurse or physiotherapist), competence supporters and competence supervisors. The working method is based on formulating clear professional requirements and criteria for these. The methods aim at creating a shared view of goals, making an analysis of activities and competence needs, obtaining competence to implement learning measures, securing the support of management, and so on. Learning is viewed as a process that must be organized, managed, supported and followed up to develop activities and improve quality. What is unique about validating professional competence in this case is that it does not take place in relation to course goals or certificates, but the requirements of working life which are defined locally.

We will try to explain how the project has succeeded in becoming sustainable. The project produced and developed methods and ways of working which municipalities and practitioners are prepared to pay for themselves without receiving external project funding. An important explanation for its success is that there have been clear project owners – a municipal association, a trade union organization, six municipalities, and later expanded to include a company in healthcare. The project has had active and interested owners who regard development work as valuable per se. Support from the managers has been a key issue for success in developing and applying the methods. The managers received training and access to a toolbox. Vocational requirements were linked to the municipality's salary policy, introduction and view of competence, which made it necessary to involve personnel supervisors in the work. The project management has been a driving force in development, but understood the value of cooperation with strategic actors in order to disseminate the methods and to have an impact on the public debate. The ambition has been to cooperate with the formal education system, particularly to avoid being perceived as a competitor and an alternative to the education system. The management understood early on the need to use learning evaluation to develop sustainable ways of working and strategies. The strategy the whole time has been to work with joint knowledge formation with external evaluators to guarantee the quality of the work and to develop a strategy to make measures sustainable.

Overall, this example shows a great awareness of how sustainable development can be organized. Knowledge of methods and strategies did not exist from the beginning, but was developed as a result of the experiences gained and reflections on these. This required high competence on the part of project management which was forced to navigate cautiously between the varying demands of different stakeholders. It involved developing a concept which has often been viewed as different and even somewhat threatening by the formal education system. Project funds were necessary to develop the ideas and working methods which could be offered to the municipalities on commercial conditions. Several thousand people increased their competence through Certified Trainee, but the major work of dissemination and strategic impact remains. Correctly handled, Certified Trainee – which proved to be an effective concept for competence development in the care of the elderly – could have a wide impact, and we consider that there is good potential for multiplier effects. Employers find it difficult to manage the supply of competence, and the formal education system cannot satisfy operational needs and quality development on its own, especially as mobility in the labour market is increasing.

THE COMPETENCE LADDER

The Competence Ladder was a state-financed programme (total: 1 billion Swedish crowns) for competence development directed at personnel working with care of the elderly (total: 120,000 persons). The aim was to improve the quality of care of the elderly through competence measures linked to the workplace, and which would be based on the needs of users and staff.

The evaluation, carried out by the Swedish Agency for Public Management, shows the value of allowing local needs to influence the distribution of funds. There was a valuable dialogue between fund providers and recipients, but the evaluators state that the administration was cumbersome and time-consuming. According to the Swedish Agency for Public Management, implementation of the Competence Ladder's mission was successful in many respects. Other evaluations and a research project show that there were innovative elements in the programme, but that traditional views of education were dominant.

The innovative elements existed principally in the six municipalities which would function as pilot and experimental. A number of interesting solutions were developed. More equal forms of cooperation were created between education organizers and the workplaces. A four-part model for collaboration was organized, where the teacher cooperated with a supervisor, a manager and participants from the workplace. In this way, formal and informal learning could be more easily integrated. The training became more adapted to the conditions of the workplace, but teachers ensured that this took place within the framework of the syllabus. Cooperation became more equal between the education and working life systems, and this made it easier to create involvement in the workplace. Many teachers were doubtful at the beginning, but later understood the advantages of having closer links to praxis (Larsson 2008).

The difficulties of this programme, as we see it, relate to how results could be used and disseminated. In a few cases, collaboration ceased when the project ended, or as a consequence of some key individuals finishing. Among the education providers, there was seldom active ownership and involvement of the group of teachers. Nor can we see that any multiplier effects were generated from this programme. It is also difficult to show that the quality of care of the elderly improved. The users were not at all involved in the work of discussing content and working forms in the training programmes.

COLLEGE

The education system has not managed to resolve the question of the supply of competence to industry – either in terms of quality or numbers. Companies have understood that they must be actively involved in order to change conditions, content and working forms in vocational education. Technical College (TC) and Care College (CC) provide an approach to the certification of vocational education and training. TC is intended to function as a form of quality assurance, showing that a number of municipalities and education providers, together with industry in a region, are developing education and training based on company requirements. Schools which have been approved, such as TC, provide education at upper secondary and post upper secondary levels, for example, different orientations with starting points in the industry or technology programme, advanced vocational education and vocational education at university level. Currently there are around 90 certified education providers. Companies play a key role in TC. They should be active both in planning the focus of education, its structure, provision of trainee places, participating in work and its follow-up. Ultimate responsibility for the training, however, lies with the municipalities. The overall aim is to create education programmes linked to regional and local industrial structures and their needs, both in the short and long-term. The development of TC can be regarded as an innovative way of running programmes.

There are no project funds in TC, as it is companies' acute and long-term need for labour which is the rationale for their involvement. There is also an important collaboration dimension in the initiative – both at the local and regional level. TC should contribute to better resource utilization through the requirement for municipal collaboration and cooperation with post upper secondary education and in-house company training. In many cases, premises, machinery and teaching resources are used by a number of different education providers.

A parallel initiative is that of Care College (CC). Municipalities, county councils and private healthcare companies, as well as trade unions, collaborate with different education providers at upper secondary and post upper secondary levels in CC. Education should be of high quality, both theoretically and practically, and the aim is to give students a wide measure of influence over content and working forms. Important ideas underlying CC are that the status of the education should be raised and that the vocational area and employers get better conditions for recruiting personnel with the right competence. In order to create a nationwide framework, a national council was formed in 2006, with representatives from employers and trade unions in health and care of the elderly. By the middle of 2010, nine regions had been certified and a number of others were on their way to becoming quality certified. Twenty-one local colleges were approved and around ten applications were being processed.

In the ongoing evaluation, it was stated that CC fulfils the preconditions to be a suitable platform for developing collaboration between education organizers and employers, and their work in healthcare and care of the elderly. Essentially what has been established is the organizational approach itself, while much of the content and concrete work remains. It is clear that CC differs quite substantially, and that the colleges which in some sense have made the greatest progress are those that have had successful development work earlier. Forms of collaboration between the parties involved need to be developed and reviewed as CCs increase their content.

Evaluation carried out of both forms of the College initiative indicate strong and growing interest among regions and educational providers to become certified. Employers have been interested in taking part in the work, both at regional and local levels, although this involves funding the cost of investments. One explanation for the interest and involvement in the project is that employers form the majority on the boards. The evaluations do not provide an answer regarding the extent to which this new form of collaboration has contributed to new thinking, increased quality or greater interest on the part of participants in vocational education. An important conclusion from the College initiative is that it is possible to obtain the support of employers for strategic work on competence development if the conditions are right and the aim is clear. Their interest is not based on access to project funds, but rather on the need to ensure a supply of competence for their own company and region. One risk identified by the evaluation is that the initiative will later require more coordination, support and follow-up, and today there is no national or regional structure capable of managing such an expansion. Another risk is that the dominance of employers in the steering group could lead to education becoming short-term, instrumental and locally oriented, and as a result, not raising participants' employability. In such cases, mobility in the labour market is not improved.

THE PRODUCTION BOOST

In Chapter 2, we mentioned the Production Boost as an interesting national programme which employee and employer organizations jointly initiated, and where the aim of achieving sustainability has been an important driving force. The Production Boost focuses on small and medium-sized industrial companies wishing to develop their production processes with the help of philosophies and tools used within lean production. Lean production builds on Toyota's production system and is described, amongst others, in Jeffrey Liker's book, *The Toyota Way* (2004). The aim is to increase the production competence of companies and thereby strengthen Sweden's competitiveness. This should take place by supporting the development of company management and co-workers. Gradually over time, the Swedish interpretation of lean has changed from a highly critical view towards importing new ideas from abroad (Brulin and Nilsson 1999) and developing a Swedish model of lean, based on employment relations in Sweden (Brulin, Hammarström and Nilsson 2009).

The concept of lean production is central. Company personnel took part in a course in lean production (7.5 higher education credits). This was combined with support and practical work on change at each individual company (total of 60 in the first programming period) through coaching. The programme should play a coordinating role in the build-up of a national structure for competence issues in production for small and medium-sizes companies. The Production Boost's first programming period was financed by national funding agencies.

The first research report showed that the programme was functioning well in many respects (Brulin and Svensson 2011). Ownership at the national level was regarded as strong, even though the roles of the employers and labour organizations, as well as the financiers, were somewhat undefined.

However, there were clear problems in creating a national structure, which can be regarded as a prerequisite for sustainability. Common to the three partnering universities was the fact that steering and management of their work in the Production Boost was largely non-existent. The work of the programme was limited in scope, with less than two full-time positions at the respective higher education establishments, and it was thus not regarded as a major project during the first programming period. The partnering universities all considered that they had more to give on the education side. All three institutions considered that they had the competence to provide lean courses in their own regions, although the Industry Centre at Chalmers had exclusive rights for this in the programme. An important issue for the future was to get the network between partnering universities to function better and with better coordination. It became apparent that the Production Boost needed to take companies' needs as its starting point, and that the local context should be given greater focus when coaching in the company. Another issue raised by the partnering universities and those who were mainly programme providers and project owners was the importance of confidence in each other and developing mutual respect. Traditionally, higher education has competed over students and commissioned education, as well as funds for research and other projects.

The group of financiers, consisting of project case handlers from the three financing organizations, had views on how future cooperation with partnering institutions should be organized, and these covered the following:

- National involvement should be ensured. Resources for implementation should be decentralized – but methods of working retained. Active partners in the agreement should feel that they participate under equal conditions, and that they can influence and shape development.

- There are opportunities for broadening the Production Boost, both by connecting other development work currently run by partnering universities, and by initiating cooperation with other universities.

- Being a party to an agreement should not only be regarded as a benefit, but should also entail responsibility for the Production Boost. Partnering universities should contribute and be involved in the work – they should be active under equal conditions as partners. Work should not only be linked to the coaches. It should also be supported locally.

- A joint identity should be established. The trademark should be safeguarded, so that all companies know the position. When work is carried out within the framework of the Production Boost, all participants should have equal conditions and opportunities to exercise influence.

These viewpoints from the financiers have been the basis for further development of the Production Boost. According to those responsible for the project, expectations have been exceeded in creating an organization in the eight regions. The original three partnering universities participated in drawing up a new programme plan. A number of other partnering higher education institutions who were interested in cooperating have now become involved. In concrete terms, this means that a number of lean courses are being implemented in conjunction with Chalmers in several regions. The expansion in the number of education providers and regional intermediaries can be regarded as a prerequisite for creating a national structure for the programme initiative. What was most difficult was that few companies were interested in taking part, and regional routines for recruiting companies were absent. The major challenge for the future is to be able to supply education and support that companies are themselves prepared to pay for without subsidies from the programme. A new 'Future Group' has also been formed, prior to a new Production Boost version 3.

This programme is interesting from a sustainability perspective. Earlier, we touched on the idea of an effective project organization and close interaction between its different constituent levels. In addition, the programme has been typified by developmental learning that has led to changes over the period, such as the involvement of a number of other universities. Another important part is the dissemination and impact of a new initiative in the public sector – the Activity Boost – which has largely been inspired by the organization and working methods of the Production Boost. In this case, it is appropriate to refer to the multiplier effects of a programme.

SOME CONCLUSIONS ABOUT COMPETENCE INITIATIVES

We have touched on a number of large programmes for competence development in working life and reported a number of interesting examples. It is not difficult to show the scope of projects or that short-term results have occurred, but it is more difficult to identify the long-term effects of such programmes. The problems which companies encounter in finding skilled labour remain, and most employers are still not prepared to finance the necessary further training of employees with their own funds. Despite the high ambitions and major initiatives, the difficulties inherent in the programmes are clear, and concern the following:

- Making the initiatives creative and innovative. The dominance of the formal education system, with its supply thinking and tradition of knowledge transfer, is strong. The thinking and structures, such as large-scale and 'bottom-up' steered labour market training, still exist in some form, where linkage to company needs and participation of individuals is not always clear.

- There are advantages in consciously combining different learning strategies adapted to local conditions, but these opportunities are seldom exploited.

- Transforming competence development into a strategic and prioritized aim, especially in small companies, where individual learning is linked to company operations. The annual follow-up by the national labour union (LO) of companies' further education and training shows that no increase has taken place; in fact the opposite has occurred, as paid training has decreased. In addition, certain groups – members of the national labour union, older persons, temporary employees, part-time employees, young people, immigrants, and so on – received significantly less paid training.

- Transforming the workplace into a learning environment, where methods for analysing operations, validation, supervision, daily learning and formal education are integrated. There are a number of good examples here, but the difficulty has been their dissemination.

- Linking competence initiatives with regional development work, innovation and growth, that is, the different initiative areas for which the Regional and Social Funds are responsible.

- Using the existing infrastructure, such as municipal learning centres, as active intermediaries, to coordinate and strategically develop the initiatives that have been taken and to have an impact on public debate. When this is not possible, new national structures for collaboration can be developed. Collaboration between partnering higher education institutions in the Production Boost is one example of this.

- Finding forms for partners to collaborate in organizing further and vocational training. The College models show that it is possible to create active ownership of competence questions for employers, and that it is not access to funds per se that determines their involvement.

The examples in this book have been chosen to enable comparisons and generalizations to be made. One comparison shows that projects which were run in isolation (such as the Objective 3 programme and the Competence Ladder) are not able to create development dynamics that generate multiplier effects. Initiatives originating from 'below' and which are coordinated by an intermediary (Certified Trainee) or with the help of a national organization (College) have better conditions to succeed in this. National programme initiatives, if they are initiated from the 'bottom up' and from 'outside', can generate multiplier effects, as in the Production Boost. These cases involve some kind of joint development work, where employers and trade unions are actively involved in the initiatives. As regards College, collaboration between the different partners is combined with quality assurance (certification) and enables requirements to be imposed on prospective participants in the programme. Traditional project logic is turned upside down, and this means that project funds are not given unconditionally; applicants must make an effort and demonstrate results in order to be approved for participation.

This section identifies a number of dilemmas and difficulties that vocational education and further training of employees must be able to resolve. One fundamental difficulty is creating collaboration between company training, labour market training and formal education, which by tradition have been very different from the ministry down to the local level. Individual projects may be successful in the short term, but if steering and coordination of the education system cannot be solved at the system level, development work will not be sustainable.

Examination from a Sustainability Perspective

In this chapter we have presented programmes and initiatives of different types. We have shown both the weaknesses and strengths in the examples presented. Can any general conclusions be drawn about programme initiatives on the basis of the three mechanisms for sustainable development? Our view is affirmative. Few or none of the programmes and projects which we have reported have all three mechanisms present. Often active ownership is lacking from the most important actors, and this is particularly clear in innovation programmes. Companies – and particularly entrepreneurs – are seldom active owners and they may also be completely absent in large programme initiatives, where projects are often run by experts or driven by researchers. In clusters, getting companies involved is easier since this form of collaboration is a natural and endemic part of cluster dynamics. However, often it is easier to find active owners for competence measures in the workplace, but even this can be difficult. Learning is often a question reserved for the staff and external education providers, especially in externally funded education initiatives.

Collaboration and joint knowledge formation is the second mechanism in sustainable development work. This mechanism appears to distinguish most of the programmes presented above, but closer examination shows that this is not always the case. Joint knowledge formation seldom exists and learning is often adaptive – rather than developmental or innovative. In innovation programmes, well-educated male public employees appear to dominate, and other groups tend to be excluded. Experts and bureaucrats play a strong role. The consequences of this homogeneity in collaboration are that the variation and differences required for developmental learning to occur are lacking. Instead collaboration tends to be conformist and supportive, rather than critically scrutinizing and innovative. When large groups are excluded and development forces are not leveraged, joint knowledge formation is undermined.

However, it appears to be easier to achieve joint knowledge formation in more focused and production-oriented initiatives, such as the Competence Ladder, Certified Trainee and College. The difficulty is maintaining collaboration when external financing and support cease. Experiences show that learning must be organized and supported if it is to be oriented to development and action. The examples of competence initiatives show that it is easier for such development to 'walk on two legs', that is, results of an initiative are easier to assess and reflect over, thereby facilitating progress in development work. As regards large and complex innovation systems, where visions and collaboration are often instrumental, it becomes difficult to assess progress and setbacks, and to learn from them. Instead we can consider this to be 'system-blocked learning', where many different actors and initiatives can only be evaluated with difficulty. The requirements imposed on ongoing evaluators and interactive researchers are increasing, and their role is becoming strategic in the development of these systems.

The third mechanism which typifies programme implementation for sustainable development – namely developmental learning aimed at multiplier effects – is what is most obviously lacking in most of the programmes presented above. The necessary knowledge, experiences, theories, strategies and support forms for organizing such learning were missing, making it difficult for project results to be disseminated, to achieve strategic impact and to promote public debate. There are, however, elements in Certified Trainee, College and Production Boost which do have mechanisms for sustainability in this respect. It is our view that the lack of intermediaries is an important explanation for the difficulties in using this mechanism. The initiatives taken so far – in the form of institutes, industrial development centres, municipal learning centres, R&D centres, universities, and so on – have seldom managed the task of achieving progress in sustainable development work. These intermediaries could have an important role as 'engines', but this would necessitate development work with this focus, a feature that has been notably lacking in the programmes we have examined.

In Chapter 2, two models for evaluation were presented – a planning-steered and a development-supportive model. Learning is crucial in the latter. Our review in this chapter shows how dominant the first model is, even in areas for which it was not intended or designed. The projects which we reported under the section on competence development show that a number of interesting attempts have been made to test an approach based on learning and development. The difficulties have been to organize, manage and create a structure for an open way of working that would be sustainable in the long term. This is a genuine dilemma, striking a balance between openness (which is a prerequisite for innovation) together with flexible planning, and a structure based on learning through ongoing evaluation that leads to strategic impact.

One important result from the review in this chapter shows that development presupposes interaction between different levels – the individual, organizational and social levels. Researchers and those responsible for development are aware of the importance of connecting individual learning to business development, but this is often difficult to achieve in practice. One precondition is that leaders and management are actively involved in the project. It is still more difficult to link together initiatives in companies with regional development. The consequence could be that successful changes at the organizational level remain isolated and do not contribute to the dynamics of regional development. The lack of intermediaries is a major shortcoming in this context.

What can the Social and Regional Funds do to deal with this difficulty and other shortcomings that we have highlighted in this chapter? Has there been any progress in making programme implementation more innovative and strategic? Can competence initiatives be combined successfully with regional development? What cooperation takes place between both funds now that they come under the same Regional Structural Fund partnerships? What does this mean, in terms of the issues that should be prioritized, and for disseminating learning between programmes?

6

Lessons from Competence Initiatives

In the previous chapter we provided a more overarching description and analysis of earlier programmes and project initiatives. In this chapter we will present results from evaluation and research regarding the Social Fund during the programming period 2007–2013. A central issue is whether this programming period has succeeded any better in making projects more sustainable. We will begin by reporting results from a survey carried out in 2010 addressed to half of all projects and aimed at employees, where the content involves competence development (see Chapter 1). The results from the survey provide a more general picture, showing patterns and relationships. In the following sections, we report a number of case studies which, in concrete and more detailed terms, show what makes a project more sustainable.

What Does the Survey Show?

We will summarize the results under a number of headings. The report also builds on a report from Statistics Sweden (Brulin and Svensson 2011).

MANY ACTIVITIES AND RESULTS

Statistics indicate that overall the programme so far appears to function in terms of the number of projects and participants. The goal of the Social Fund was a total of 4,000 projects and some 315,000 participants. However, it has been difficult to include projects in the programme area aimed at people outside the labour market and vulnerable groups, including people on long-term sick leave. This difficulty can be interpreted as indicating weak ownership of the project on the part of the organizations. Overall the programme appears to reach out to men and women of different ages and regions, both Swedish and foreign-born, in companies of varying sizes and in different industries. The well educated appear to get more resources than the lower educated, which conflicts with the goals of the programme.

How can an assessment be made as to whether all activities in the projects have led to expected results? Reviewing the evaluations and the documentation, it is easy to see that the projects have led to a number of results. A large amount of training has been carried out. A number of methods, instruments and tools were developed in the projects, covering mapping of competencies, guidance and counselling, support, collaboration and validation. New forms of practice were tested and developed in the projects. Often there was an ambition to combine individual learning and changes in operations, especially where managers were involved, but the strength of this relationship was unclear.

What results did the project managers consider that they had achieved? We compared responses between projects that had been ongoing over both longer and shorter periods. It turned out that more results were achieved the longer a project had been running, which indicates that the projects were delivering. Project managers had a better and deeper understanding of more of the results compared with the leaders. Those who worked in the public arena were more positive to the results achieved. This picture of a large number of activities leading to results is confirmed by the interviews, meetings and seminars which we have participated in, and existing documentation and evaluation.

DIFFICULTIES IN THE PROJECTS

There are problems and difficulties to be overcome in organizing and administering an initiative of this scope, amongst other things, as a consequence of economic turbulence and resulting layoffs and redundancies. It takes time to initiate, plan and quickly get started with large, complicated projects and to complete them on time. Individual projects must be suspended when conditions change rapidly. Large strategic projects require collaboration between different actors and organizations, which makes decision-making cumbersome and lengthy. Forty-two per cent of the respondents considered that there were problems and difficulties in implementing projects. From the responses, it was evident that problems and difficulties in the projects were common. The problems can be grouped into the following areas:

- managing project funds, that is, the bureaucracy involved in reporting and accounting for use of project funds;

- changes in settings – amongst other things, redundancies and lay-offs – which made it difficult to implement competence development as planned;

- shortage of time, that is, competition with daily activities, was perceived as the major problem in implementing a project as planned;

- weak project management, bad teachers and training not customized to company needs;

- a lack of motivation to participate amongst employees was referred to as an obstacle by some. Among some groups of employees, there was a widespread feeling of tiredness over change and projects.

In summary, we can state that most of the difficulties were connected with changes in conditions and a lack of time. Here we will focus on the causes of problems and difficulties. Problems were, amongst other things, connected to how projects originated. A number referred to poor preparation as one explanation for the problems: 'The application was badly written, and we felt there was a lack of information from the consultant helping us' (project managers). When management took the initiative to start projects, there were fewer problems compared with a situation where projects were initiated by an external person (consultant, education provider or researcher). The questionnaire could debunk the myth that projects are in general initiated by consultants. In more than half of the cases, management had taken the initiative in starting a project, but it was a project manager who had planned and been the driving force, once the project started. Another interesting result is that employees were seldom active at the start of a project. This applies particularly to the trade unions. The trade unions only had a strong driving role in 1 per cent of the projects. Here it turns out that the influence of the trade unions has decreased over the programming periods.

Rapidly changing external and internal conditions for development work reinforce the idea that a project must be able to change course over time, particularly as regards implementation. However, this requires close and continuous cooperation with the European Social Fund (ESF) office, so that those responsible for projects can receive fast and clear answers on what is permissible. The importance of the project's prehistory is something we have been aware of. Earlier studies of the Social Fund showed that the reason for applying for project funds was important for implementation and achieving results. Applicants who were motivated by 'opportunistic' motives achieved worse results. Our survey shows similar results. Workplaces without competence development, apart from the project, tended more often to give opportunistic reasons for their participation. The ambition of achieving change in work organizations and methods of working was lower in these projects.

If there was ongoing work on competence development in the workplace, implementing the project was easier. Workplaces which had previously participated in projects had higher ambitions of achieving change, for example, in the area of gender equality. Support within the company turned out to be a key issue. Managers thought more often than consultants that there was an ambition to change working methods and organization – for example, delegating responsibility, introducing job rotation, developing work teams or creating broader work content. When management took the initiative in starting a project, linkage to changes in operations were clearer, especially when there were obvious shortcomings in the competence of staff as regards quality, managing change, cooperation and taking responsibility. If competence development is run in the workplace, then competence development is more clearly linked to changes in operations.

The importance of managerial involvement was also apparent in the implementation of competence measures. If there was support from supervisors and managers, projects more often led to changes in operations. Workplace learning presupposes support from management and leaders to function. The survey also showed that supervisors were important in strengthening vocational competence, as was the use of validation. Validation becomes particularly important when the aim is to change working methods or operations. Our data shows the general importance of active ownership, where management and/or politicians support ongoing development work through their actions.

Workplace learning is not without its problems. If the leader or project manager is active in the implementation of training, then participants' company-related competence will increase, but their general employability is considered to become worse. This is an interesting result from the survey that needs to be followed up. The results show the risk of allowing companies themselves to decide content and how competence development is organized. More generally oriented training, which is important for creating employability, turned out not to contribute as clearly to company-specific competence or quality awareness. The survey also showed another interesting result, namely the interaction between different competencies. This concerned, amongst other things, questions about motivation, the overall picture, professional expertise and interest in development work, where learning processes appear to create a dynamic driving force amongst participants to learn more and apply their knowledge. Those who responded that participants had become more interested in development work agreed more often that the project had contributed to increasing the company's competitiveness. The survey can in fact show a perceived linkage between the individual's learning and the development of operations.

CONTENT AND IMPLEMENTATION

The survey was based on studies carried out earlier in the Social Fund. It provides unique opportunities to make comparisons between different programming periods. What similarities and differences do we see? Studies from both programming periods show that project management and those responsible for projects experienced good results both at the individual and operations level. About 90 per cent in the later survey agreed (strongly or partially) that participants had increased their competence. This applied particularly to participants' interest in new learning and enhancing their professional expertise (95 per cent). The results were also experienced as positive (with similar figures) in terms of operations development. These high values from studies of two different programming periods must be interpreted with caution. We know from experience that project management and those responsible for projects tend to give positive assessments of their projects. Bias towards over-valuing effects from the projects seems to operate as there were high scores on the response scale. The responses reflect a strong belief in projects and what they should lead to. The responses become more interesting regarding concrete changes, for example, changes in operations or the number of new jobs created, and then the assessment becomes different and less positive.

The surveys reveal shortcomings in participation when initiating, developing and implementing projects, especially during the later programming period. Here there is a clear difference between the programming periods. In the earlier period, participation was a requirement, which led to much focus. There is nothing preventing an authority from introducing this requirement in its call for tenders in the current programme, but this has not happened. This example shows how difficult it is to bring in experiences from earlier programming periods when this is not explicitly stated in the programme document. Trade union participation in project development and implementation appears to have been lower in this programming period. This may be partly a consequence of withdrawing the participation requirement in project initiation, but it may also be because the union now has fewer resources to work proactively and/or they are not prioritizing development.

During both programming periods, courses (in and outside the workplace) were the most common means of organizing competence development. Common to both programming periods is the lack of experimentation and new thinking over the organization of competence development. Redundancy announcements in the current programming period contributed to the rapid start-up of competence development and because of this, the choice of well tested forms.

An interesting question is what would different learning strategies look like in the different programming periods, and to what extent would they differ? The similarities dominate since the training initiative in different forms – both in and outside the workplace – dictates in both programming periods. There are, however, certain differences. The later survey shows that the use of validation became more common during this programming period. Awareness of the importance of using the hidden competence of employees has increased and new methods are now available. Validation is often linked to participants using their new competence at work. The results confirm research findings showing the importance of education as an integral part of core operations and the company's long-term strategy. Validation can thus play an important role in linking learning to development work.

It is too early to study how different methods and learning forms affect results during this programming period since so few projects had been completed at the time of the survey. One interesting observation, however, is the weak relationship between different methods on the one hand, and project aims and expectations vis-à-vis results on the other. The lack of clear and systematic relationships in this respect indicates shortcomings in initiation where routinely a certain method appears to have been chosen for training which is not linked to any specific aim in the project. The linkage between approach, execution and goals is, as a result, unclear in most cases. The shortcomings may be partly a consequence of the fact that no competence audit or business analysis was carried out, or that little knowledge of learning forms and methods appropriate for a particular purpose exists. An overall conclusion from the later survey is that more time should be devoted to preparation, initiation and analysis in the early stages of a project. Sixty-nine per cent responded that the project made additional initiatives possible, but the question is what does this mean? Does it mean more of the same thing, or something new to be tested in the project?

Long-term Effects

Overall our assessment is that activities and results are not the major problem facing the Social or Regional Funds. A large number of activities were started and a number of results achieved. Instead the key question is what long-term effects can project results be expected to lead to. Here it becomes more difficult for us to make an assessment since few projects have been completed. Nevertheless, we can critically examine project organization based on how the projects have worked on strategic impact, and what multiplier effects they aimed to reach. We will start off by providing some examples of how different projects focused on long-term aspects and sustainability. The first example should illustrate how strategic impact can be transmitted through a project where a trade union is the owner. In this case it is very easy to show multiplier effects of different kinds. The second example deals with six contractors collaborating with a large customer to streamline production under the management of an intermediary – in this case, an industrial development centre. The example illustrates the importance of active ownership and clear steering of the project, but also shows how collaboration is dependent on an active intermediary. The following two examples apply to the social economy and how better conditions can be created in projects for more long-term strategic work. The first case deals with how a training project leads into strategic cooperation between different actors in the social economy. The second example is unique in that it shows how a social company was developed through innovative ideas which were commercialized in very different markets. The final example deals with municipal collaboration over managing the supply of competence in the future. The project has been reorganized to strengthen steering and ownership, and provide better conditions for sustainability in development work.

A LOCAL PROJECT BECOMES NATIONAL

There are examples, but they are extremely rare, where the trade union plays a proactive and strategic role in local and regional development work in the Social Fund. Different projects run by the Metal Union in Sweden are amongst the few exceptions. This deals with a total of five projects where more than 1,000 people took part in competence development from around 35 small companies. The project was aimed at small companies needing competence development. The companies met the trade union and discussed what competence development was necessary for them to be able to grow and meet global competition. Based on these discussions, the project built a platform with educational organizers to enable the companies to provide joint education for their personnel. Cooperation covered procurement with a framework agreement, and customized education.

Instead of calling a large number of education providers, the companies now had a project coordinator to manage this. The project functioned effectively as regards content, implementation and cost-effectiveness. New forms of cooperation have also been created between the companies as a consequence of the training. Both the companies and the Metal Union had discussions on how methods and working approaches developed in the project could be used as a basis for permanently organizing their training: 'In the current situation, we are thinking about what such a platform would look like. Possibly we could form a joint association. We have submitted a new application to the Social Fund to build up a permanent operation' (project managers). These five projects are interesting for other reasons as well, namely the strategic impact achieved at national level. One consequence of this regional project is that the Metal Union decided at the central level to be more active in the Social Fund and to monitor tender announcements more closely. A representative from the Metal Union has been appointed in each ESF region. Together these representatives draw up development strategies, plan future projects and develop national collaboration in the Social Fund: 'We believe that we can raise the competence of our members. But it also involves creating sustainable working life in industry and society as a whole' (person responsible at the Metal Union's Head Office). A trade union representative takes the initiative to start a project that later turns into five projects. Perhaps this is not so unusual, but the project reinforces ongoing activity in one of our largest trade unions. It is part of a long-term strategy dealing with the new role of the trade union, namely to be proactive and strategic as regards competence development. The Metal Union is now working with a number of applications to the Social Fund, both at regional and national levels. An application has been submitted for a national call for tenders and this has been granted in competition with a large number of projects. At the central level, the trade union takes on the role of coordinating and integrating this work. Locally, departments are responsible for contacts with companies interested in participating in different projects. There is yet another dimension to strategic impact at a national level, but so far we have only been able to see its broad outlines. Possibly the involvement of the trade union in questions dealing with learning and development of operations could be regarded as part of a Swedish contribution to a European model for sustainable working life. Such a model can build on the parties working together for a working life which covers good working conditions and efficient production, at the same time as it generates growth and rising standards of living. This would then be a continuation and further elaboration of the Metal Union's widely circulated ideas about 'The Good Work' presented during the 1980s. In the new version, the Metal Union talks today about sustainable working life. This project clearly shows how multiplier effects can be created when there is a national organization to back up and leverage local experiences. In this way, work supported by enthusiasts will be institutionalized and conditions for sustainability will increase.

COMPETENCE DEVELOPMENT FOR SUB-SUPPLIERS

The aim of this project was to strengthen the competence of employees in six smaller companies on the basis of needs identified through mapping in a pre-project. Mapping in the pre-project showed that there was a lack of vocational competence in areas such as welding, lasers and programming. There was also a lack of professional competence on the part of those responsible for purchasing and project management. Participants needed to strengthen their vocational competence in TPS (Toyota Production System) in order to be able to meet new and increasing demands imposed on them today and in the future. By strengthening employee competence, company competitiveness would be increased. All six participating companies stand at the crossroads of a new way of working. The requirements which BT (a large company in the Toyota group) and other customers impose on them requires structured work with TPS, which imposes new competence requirements on all co-workers. TPS requires knowledge of a number of different methods and tools, but it is also a basic philosophy for efficient production with requirements for ongoing improvements, high quality and cooperation.

The project will develop forms for how companies can continue to work with competence development after project completion. The mapping of competencies, done in the pre-project and to be implemented at the end of the project, should be a working approach that can be used in development dialogues, and to develop new competence-raising measures. The idea is to apply the concept of lean production methods to also bring about permanent improvements in the project. In the steering and project groups, new tools and methods will be employed which today are used for managing deviations and root cause analysis in production. The method systematically breaks down a problem until a solution is found. The learning evaluation procured should support this work. The procurement contains a requirement that the evaluators propose improvements in the training and activities included in the project.

There are a number of aspects which we consider to be particularly interesting in this project, which we are currently evaluating, hence the results are still provisional. The results of the project will be critical for the companies' capacity to survive and develop. If they lose a major customer such as BT, then their survival will be at risk. The importance of the project can be seen from the fact that production management is actively involved, amongst other things, in the steering group, but above all in implementation at their own company. A representative of BT is a member of the steering group and clearly emphasizes the necessity of fast and real improvements if the companies are to remain suppliers. Here we see active ownership, both from the customer and company management perspectives. Essentially, external pressure for change means that the project and competence initiatives are given strategic importance and attention (cf. Ellström and Kock 2009). The results of different evaluations of training are continuously monitored and the requirements for improvements are forwarded when results deviate from expectations. The ambition of continuously making things better is part of the lean philosophy and appears to have had an impact on the project culture.

An industrial development centre (IDC) has played an important role in bringing about this collaboration between suppliers and a major customer. The IDC has functioned as an active intermediary, both as a broker and a driving force. Without the centre's proactive and strategic work, collaboration between the companies would not have materialized. Neither individually nor together would they have been able to organize their collaboration, nor would they have had the time or resources to apply for project funds and submit an application. In the immediate crisis that afflicted the companies and which led to lay-offs, they did not have the capacity on their own to organize strategic development work. They needed support and practical assistance with organization and collaboration. The example shows what regional and competence development can achieve if it is introduced in the right situation and backed up by management, with external support. Most of the companies in this county are located in small towns, and they are important locally for its future development.

It is still too early to determine what the long-term effects of the project will be within the companies. However, there are a number of indications that conditions for sustainable development are good. Everything seems to flow when the right conditions exist and when the work is well managed by an effective project organization with well-developed interaction between the actors. The IDC can function as a broker and an engine in development work that leads to multiplier effects in a regional arena. It becomes an intermediary facilitating learning and cooperation between different actors – customers, suppliers, education providers and researchers. Projects and collaboration, however, do not solve all problems. There were seven companies at the beginning of the project, but one has now outsourced its production abroad.

COMPETENCE DEVELOPMENT IN THE SOCIAL ECONOMY

The social economy has had a number of projects approved by the Social Fund, amongst other things, within the framework of a national call for tenders. Projects often involve associations and organizations working with vulnerable groups to strengthen their employability through different forms of support and competence initiatives. The idea is that the social economy, through new forms for activating work and support, will strengthen these groups in new and better ways. We will describe one such project, where the project management and steering group themselves reflected on sustainability and the difficulties that arose, as these are typical for similar projects where competence initiatives should lead to development. The project, Competent Social Economy, aims at strengthening the social economy's personnel in the County of Stockholm so that the associations can retain their employees, expand the business and later employ more people. Another goal of the project is that public employees receive competence development in how, by using new forms of collaboration and with the help of new actors, they can solve problems in society in a new way. Another starting point in the project is to find new financing forms for the social economy in the future. Coompanion Stockholm County, which plays a coordinating role in the social economy in the county, is the project owner. The project owner carries out some training under its own auspices, but the majority is procured.

The evaluation showed early on that the goal of training 1,000 people in the social economy was the mobilizing force for the whole project. The risk is that focus ends up on activities and their outcomes, and not on the long-term effects for the social economy. It was also difficult to fulfil the quantitative training goals, which contributed to the overall aim (strengthening the social economy) fading into the background. At a steering group meeting, where evaluators participated together with project handlers from the Social Fund, the specifics of the training goal could be organized so that other and more strategic parts of the project could be discussed.

Awareness has grown subsequently in the steering group on the importance of working with strategic impact. Afterwards it was understood to be necessary to take advantage of the results from the project and find ways of further developing collaboration models in the region between the social economy and important actors. At a later steering group meeting, discussions were held on how long-term development support could be organized, and which actors and organizations were affected, as well as which of them could function as active project owners and intermediaries. If the project can contribute to better coordination between different actors and organizations in the social economy, then it has contributed to and created conditions for increased sustainability. Different actors were identified and invited to participate in the working group in order to establish relationships, agree on the distribution of responsibility and formulate strategies.

This project exhibits a typical pattern, where there is a focus on quantitative training goals and a steering group with an unclear mandate and varying degrees of involvement. It meant that the overarching aim and strategic work was not prioritized. Thus the conditions for creating developmental learning to generate multiplier effects did not exist at the beginning. At the same time, the example shows something even more important, namely that it is possible to highlight problems and try to resolve them. In this work, learning evaluation can function as a support and as a catalyst for changing work and its direction. There was strong involvement amongst participants in the social economy, but the preconditions for using the results were often poor. A project which takes the initiative to coordinate the development of a platform for the social economy in the region can in the long run be of major strategic importance. In this way an intermediary was created to organize meeting forums, mediate contacts and function as a driving force in the regional work of developing a strong social economy.

THE BASTA EXAMPLE

The Basta work cooperative was inspired by the cooperative for drug addicts in San Patrignano in Italy, where 700 former heroin addicts ran a financially successful company. The founder of Basta decided to start a similar enterprise in Sweden. At that time the social economy was still relatively unknown in Sweden. In 1994 Basta received its first addict. In 2008 the business had a turnover of 50 million Swedish crowns and around 100 employees. A number of Social Fund projects provided support. These included Yes-education, which is a one-year vocational and entrepreneurial programme for marginalized groups. The project started in 2002 and was later supplemented by a vocational and validation programme for newly arrived refugees from the Middle East. The focus is on woodworkers, tilers, horse grooming, dog trainers and other occupations. Other initiatives involved the participation of users from a university training programme, where a number of user organizations, associations and higher education institutes now function as partners. One project involves microfinancing, where different savings banks, the Stockholm School of Economics, the Public Employment Services and others participate. Transnational work is regarded as important, both for project development and learning.

The pedagogical approach should be 'liberating' for participants, and be based on their experience and a strong belief in their ability. Working methods are based on openness and dynamism, as well as shared and equal responsibility between students and teachers, where gender equality is strongly emphasized. The environment should be similar to what participants are used to, and create security in a setting where 'failing' is permitted.

The programme leaders emphasize that Basta is not a treatment centre, but a social company run by former addicts for people who wish to overcome their addiction. Most of the people coming to Basta are men in their 40s, with an average of 20 years of drug abuse and 12 years of prison behind them. Here rehabilitation is run entirely without traditional treatment methods, pedagogues and experts; the idea is based on the fact that all who come here do so of their own free will. Participants are supported with somewhere to live, a salary and work. Ninety-five per cent of those who are employees come from the target group and have themselves been rehabilitated through Basta. They should serve as a model and inspiration to newcomers. An evaluation shows that participants had a greater belief in their own capabilities and that discussions in the classroom made it easier for them to express themselves. The evaluation explains the success as due to flexible teaching that is largely adapted to participants' needs.

The Basta collective is interesting from our perspective on development as it focuses on long-term effects. Here developmental learning is strong and has led to multiplier effects. Since more people come to Basta and want to stay and build up the company, it must be continuously developed. It is easy to identify the development forces in different areas within the cooperative. A pedagogical approach developed for addicts was disseminated to students who, tired of school, apply on their own initiative for a place in the programme. Basta began accepting young people who did not fit into regular upper secondary school, and in autumn 2007 started a vocational and validation programme for people from the Middle East. Basta also sells its education and training to the social services, prison and probation services, and its education places in Yes-training to municipalities. Users also participate in university programmes for social workers within the framework of a Social Fund project. The different projects provide experiences which are analysed and lead to new projects, and above all functioning operations that do not require project funding for their survival and development.

Basta has succeeded in managing the transition from public support to operating in a competitive market. Companies in Basta are run on commercial conditions, completely without grants and in competition with other care providers, but without any profit requirement. The business has also expanded its geographical coverage. One example that can be mentioned is of a business built up in a Swedish city with 25 full-time employees; and these ideas have also spread to another city. The ideas that have been tested are innovative and range over a number of areas. A shared feature is that experimentation is combined with support from strong partners. The work is activity-oriented, but combined with systematic learning – amongst other things, through different evaluations which have led to publications analysing operations. Those responsible consider that financing from the Social Fund has been vital in providing time, resources and support for development work. Funds have functioned as a kind of venture capital, something which does not exist in the social economy. Project funds have enabled an experimental and pragmatic approach to be taken. The aim has been clear – not to be dependent on project funding, but to develop services that are in demand and which can be sold on the market. 'Everything that is done should be for real' is the motto. Work has taken place in small partnerships, where the creativity and involvement of participants can be maintained.

MUNICIPAL COOPERATION IN THE SUPPLY OF COMPETENCE

The Generation Shift is a large Social Fund project aiming to manage the supply of competence for municipalities in the future. In Sweden as in other mature welfare states, millions of municipal employees will have retired within a decade. Of these, a large proportion are managers and supervisors. Ensuring the supply of competence involves finding ways and forms of working to attract, recruit, introduce, maintain and develop competence. The overall aim of the project is to facilitate generational change in municipalities through competence development, and at the same time make the municipalities attractive working places. A mobilization phase has been carried out where eight municipalities have together implemented a number of activities and planned an implementation phase. There is a steering group for the mobilization phase consisting of municipal directors and personnel heads in participating municipalities. There is one sub-project manager in each municipality who, together with the project manager, makes up the project's working group. This description aims to show how work was done to strengthen the project organization, especially the role and responsibility of the steering group. At the same time, the example shows how learning collaboration can be organized.

At an early stage, the project had not established firm structures; it lacked active ownership in a number of the municipalities. The municipality which should function as the support recipient did not wish to take on this responsibility, so another municipality took up the role. Distribution of responsibility and work in the project organization was unclear, and much rested on the shoulders of the project manager. There was a lack of interest and involvement from some of the members of the steering group, and it was unclear how feedback to municipal management and politicians would work out. When the project manager felt that the conditions for implementing the project did not exist, she turned to one of the Social Fund's process support options. This led to the steering group and project management spending two days going through the vision, aims and goals of the project. The steering group discussed and formulated the aims of the project and drew up its priorities. In this way, they were able to take command of the project.

One problem, in fact, was that the project application had been drawn up by a group of consultants who had not got support for their ideas from those responsible in the municipalities. Another part of this meeting involved clarifying roles, tasks and distribution of work and responsibility in the project organization. The steering group clearly emphasized that they wanted to play an active role and that their responsibility was to create the conditions for active ownership in the municipalities, which was considered vital for the project to lead to long-term effects. In the municipalities, there was an awareness of the importance of flexible competence at the top level, but there was little systematic work to prioritize the question and make it an integral part of personnel and strategy work.

From the minutes of a board meeting before the implementation phase of the project, the importance of learning and collaboration was emphasized:

> *The steering group's programme statement prior to implementation stated that the project in terms of methods should use the competence and good examples existing in the participating municipalities in order to stimulate learning, and also monitor what exists in the surrounding world. A guiding principle of the project is collaboration between the municipalities in the project. By means of the collaboration started in the mobilization phase, the project laid the foundations for future collaboration between participating municipalities. This was viewed as an innovative approach, where learning and exchange of experience in the project contribute to competence development. Learning is an active process in the project, and means that participants are open to new knowledge and are genuinely curious. Innovative learning takes place in interaction when people with different backgrounds and experiences meet to develop a common purpose for an assignment or a question.*

In the workshops the project created a forum for learning between participants from different municipalities. The work of creating strategic impact was led in the first instance by the steering group, working group and project management. All those involved will disseminate all the good examples which the project develops. Learning and awareness of the importance of organizing collaboration has developed in the context of the difficulties encountered in the project. The same minutes also recognized the difficulties that had existed in the project organization, and what was required in the future, covering, amongst other things, the following:

- the time taken to become a steering group;

- the importance of clear expectations and assignments;

- the importance of clarifying roles; how 'hands-on' should the steering group be?

- the expectations placed on the project group by the steering group must be clear and communicated;

- meeting discipline and playing rules must be determined at project start-up;

- the importance of there being a mix of competencies in the steering group.

At a later steering group meeting, members were able to discuss what the project could contribute in the long term in different municipalities and what obstacles could be encountered en route. Expectations were high and they applied to the following: more strategic, structured and long-term work on the supply of competence; developing cooperation with other municipalities; finding forms for individual and organizational learning that are systematic and prioritized. When someone finishes, the person with knowledge should be 'debriefed', but at the same time mobility is recognized as a part of renewal and the further development of operations. In addition, projects should be a means for the municipalities to manage the new requirements arising from changes in the external world and new forms of steering.

The conditions and obstacles that were highlighted above all concerned the importance of broad and deep participation, as well as strong support at management level and amongst politicians. Participation presupposes that the project is understandable and attractive for many, and that support requires the project to be flexibly organized, so that it can be applied in all the municipalities. The vision is that the generational change should be solved in the municipalities involved in a few years.

What conclusions can be drawn from this project, and how are they related to our three mechanisms for sustainable development work? The aim here is to assess how effectively the project functioned and whether any long-term effects were achieved. Some of the important conclusions we can draw so far are:

1. It is difficult to cooperate and it takes time to develop relationships, shared views and responsibility, particularly if the project has been initiated externally and there has been little time to prepare the groundwork.

2. It is important to spend time on formulating goals where the steering group can discuss, try different approaches, reflect and determine their standpoints, and repeat this process when membership of the steering group changes.

3. It is valuable to sort out the distribution of work and responsibility in the project organization, where the mandate and feedback between representatives in the steering group and municipal management/ politicians is a key issue for sustainability.

4. It is also very important that somebody external to the organization can provide support in this learning process between the participants. From the beginning, process support helped with this, but in the future this will be a task for learning evaluation.

Essentially, this example shows how a project does not follow linear and predetermined logic. Instead, development takes place by learning how to handle the difficulties and dilemmas that occur en route. This presupposes flexible planning, clarity over roles and responsibilities, being able to learn from earlier mistakes, using support from external sources, acting proactively and reflectively, and an awareness that collaboration is both demanding and complicated. Such a perspective means that development can be more realistic and sustainable. Before the implementation phase, the steering group clarified each municipality's commitments, the role of working groups, as well as the distribution of areas of responsibility for different spheres, and this shows that learning has been transformed into action and led to the creation of a project organization which facilitates professional steering and active ownership.

Some Concluding Comments

The majority of programmes implemented have not succeeded in demonstrating that they have produced long-term effects, for example, as regards employment, growth, innovation, or inclusion in the labour market (see Chapter 5). What can we expect, then, from the Social Fund? Isn't it too early to require long-term effects from the programme? To some extent, but nevertheless reasoning about the usefulness and value of the project in these terms, especially its long-term focus and sustainability, are central goals in the Social Fund. The examples presented above can provide a basis for such a discussion, but in that case our starting point is *indicators* of effects, rather than well-documented examples.

The Metal Union project has meant that cooperation between labour market partners has been established, and can be expected to continue at the regional level, possibly even without external project funding. The project led to the creation of a regional infrastructure for adult learning. This includes a web platform, establishment of relationships between the trade union and a number of companies, collaboration with different education providers, systems for procurement of training, and so on. At the national level, we can see a clear effect from the project. The central office of the union has started working on competence and development issues in a strategic way. A national project has been started. Work on development could lead to the revitalization of the earlier well-known initiative 'The Good Work'. The union has created a new, national organization, enabling it to be more active in Social Fund projects. The inspiration for this has been the regional work in the Metal Union which we have reported. This project is a good illustration of our criteria for sustainable development work, namely developmental learning leading to multiplier effects.

The lean project is an interesting example of how strong and acute external pressure for change stimulates the involvement of management. Suppliers were at the very bottom of BT's list as regards quality assessments, and they risked losing their largest customer. The example shows the importance of customer involvement in development work and contributing their competence, which in this case is unique because of the connection with the Toyota group. An effective project organization, the ongoing requirement to make project and development work more efficient, an active intermediary and possible regional multiplier effects – all this makes the project's progress very interesting to monitor in the future.

Examples from the social economy are interesting in different ways, but in both cases relate to the importance of working strategically and over the long term. The first case showed how awareness grows and project owners try to strengthen their role as intermediaries and coordinators in regional development work. In the second case, strong development dynamics were driven by an increase in applicants from outside the business. New job opportunities must be created and innovativeness is high in terms of finding business areas.

The project with the eight municipalities illustrates the importance of creating conditions for active ownership and professional steering. Initiation of a project is important, and if there are shortcomings in this phase, they must be rapidly corrected. This is not done on one single occasion, but must be done over and over again, and be based on the involvement of participants. Creating inter-organizational learning between municipalities which have not cooperated previously requires a project organization with clear distribution of responsibility and work.

Which Findings Can Be Generalized?

What is specifically Swedish about the findings presented in this chapter? Very little, in our view. There is extensive research from different parts of the world that supports our findings from Sweden (Malland et al. 2011). In fact we would argue that Sweden is a highly illustrative case.

The importance of combining individual and organizational learning is a continuous theme in the research literature. The application of professional and occupational skills must be seen from a holistic and contextual perspective, and this involves the use of mentors, support from co-workers in a community of practice, actively interested supervisors and managers, time for learning and reflection, access to teachers in the workplace (physically or virtually) and the use of e-learning.

Another central finding is the usefulness of integrating formal, non-formal and informal learning. There is a shift from schools to workplaces. The workplace is seen as a highly important arena for learning. The more narrow term 'training' is increasingly being replaced by 'workplace learning'. By using the workplace as a learning arena, the outcome of a learning activity is considered to be more work-related and useful for the organization. A study of Vocational Education and Training (VET) in Korea can illustrate some of the themes and findings presented above. A comprehensive approach is taken to lifelong learning that includes active ownership and partnership cooperation by strategic partners, according to the Triple Helix concept. In Korea, VET is seen as an important mechanism for innovation and growth. One initiative for a lifelong VET system was directed towards under-represented groups, such as workers in SMEs, non-regular workers, the unemployed and low-skilled people (Choi 2011). The focus on SMEs is related to the increasing productivity gap between large enterprises and SMEs. Two pilot activities have been launched by the Korean government. It is possible for individuals to accumulate learning credits based on various learning experiences and receive new opportunities to acquire academic certificates. An online training scheme has also been introduced for the provision of vocational training. The number of participants in this programme increased from 27,000 to 740,000 in a few years (Choi 2011: 246). Efforts to establish a Korean qualification framework have also been introduced. The partnership approach is central in these programmes. Different consortia are organized, including large enterprises, SMEs, public training institutes, universities and employer organizations. At the national level, there is a VET partnership between labour, management and the government.

In Australia, competence-based training is used as a central platform, as part of a national initiative. The focus is on industry-specific skills rather than traditional course inputs or content, in order to promote organizational capacity-building. Different programmes and projects have shown that competence-based training can encourage workplace participation and commitment, promote professional identity and career development, reduce staff turnover and, in some instances, increase workplace productivity. One critique of this approach is the omission of teachers in the introduction of training programmes (Clemans and Rushbrook 2011).

In the United States, the approach to education has historically fluctuated between an emphasis on general education and more vocationally oriented education. Despite the growing recognition of the relationship between work-related learning and economic development, parents prefer college preparatory programmes for their children. Work-related learning within the United States is highly decentralized and pluralistic, which leads to ambivalence and uncertainty about the effects on individual job performance and organizational productivity. There is also a change from an instrumental perception of work-based learning, where specific skills are learnt, to a more complex and multifaceted understanding of learning. The relationship between work-based learning and higher education is debated and a more integrated approach is advocated. In summary, work-based learning has come a long way since the early days of trade apprenticeships, with an emerging rapprochement between work-related learning and general education. This development is mirrored by growing reliance on partnerships between industry and educational institutions and agencies (Dirkx 2011).

However, there is also a risk in workplace learning – skills can be seen as distinct from innovation. Skills are about what is already known, while innovation is about knowledge yet to come. The Canadian programmes for skill development are separated from the innovation strategy, which occupies a central position. This leads to new confusion and ambivalence, especially about the state's responsibilities for increasing workforce skills (Fenwick 2011). What will happen if the state abdicates this role? This will be a major problem because we know that, for most employers, workers' learning is not a priority but a low-order decision. Ideas and expectations about workforce development will seldom be put into practice in large and complex organizations (Evans, Waite and Kersh 2011).

The relationship between universities and workplaces is critically scrutinized by Costley (2011). Work-based learning is directly related to participants' real-time work activities, supported by new technologies for e-learning. The focus is on the learners themselves and self-directed learning. It is carried out within their particular organization or professional area, not within the university but with linkages to it. It is a challenge for the universities to deal with these new demands for workplace learning. A partnership approach is seen as one means of dealing with the dilemma between the freedom of the university and a more practical and short-term attitude among companies. It also has to reconcile the dilemma between learning for the individual and for the effectiveness of the organization. Traditional supply-based education must be complemented by a demand-based approach, facilitated by dialogue at a local level between different stakeholders such as education providers, employer and employee organizations, professional institutes and researchers (Evans, Waite and Kersh 2011).

Learning is seen as an important instrument for dealing with the demands and threats from globalized markets. The institutional framework can either support or hinder projects which try to develop companies and strengthen individuals. In Germany, globalization might be regarded as a threat to its long-established dual system of apprenticeship, whereas the UK sees it as a rationale for a more flexible labour market. There is a risk that this Anglo-Saxon model of capitalism will lead to short-termism and polarization of the labour market, with many low-skilled jobs (Fuller and Unwin 2011: 46). What does all this add up to? It points to the necessity of analysing local projects in an institutional context in order to determine which of the changes achieved will be sustainable.

The change processes presented in the literature are often characterized by formative interventions which are radically different from the linear notion of intervention used in controlled experiments. Interventions are seen as part of a collective activity system which is composed of contradictions, tensions and oppositions (Engeström 2011: 98).

Sustainability in the Social Fund

A clear result presented in this chapter is that projects contribute strongly to opening up development issues, and thereby create development dynamics. The interest of management and politicians in development increases if they are involved at an early stage of the project. Their involvement and interest is the most important prerequisite for sustainability. Sustainability is connected above all with the context in which the project originates and the applicant's motives for participating. If the motive is linked to a combination of individual and business development, then the conditions for sustainable development are more favourable. There is then a larger element of long-term thinking in the initiative, especially when the project builds on earlier experiences. The scope for active ownership increases under such conditions.

An important prerequisite for sustainability is how the implementing organization functions in relation to the applicant. Studies from earlier programming periods show the importance of project case handlers having time to get involved in a project, and this conclusion is confirmed by the results from this programming period. This involves not only support and assistance over administration, but also that the relationship may have 'disturbing' elements, that is, a questioning approach that leads to new ideas and higher ambitions. This can be regarded as a part of developmental learning. In an earlier project period, interaction between project case handlers and applicants functioned as a 'value-added dialogue', where ideas were discussed and developed. This could also take place through different projects meeting each other to further elaborate their ideas and working methods. In this way, the conditions are created for joint knowledge formation and collaboration between authorities and different actors and organizations.

One problem with the Redundancy project, which was launched to counteract lay-offs in connection with the economic crisis, was that requirements were lower and the dialogue concerning project initiation was less complete. The consequence was that the ambition of the project was lowered and solutions became more traditional.

The sustainability of project results and its capacity to survive (by implementation and changing gear) are, as stated earlier, connected with ownership and steering. The problem tends to become bigger in this programming period as there has been a shift upwards in clear ownership for many projects where large state actors are involved. Many of the collaborating actors in Social Fund projects have become more centralized in recent years, the consequence of which has been that the clear owner – if he/she exists – is often far removed from project implementation. The regional and local levels have in a sense been 'stripped' of their opportunities to make decisions regarding their own operations. The government's letter of instructions to the authorities providing the preconditions and frames for their work is today determined at a greater distance from daily operations compared with a few years ago. Today there are neither regional County Labour Boards nor social insurance offices that have power over their own development and the possibility of transforming project results into mainstream activities. Having a regional or local head of an authority in a steering group is no longer a guarantee that project results will have an impact on the organization, however good the project actually is.

7

Innovation and the Regional Fund

One of the very large programme initiatives with increased focus on innovation is being carried out in the Regional Fund programmes 2007–2013. This programme initiative also illustrates the difficulties of evaluating what can be obtained from large programmes aimed at increasing the focus on innovation in more than 250 EU regions. It is difficult to evaluate whether to use the planning-steered developmental model or the development-supportive evaluation model. With the planning-steered developmental model, it is not only difficult to determine performance, but there is also the risk of steering incorrectly in implementation and use of resources. Nor can definitive results be demonstrated from the programme initiative with the development-supportive evaluation model. However, the initiatives and activities that should lead to changes in structures and processes can be shown, and thereby the foundation for innovation and sustainable development is identified and can be examined.

In order to be able to evaluate how well the focus on innovation has succeeded in the Regional Fund programmes, it is first necessary to know what the aims of this focus were. An advisory document dating from 2006 from the EU Commission stated what the Commission wished to achieve in its initiative for regional innovation policy (European Commission 2006b). The advisory document is not mandatory, but intended to provide the basis for member states to plan their programmes, initiatives and actions.

It can be stated that the arguments of the Commission 2006 for increasing focus on innovation generally mirrors the discussion which we reported in Chapter 5. The idea is to use the Regional Structural Fund to overcome the European paradox. The fund should finance experimentation within the field of innovation. The Commission states that there has been a transition from linear models to an innovation systems approach, which in its turn is being challenged by new views on innovation processes, user-led innovation, orchestrated innovation, and so on. The document argues that innovation depends above all on collaboration between producers, users and mediators of knowledge in the regions, that is, knowledge spillovers. Increased focus on innovation is very much to be aimed for, at the same time as the importance of experimental pilot projects in the EU is emphasized, since the forms for running innovation processes change rapidly.

Innovation is regarded by the Commission as a process of continuous development. Well-run innovation approaches, it was thought, would really be able to act as a catalyst for regional growth, but exactly how this should be achieved was still an open issue. For this reason, the Commission proposed that experimental pilot projects should be financed on a large scale to create critical mass in initiatives in regional innovation settings.

The Commission was aware of the extent to which the implementation strategy proposed for the Regional Fund was highly risky, but with 'continuing evaluation' – which in later advisory documents became 'ongoing evaluation' – the aim was to ensure the quality of the initiatives and to generate a sound basis to be able to reorient direction. Well-implemented evaluation generates knowledge which should make it possible to build further on experiences from the pilot activities, in order to disseminate them to other areas. The results should thus be regularly fed back to the managing authority responsible for the operational programmes. The results of experiments would, it was thought, provide the foundation for new focal points on initiatives from the Structural Funds, preferably in the direction of more innovative measures.

The Commission's focus on innovation prior to the new programming period 2007–2013 can be summarized as follows. It was not known exactly how increased focus on innovation could be achieved, only that it should be based on a powerful initiative for regional experimentation in new forms and approaches. Different opportunities for linking and increasing knowledge spillovers and learning between science, companies and public institutions should be tested. The aim was not to transfer scientific knowledge and research findings; the ambition was in fact to integrate different kinds of knowledge, and praxis about commercialization with theoretical knowledge. The question we raise in this chapter is whether a member state such as Sweden can be said to have lived up to expectations. What has been achieved and what conclusions can be drawn from the programmes so far? Is it possible to argue that the initiative has 'paid off'?

Can Innovations Be Evaluated?

Let us first approach the question of whether it is possible to evaluate innovation programmes. Alasdair Reid (2010), Director of the Technopolis Group, examines the prerequisites for evaluating measures taken to increase focus on innovation. Reid maintains that, irrespective of which estimate is used, initiatives for increased focus on innovation during the programming period 2007–2013 have meant at least a six-fold increase in investments in Research and Development and Innovation (RTDI) in comparison with earlier programming periods. What has been carried out in the regional operational programmes represents, in other words, an exceptional initiative in increasing innovation.

ONE-DIMENSIONAL FOLLOW-UP

Reid's view is that it is absolutely essential to improve the evaluation of regional innovation policy. This is an interesting discussion which we will take up in the next two sections (see Reid 2010). There is a great need to improve the evaluation of innovation to provide more and better evidence that the costs and benefits of government support for innovation really do provide value in relation to investments made. In the more advanced member states, evaluation has now started to move beyond a simple examination of performance through follow-up of indicators, and becomes an integral part of the learning approach, with feedback on policy decisions and in programme design. There is no 'magic bullet' that can be fired to ensure good evaluation and proper knowledge formation. There is no single method that will give us the answers to the most important questions in an evaluation and which can be applied in all types of studies. We have to live with a combination of methods which are chosen to satisfy needs in the individual studies. However, one problem in this context is that the authorities responsible for implementation generally devote too much attention to technical and administrative aspects. Too often, they are not deeply concerned with whether initiatives and projects really contribute to greater focus on innovation. The major problem with the earlier mid-term evaluation was that it often privileged a financial perspective or a quantitative outputs perspective. It did not really take into account the qualitative impacts and it did not measure impact on regional growth and development. Much of the one-dimensional evaluation culture remains, despite the fact that mid-term evaluation has been discontinued (Reid 2010).

EVALUATING INNOVATIONS

But it is difficult to evaluate innovation focus. Innovation is complex and a highly risky venture; there is no guarantee that public funds invested in a project will generate innovations. Innovation can only be assessed in the long term, at the same time as policy-makers and society require follow-up and evaluations that report on short-term results. Innovation is not developed linearly and leads to complex and multifaceted effects which cannot be identified in a simple way. Often a linear analysis of consequences is impossible. The time dimension is crucial when assessing the consequences of research and development, and innovation programmes and initiatives (Reid 2010). The problem is that the indicators used have not been developed to catch the system improvements and change of preconditions which research shows are crucial for increasing innovative capacity.

Simplified models that try to identify direct causal relationships – amongst other things, as returns on investments in R&D – are nearly always misleading. An innovation hardly ever occurs in isolation, but almost always in the context of structured relationships, networks or in a broader social and economic context. Nonetheless most R&D evaluations use a simplified input–output result model. Often an attempt is made, using a one-dimensional approach, to understand what happened as a consequence of an intervention and then link this to programme goals.

Such an approach raises a number of methodological issues. The first and possibly most important deals with how much 'prestige' should be given to a programme or project; this allocation problem is very complex. How is a decision to be made on how much of a change in a variable is due to the initiative? The problem of allocation is made worse by the problems concerning overstatement of results. What is administratively defined and funded as a project often does not fit in well with support recipients' ongoing development work. The trend towards overstating results makes all attempts to understand and identify the effects of an administratively defined project difficult Given the complicated nature of innovation processes and the tendency towards bias in project reporting, it often becomes completely impossible to separate the impact of other projects on the project evaluated. A classic example of this phenomenon is the double counting of effects in the number of jobs created. Thirdly, the problem of tracking 'average' results – the fact that commercially successful R&D and innovation projects normally only make up a very small proportion of any portfolio of projects funded by an agency – needs to be taken into account. Measuring impact in the short term (six to twelve months after the end of a programme) implies applying different indicators than an impact assessment done two years or more down the line, when the 'economic effects' should become visible.

Measuring effects in the short-term, six to twelve months after completion of a programme, involves using indicators without carrying out an analysis of consequences. There have been hardly any new products that have had a commercial impact on regional growth within a year or two after a programme has finished. It is thus more reasonable that an evaluation examines secondary effects as well as direct effects. It is also necessary to investigate whether funds have created permanent changes in processes and praxis concerning the implementation of innovations, for example, in situations such as whether a company has developed new methods or tools to identify innovation projects, or whether methods for handling innovations have been improved.

The answer to the question of whether innovation focus in the Regional Fund can be evaluated must be negative if one accepts Reid's summary of the research situation and the evaluation discussion. Nevertheless we find ourselves in a situation where substantial resources have been, and will continue to be, invested in increasing focus on innovation. In some way we must be able to determine if these investments have been, and will continue to be, made in a meaningful way, and if they could possibly bear fruit in some respect.

Focus on Innovations in the Regional Fund

In Sweden, the focus on innovation in the Structural Fund has meant that the area of regional innovation environments has been given a stronger position in the eight Swedish Regional Fund programmes. In these, it is argued that financing from the Structural Fund should be used to support the growth of a more innovative and knowledge-based working and industrial life.

More specifically, it is argued that this involves developing and strengthening regional innovation environments and promoting innovation-based entrepreneurship. The programmes should support projects which improve the conditions for industry to develop new, attractive products and services with high value-added for introduction to the market. In particular, the aim is to increase the return from scientific knowledge and research by ensuring that projects contribute to developing regionally innovative environments and clusters that facilitate collaboration between universities and university colleges, companies and authorities. The capacity of companies to assimilate research and technological development is regarded in the programmes as vital in contributing to increased growth driven by innovation. Developing working methods and approaches that improve the transfer of knowledge in industry, and also between industry and the research community, and other actors, should be an important element in innovation projects. This covers everything – from support in starting companies where an idea is the seed that can be transformed into an innovation – to joint development of new knowledge between established industry and researchers. The programme initiatives in many respects are based on creating knowledge spillovers and dynamic collaboration with industry that goes beyond a mechanically functioning innovation system.

Ongoing programme evaluation shows that a surprising amount of resources (given the Commission's expectations on experimentation) have gone to R&D-based innovation projects with existing companies and industries. The aim of these projects in the first instance has been to develop knowledge, competencies and solutions which can provide the platform for existing companies to develop their processes and products.

An illustrative example of such a project involved developing knowledge on the causes of stoppages in the production process of the paper industry and how these could be reduced. The stoppages led to high income losses for the companies. If these stoppages could be eliminated entirely, profitability would increase substantially. Companies in projects of these types are mainly interested in obtaining more knowledge and proposals for solutions, and wish to use this knowledge to make necessary changes in their production processes. This means that the impact of a project on a region's industry is that it becomes more rationalized and the competitiveness of existing activities are strengthened, as opposed to becoming more innovative.

But in rationalization processes, many good ideas that could well become innovations also lie hidden. Such 'hidden and overlooked' results have a tendency to disappear when results and effects are reported. In addition, such initiatives are of great importance in strengthening existing companies, both those directly involved as well as those indirectly affected, such as suppliers.

The importance of using public programme initiatives to encourage existing companies to leverage knowledge formation processes in their 'home areas' should not be underestimated. The observation made by Markusen (1996) some decades ago that industry and R&D policy should increase the friction for global gliders – large companies ('sticky places in a slippery space') in an increasingly 'slippery' world – still applies! Global gliders or sticky clusters is the issue (Brulin and Ekstedt 2005). The main task of the initiatives in innovation systems is first and foremost to ensure that global companies stay. This is one of the main conclusions of the large evaluation of the much-discussed Finnish innovation system (Evaluation of the Finnish National Innovation System 2009). Possibly, it is only in the light of the extent to which innovation programmes tie in large companies to a country that they can be evaluated. All other discussion is empty rhetoric intended to conceal the fact that initiatives in the innovation system are nothing more than disguised R&D support to important companies to persuade them to stay.

In this respect, however, Regional Fund projects deviate from innovation system initiatives by expressly focusing on knowledge spillovers between research and companies. Regional Fund projects do not aim to create innovation from research findings and scientific knowledge, but are prepared to provide support for all forms of learning and collaboration between the academic world and industry – joint laboratories, incubators and technology parks, student work and degree projects in conjunction with industry, and so on. In other words, this deals with initiatives that can fundamentally transform traditional universities and university colleges, especially because of their size. One effect of the Regional Fund could be that the 'entrepreneurial university' really begins to take shape. Many different forces appear to work against European universities becoming more like their American counterparts in their focus on commercial applications, and here the Structural Funds can play a crucial role.

HUGE INITIATIVES!

Large project initiatives are run with a focus on innovation. In the programming period 2007–2013, the Regional Fund will have provided co-financing of more than 40 per cent of the total amount – about 20 billion Swedish crowns – in the priority 'regional innovation environments', that is, about 8 billion Swedish crowns. These are large sums compared to what would be channelled into the innovation system through the Swedish Governmental Agency for Innovation Systems (VINNOVA) and to traditional research by such bodies as the Swedish Research Council. The transition to large projects, owned by universities and university colleges, may have meant that the agenda of researchers – scientific articles, research positions and patents – to some extent determined project agendas. Innovation may be better promoted if ownership of the project is not confined to the research community. The three universities in northern Sweden have become the largest recipients of financing from the Regional Fund. In southern Sweden, it has become more common that other regional actors run this type of project.

In ongoing evaluation in the three programmes in southern Sweden, the evaluator (Sweco Eurofutures) notes the work on broad partnerships, rather than university and university-owned projects, in preparing the way for new industries and innovations. In addition to public actors, non-commercial organizations and private companies are often involved in these projects. The aim is to support the growth of new technology or market areas. This deals with innovative areas in the borderland between different industries and technologies. Some examples are different types of 'Clean-tech' industries, services linked to the health and medical care sector, new combinations of IT services, and so on.

HUGE DIFFICULTIES!

The initiatives are comprehensive. Despite this, it is difficult to show results that lead to sustainable development (Brulin and Svensson 2011). Large strategic projects are not always more efficient than small projects. There are clear indications that large projects often have lengthy start-up phases, and ownership is unclear, as are goals and tasks. The requirement to clearly report how work will be carried out so that research will lead to innovations appears to be excessively weak, as is evident in reports from the ongoing evaluation of programmes and projects.

Instead, work should be directed to developing projects that build on close cooperation with companies. It would also be desirable that representatives from industry involve themselves more in Structural Fund partnerships and in the monitoring committees. Prioritization of projects should be done together with specialists and experts so that it is the extent to which there is focus on innovation in projects that determines whether a project should be funded. Another question that can be put is whether the transition to large strategic projects targeting innovation has selectively favoured male participation during this programming period. Indications exist that the transition to large projects functioned as a return to the earlier status quo in terms of gender power structures in project leadership.

Different evaluation reports illustrate the problems that appear to be typical of a number of large projects. The DARE project is part of the VINNOVA 'key actor programme' and is partially financed by the Regional Fund. Over eight years, the project will have a turnover of about 150 million Swedish crowns and will consist of about ten sub-projects. The aim of the project has been to strengthen the commercialization of research findings and the transfer of knowledge between industry and the academic world, to increase the contribution of universities to growth and innovation in the northern region. Problems in the project can be summarized as a lack of active ownership, weak steering and unclear project logic: long-term goals, 'stage' goals and milestones which are not related in a convincing way to show how they can lead to results and long-term effects. The steering of projects as a whole has been weak from the start, the sub-projects have not collaborated and synergies have not been created. Linkage to industry has been too weak, and projects have not received support from companies, as potential entrepreneurs have had little confidence in them.

Even though the Regional Fund programmes appear to be working with the right things – solving the Swedish and European paradox of lacking knowledge spillovers between research and industry – it is not always done in the right way. The problems may have been due to the project having the wrong owner and thus a lack of active ownership. Projects became too large and the requirements from the financiers – VINNOVA and the Swedish Agency for Economic and Regional Growth – have been too weak. The lack of a clear evaluation culture in earlier programming periods may also have contributed to the unawareness of universities and university colleges that the project must work and deliver in accordance with its goals. Routinely funds have been allocated to fairly traditional activities, instead of focusing on collaboration and joint knowledge formation between the scientific community and industry. Obtaining such knowledge spillovers, as we have shown in Chapter 5, is not easy. Setting up innovation systems where three different spheres – the academic, authorities and industry – should 'mesh' with each other sounds promising, but is not in itself a solution. Initiatives which create more cluster dynamics are required.

The difficulties of developing commercial products and services from development projectsare not unique, however, to public innovation systems. Large Swedish companies also share this difficulty. Studies in the pharmaceutical industry and engineering companies such as ABB and Ericsson indicate random factors, unpredicted events, and many long delays in the development of classically successful products such as Losec, Pharmacia's anaesthetic and semi-conductor switchers. The challenge is that innovation processes are currently being run in many different forms, and this means that there must be significantly greater openness in how innovation projects are organized. It is not sufficient that projects organize mechanically functioning systems. Orchestrated and user-led innovation indicates new forms for running innovation processes.

What Is Really Significant Cannot Always Be Measured!

Do the initiatives of the Regional Fund make a difference? Do the projects lead to innovations, new companies and jobs? Can the value of initiatives be evaluated? The Robot Valley is one example of a public innovation programme making a difference. The project is owned by a university, but also has strong representation from industry. The initiative was launched in 2004, together with the company, ABB Robotics. 'Bestic' is an example of what has come out of the project. It is a feeding robot for people with functional arm/hand impairments. The robot has an arm that holds a spoon/fork, picks up the food and lifts it to mouth height. It is steered by a small control panel at the edge of the table. The inventor, who is an engineer running a small family company, got in touch with the Robot Valley five years ago about his idea, which at that time was an undeveloped prototype. A group of robotics experts in mechanics and design from the Robot Valley project took on the task of supporting the inventor. The product needed better design, better electronics and presentation material. The Robot Valley linked the inventor with engineering students who contributed to its development. Partners to produce components for the robot were then identified. Venture capital for production and market launch were applied for. The Robot Valley's personnel have a background in industry, and cooperation takes place with engineering programmes in the region. Different R&D projects are run together with small and medium-sized companies. An important asset is their links to higher education. The Robot Valley project plays the role of a broker where researchers, students and companies are linked together. The Robot Valley fulfils a filtering function, enabling innovators to receive both financial and technical support.

It is difficult, nevertheless, to determine the usefulness and profitability created by the projects. The application of the planning-steered developmental model risks reducing rather than increasing clarity. Within this framework, projects are required to submit detailed reports of the number of innovations, prototypes, spin-offs and company start-ups, jobs created, and so on. This is a type of follow-up that can hardly be appropriate for a three-year innovation project. The actual time frame from idea to innovation is substantially longer. The route to market launch is always full of surprises and unexpected difficulties. The element of chance and unforeseen events is high. The requirement to state how many new jobs and companies an innovation project should achieve as goals over three years is not possible. It is not even possible over a ten-year perspective. What should really be assessed, if the aim is the achievement of sustainable innovative development – in terms of changing structures, clearer ownership, collaboration through joint knowledge formation between the academic and corporate worlds, and so on – can hardly be operationally estimated.

The problem of the planning-steered developmental model – by giving the impression that it is possible to measure and control how successful innovation projects have been – in the best case is that it contributes to 'misleading' disinformation, and in the worst case, a smokescreen of confusion. These smokescreens probably hide a large number of symbolic activities, meaningless actions, grandiose initiatives and highly ambitious plans. The indicators assumed by the planning-steered developmental model to be accurate – in terms of capturing results in the form of innovations, product ideas, new companies, and so on – give an illusion of controlled rationality. In an earlier chapter, we have shown that a shift has taken place in evaluation models towards development-supportive evaluation. Instead of focusing on what has been done, ongoing evaluators and interactive researchers try to determine how things could be done so that activities and actions are likely to lead towards goal attainment; how the preconditions for innovation are changed.

In the following three sections, we examine what results and long-term effects can be identified by interactive researchers and ongoing evaluation in three different types of innovation projects. The first example concerns increased cluster dynamics and entrepreneurship in six innovation systems in the north of Sweden. The second example relates to the final recipients of support, companies in northern central Sweden. In what way have they benefited from being involved in Regional Fund innovation projects? The third example of increased focus concerns the major initiative in 12 venture capital fund projects. These examples illustrate how attempts have been made in programme implementation to satisfy the Commission's requirements for experimenting in order to achieve greater focus on innovation. They also show how attempts are being made to build structures to promote knowledge spillovers and change attitudes in the direction of more dynamic collaboration between research and surrounding industry. Whether these measures will really deliver innovations in line with the ambitious goals set up is still too early to determine. The time frame so far is too short, but the Robot Valley has evidently been delivering an innovation project for more than a decade, making a contribution to regional development.

Innovation through Clusters and Entrepreneurship

Important parts of Regional Fund projects deal with trying to make 'innovation systems' more dynamic – to resemble clusters more closely. Six attempts to create cluster dynamics in three innovation systems in the north of Sweden have been evaluated. These relate to innovation systems in the areas of biotech and tourism, forestry and wood, sports/outdoor recreation and alternative energy/energy efficiency. These are industry and research areas which have been identified as priority areas for initiatives in Regional Fund programmes.

Data collection was carried out with the help of focus groups. Ongoing evaluators went through the aims and goals of the innovation systems, activities, participating players, financing and organization. The initial analysis showed that it involved 'making clusters from these innovation systems'. This was done, based on what is considered to be the five success factors for clusters – aims and goals, driving force and involvement, operations, critical mass and organization (Brulin and Svensson 2011). In what follows, we look at the results of this study.

A smaller group of core actors, who had been involved in starting the activity, led the work in the six innovation systems. The reasons for developing an innovation system varied, but they all came from the academic world and the public sector. In two cases, the academic world and companies were joint initiative takers. Project support from the Regional Fund led to a change in the overall idea, as it was broadened to encompass new areas. One innovation system went from the development of forestry materials and the forestry industry to also working with alternative energy production based on forestry materials and to alternative areas in biotechnology/medical technology. A distinguishing feature was also that the main focus in the innovation system shifted from research and production of scientific knowledge to business development and commercialization. In the following sections, we briefly review a number of key factors important in creating successful innovation systems.

ACTIVE OWNERSHIP

The innovation systems studied all had a lack of active ownership. The underlying ideas of the innovation systems were organized by those taking the initiative. The review above shows that the internal core needed to become better at communicating the ideas of the innovation system and obtaining support from outside the 'inner circle'. Initiatives were required to increase activities and the involvement of ownership, almost without exception. In at least two of the systems studied, activities concerning ownership have clearly increased. In these cases it was decided that activities and initiatives should involve all the members. Significantly more cluster dynamics have started sprouting.

COLLABORATION AND JOINT KNOWLEDGE FORMATION

In four of the innovation systems, there was a research platform to provide the foundation. The initial task involved strengthening the research platform and creating links to industry. Ongoing evaluation shows that the innovation systems were initially strongly influenced by the agenda of researchers and the scientific community. Gradually, the foundations for joint knowledge formation became evident and collaboration over solutions to different problems emerged. It has taken time for the researchers to understand that they should be involved and apply knowledge, and disseminate research findings about new/improved processes or products and services. Joint knowledge formation has also taken place through individual companies receiving assistance from the research platforms to test and assess proposals for new products and processes. There have also been examples where research results have been commercialized by other companies, licensing arrangements, and so on, with the support of incubators and companies specializing in business development.

Ongoing evaluation shows that funding from the Structural Funds played a vital role. This has been crucial both in building up the organizations and continuing many of the activities. There is some uncertainty concerning future financing. In the worst case, it may turn out that the initiatives designed to get the innovation systems to function more as dynamic clusters were merely a one-time phenomenon without lasting effects. At the same time, there is much to indicate that seeds have been planted that will enable joint knowledge formation to grow, and the scientific community sees new opportunities in both commercialization and entrepreneurship.

KNOWLEDGE SPILLOVERS

Activities in innovation systems have gradually become more interlinked to industry. In innovation systems where the original initiative came from the academic world, the start-up phase has been significantly longer. If at the start a research platform existed in an area, it has taken much longer to get existing industry to see the opportunities inherent in collaboration. It meant that researchers in these innovation systems needed to look for ready-made ways of using their research findings amongst members or, sometimes, to create completely new companies based on their research findings.

A number of researchers in the innovation systems did not see themselves as entrepreneurs. For instance, the biotechnology cluster in Upper North started a project to make researchers the main owners of a company, CMTF

Business Development AB, where commercialization of research results has started. The company has made it simpler and more interesting for researchers to get involved in commercialization.

PROMOTING ENTREPRENEURSHIP

The Innovation Alliance project is an illustrative example of how work should be done to promote entrepreneurship. Actors and financiers supporting innovation have gathered here. The project's task has been to support individual innovators to develop ideas for new products, services and companies. An ongoing evaluation shows that the Innovation Alliance is gradually improving the effectiveness and environment for innovations and product renewal by creating a coherent innovation process, with support and advice for the region's innovators. In the project the incubators were able to play the role of catalysts in the early stages of an integrated innovation process. Early stages involving pre-study meetings about business development, trademarks, finance and design have been followed by support in the financing phase and launch to market. Examples of supporting activities are guidance, coaching and mentorship which are targeted at new companies established by innovation and also entrepreneurs with new ideas in already established companies. Support in the last phase, the growth phase, is provided where an innovation has been developed into a final product or service but where commercialization remains. Examples of support and services in this phase are guidance, coaching and dissemination of opportunities to access venture capital.

Within the Innovation Alliance, the cooperation partners have developed joint decision-making processes for financing innovation support. According to the ongoing evaluators, this has been the foundation for guidance over competence enhancement and more extensive feedback. In providing guidance, the Innovation Alliance has worked with, amongst other things, CONNECT's tool, 'Springboard'. Springboard enables entrepreneurs to present their business idea to a panel of experts. The panel helps with advice and tips on how a growth company should act in order to grow rapidly and develop. The panel is unique in the sense that different people are invited to participate depending on which company is giving a presentation. Springboard can be regarded as a 'turbo' that can be specifically applied when a company really needs support to grow. These tools from the Innovation Alliance have become a part of the overall innovation process.

The activities of the Innovation Alliance have also inspired and informed many regarding the scope for innovation. The aim has been to get more people working together on their ideas and to enhance their learning about innovation processes. In the inspiration phase, special measures have been directed at women and immigrants. Special efforts have also been made to encourage the development of business ideas in the service sector, and also healthcare and care of the elderly. Potential innovators have received help in assessing their ideas – to determine whether they can be protected or not, if there is a market, if the technology works, and so on. Thereafter the originator of the idea receives help for its development in terms of marketing, design, agreements, financing, and so on. The owners of ideas are responsible for how their ideas are developed through the whole process and receive support in terms of competence for the further development of the idea. Processes should have a clear market focus, with an orientation on the customer's customer, the entity that finally pays for the idea.

Many evaluation questions remain to be answered. Initiatives in innovation and entrepreneurship have become something of a mass phenomenon and may be able to release the hidden potential of businesses. At the same time this mass phenomenon poses a risk of locking up creative individuals in regions and communities where there is no realistic future, at the same time as there is a demand for these people in expanding urban areas. Returns in the form of real new business ideas that can be commercialized, that is, innovations which the initiatives will lead to, cannot yet be determined. It will be difficult, if not impossible, to determine whether the cluster dynamic innovation system or the Innovation Alliance was the key factor.

Involving Companies

The fundamental question in different evaluations deals with the participation of companies in innovation projects. Has participation contributed to the growth of companies? Has participation in Structural Fund projects meant that companies have invested more in R&D to develop new products and services? The question, in other words, is whether the Regional Fund has contributed to greater focus on innovation in companies.

A number of companies in the initiative area of regional innovation environments were identified. The selection process resulted in a list of 20 projects, of which 12 had the explicit goal of supporting innovation processes in order to create new commercial products and services. The other eight were also evaluated as interesting from an innovation perspective. In those cases where projects had ongoing project evaluators, contact with the project was preceded by a dialogue. Initially, the evaluators turned to six pilot study projects to identify hypotheses. In these projects, close to 30 companies were contacted.

The starting point for the evaluators' questions was the importance of the company's relationships with its surroundings, other companies, knowledge institutions, consultants, and so on. The idea is that innovations occur through the exchange of knowledge, thoughts and ideas. The basis for such an exchange lies in the contact networks existing between companies and other actors in their surroundings. If such networks are lacking, then the preconditions for knowledge spillovers are also lacking.

BENEFITS FOR COMPANIES

Two thirds of the companies were service-oriented. They covered computer consultancy, clean-tech, multimedia and design, and energy consultancy. One third was manufacturing companies, in the paper industry, machinery manufacturing and manufacturing of electrical apparatuses. The companies varied in size, but the majority was small companies with low turnover and few employees. Their average turnover in the most recent financial year amounted to 4 million Swedish crowns. The majority of the companies had between zero to four employees.

Slightly more than half of the companies stated that the innovation project had satisfied their expectations. Fifteen per cent felt that their expectations had been exceeded. The others had no specific view on the question. The majority of the companies stated that the project's main contribution was to provide access to networks and new contacts. Other important contributions were improved working processes and competence enhancement. Some companies stated that the project had contributed directly to the development of new products and services.

Amongst the 83 companies interviewed, 15 stated that the project had contributed to a new product/service. In these cases, the companies stated that the development of these products/services had been directly related to their participation in the project. A further 19 companies thought that the project had contributed to speeding up the process of developing or improving products/ services. In these cases the companies argued that participating in the project had been useful, but that the development or improvement of products/services would probably have taken place anyhow. Where the project had contributed to speeding up the process or improving products/services, it cannot be excluded that this would have occurred anyhow, albeit over a longer period.

PROJECTS WHICH HAVE CONTRIBUTED TO INNOVATIONS

In total, there were seven projects which together had contributed to the new products/services, but two thirds of these originated from three projects. Examples of new products developed by the companies were different types of robots – a feeding robot, a car robot for hospitals, and so on. Other examples were a mechanized cleaning mop and intelligent textiles for use against pressure/bed sores. Amongst the new services were a number of digital ones covering monitoring, net-based testing and web applications. One example of a company that had developed a product from its participation was in the 'The Paper Province' cluster. The company owner considered that as a result of this innovation project, the company had felt able to take the next step to develop its own product. The company was aware of the breadth and status of the project and was able to invest more in the product when it joined the cluster. This opened the doors to the customer base necessary for commercializing the product. It was also possible to take part in industry-specific meetings.

In general, all the companies emphasized networks and greater contact opportunities as the main contribution from innovation projects. This mainly involved increased contacts with other companies in the same or closely related industries. Some smaller companies mentioned external world monitoring as a benefit from participating in the project. Innovation projects are viewed as a channel for rapidly updating information about competing companies and developments in the industry. It is reasonable to expect that factors such as these are of greater importance to small companies than medium-sized and large ones. External world monitoring and building networks are important tasks which, because of time constraints, often get neglected by small companies in a start-up phase.

A number of companies expressed the hope that the contacts would lead to new cooperation, new ideas about their own business and increased growth. Business in general and innovation work in particular is always typified by uncertainty: companies can never be certain that the results will turn out to be what they want or have planned. For this reason, confidence is important as it reduces perceived uncertainty, and this has a positive impact on the company's willingness to be open and to share information and knowledge. The fact that the project contributed to the creation of new contacts and confidence must be regarded as positive, and as a fundamental precondition for developing innovations.

IMPROVED WORKING PROCESSES

In addition, a number of companies considered that the project had contributed to improving work processes and the development of the company, partly through advisory services, but also through seminars and workshops on important questions such as working on a board, company valuation, information on investment opportunities, personal development and business coaching. Three completely new companies were created. In one case, three companies started a new company together with the aim of integrating their respective competencies in the environmental area. The three companies believed that they would not have met if they had not participated in the project. In a second instance, the project had contributed to speeding up processes and helped start a new company. In the third case, an American company relocated its operations to Sweden.

The main focus of the programme was on building up contact activities. This raises difficult questions about how essential these activities are for bringing about innovation, and thus how much of the Structural Funds should be used for this purpose. An equally difficult question is the time period for achieving results from product and service innovations. What investments and what time horizons are reasonable?

CHARACTERISTICS OF SUCCESSFUL PROJECTS

The contribution of projects to increased focus on innovation was generally unequally distributed. It has not been possible to identify any innovations in seven of the projects examined. This can be viewed in the light of the fact that nearly two thirds of the projects (about 900), according to the priorities decided on, should contribute to real innovations. It is always possible to discuss why a larger proportion of the projects could not demonstrate innovations. One reason is that at the time of the study the projects had not been completed. A counter-argument is that, in most cases, large projects have had a pre-history. Despite no innovations from a number of the projects, it could be particularly interesting to study the characteristics of those projects that actually contributed to innovations. In what follows, we will look more closely at what key factors for success can be identified amongst the seven projects that directly contributed to the companies' development of products/services.

Industry-oriented projects proved to have the greatest success in contributing to innovations. When reviewing working methods in the seven projects which had directly contributed to the development of new products and services, it appears that these projects differed from the rest of the sample population in two ways: firstly, they worked more with business advisory services and the development of other company services; and secondly, none of them worked with training or general knowledge development. The majority of the projects were part of larger strategic initiatives that had been ongoing over a longer period, sometimes many years. Innovation processes often have time horizons of more than three years. In other words, the successful projects always had a pre-history.

It has not been difficult to compare innovation projects from the Regional Fund with those of VINNOVA which, amongst other things, provides ten-year development financing through its Regional Growth Through Dynamic Innovation System programme. In practice, a number of the larger Structural Fund projects had links long before the current programming period. At first glance, this might appear to be in conflict with the requirements of the Regional Fund for innovation in their projects. In practice, however, applicants usually find a new angle in a project, so that this obstacle can be overcome. Since financing from the Regional Fund had often taken place in parallel with co-financing from bodies such as VINNOVA, county councils, county administrative boards, regional associations, municipalities, and so on, it was impossible to relate a given result to specific Regional Fund financing.

ESTABLISHED INTERACTION BETWEEN HIGHER EDUCATION AND INDUSTRY

One observation was that projects that are properly embedded in an existing industrial structure have a greater likelihood of achieving successful innovation. The structures may, of course, have been built around one or more larger 'locomotive companies'. An advanced larger company (from a regional perspective) can be regarded as a resource, which as far as possible should be used to advantage locally. The possibility of interacting with existing industry was important for potential innovators in the project. If the project could provide such an arena, it would be able to make a positive contribution to the development of innovation. From the perspective of large companies, well-run projects can be interesting in providing a well-functioning supplier structure. In order to develop the right forms of collaboration with industry, it is desirable that people with a background in the industry are involved, amongst other things, in steering and reference groups, or in other ways. All three projects which had directly contributed to the major part of new products and services had collaborated with both industry and higher education.

Such linkages facilitated collaboration between the companies and qualified researchers in research projects of relevance to the innovation. This might also involve using PhD students in industry, who direct their research towards current innovation projects. Another form of collaboration is where a first degree is preceded by a development project as a part of degree work. One of the most important tasks of project management from this perspective, then, becomes the role of broker. Innovators are navigated to both the academic world and to contacts in industry, and the project contributes contacts and knowledge about higher education environments and company networks. A closely related task for projects is to provide innovators with guidance to financing. In the early stages of development, there are a number of different routes for innovators to finance development work – once again projects can contribute knowledge and contacts.

INFRASTRUCTURE FOR INNOVATIONS

Special access to laboratory environments to carry out tests and experiments were regarded as valuable from the perspective of promoting innovation. The possibility of using laboratories and other similar facilities was the main inducement for some companies to take part in projects. A number of companies where projects had directly contributed to new products or services highlighted access to marketing channels as the project contribution. It is not surprising that many of the companies interviewed put a high value on marketing activities provided by the projects, such as trade fairs. A well-known fact is that often further capital is required to bring new products or services to the market compared with the cost of innovation processes. Some of the companies cited the project's role as a broker in mediating international contacts through the project owner or manager.

CONCLUSIONS FROM THE STUDIES

In this section, we summarize some of the results from the evaluation studies. This shows that the selected projects in the programme in central Sweden contributed to innovations in some of the participating companies. It has been difficult to make an assessment of the innovativeness of the products and services. It has also been difficult to make an assessment of the real opportunities for commercializing products/services, since only a couple of them were on the market at the time of the study. In these cases, the project contributed to speeding up innovation processes. In cases where the project had directly contributed to the development of products and services, relatively concrete and solid measures were involved – test labs, relevant current contacts, essential competence and marketing. An overall conclusion is that the projects which appear to be the most successful are those that have achieved knowledge spillovers and integrated knowledge between the academic and corporate worlds.

One observation is that regional innovation projects take place in a small world. It is not unusual that the same people and companies are connected to a number of different projects in the region. The risk is that symbiosis occurs between projects and participating actors. Thus, it is important to regularly review all long-term regional development projects. Reassessment should take place in relation to the goals set up and the initiatives' relevance to the preconditions in the region and the surrounding world. Ongoing project evaluation in the larger projects has not really fulfilled this function. It has had far too supportive a function instead of being critically constructive, as current goals in the initiatives have been taken as given. The critical constructive task in ongoing project evaluation thus appears to have been far too weak.

A question for further discussion is how cost-effective the projects have been. It can be stated that large amounts have been invested in projects that aim to support innovation. The quality of project implementation varied. There are working methods and models which make the creation of innovation more likely. Successful projects ought to be more widely used as models for initiating and prioritizing new innovation projects.

Ensuring that projects work on the basis of well-tried models would significantly increase their cost-efficiency in comparison with the frequent use of unplanned recurring 'trial and error' approaches. Substantially more systematic learning and exchange of experience between projects is needed. Ongoing programme evaluators in northern central Sweden also state that projects are initiated without any clear transfer of knowledge from other similar initiatives, earlier experiences and other regions.

Another question for discussion is whether project presentations are sufficiently good to have a demonstrable impact on development in the region. It is a well-known fact that there is a major leap between creating knowledge that has the potential to become an innovation and successful commercialization of knowledge leading to a real innovation. Earlier studies have shown that the majority of innovations never become successful commercial products/services. As a consequence, projects are required to contribute a large number of new innovations to establish credibility that the work results in products/services that are commercially successful. In addition, this requires the existence of an industrial structure in the region that can benefit from innovations, in such forms as being able to produce or distribute the products/services.

In many cases, innovations have been niche products/services, where the potential market can undoubtedly be global, but where volumes will probably be relatively small. In a number of cases, the question is whether the main value of innovations lies in improving existing products or production processes. This development work, of course, can be of great value for industry in the region. For the individual company, innovations might make all the difference between being competitive or threatened with closure.

It has been difficult, however, to show a direct relationship between innovation and more important increases in employment in northern central Sweden. The value of this type of project possibly lies more in creating conditions to safeguard industry and employment by increasing or maintaining competitiveness. Another value is that projects contribute to more knowledge amongst the participating actors, which can be expected to contribute to maintaining or increasing competitiveness. From this perspective, the expectations to be imposed on this type of project must be discussed, as well as their importance for regional development and growth in both the short and long term.

An Initiative in Venture Capital

In the programming period 2007–2013, a full-scale experiment is being carried out to increase innovation focus by means of an initiative covering 12 nationwide regional co-investment projects. This experiment will consume nearly 10 per cent of available financing from the Regional Fund. As an experiment, it must be regarded in all respects as fulfilling the Commission's expectations for pilot activities to increase focus on innovation. The co-investment projects should, together with private co-financiers, invest equity capital in small and medium-size companies (SMEs).

The background to the initiative is interest on the part of the EU Commission, and from national and regional actors, to use revolving financing instruments in the Structural Fund, in the form of venture capital, with the aim of satisfying an identified lack of capital for financing SMEs with growth ambitions. Revolving finance means that the projects aim to secure an increase in value so that when the holding is sold, it can be reused. Capital in the projects that has not been invested in portfolio companies at least once by at latest 31 December 2014 will have to be repaid by Sweden to the EU Commission. Available capital that does not need to be repaid will stay within the region. During the project period, capital can be redistributed from the venture capital projects to other Structural Fund projects.

Ongoing evaluation researches the initiative's progress and contributes to learning about the its implementation, results and long-term effects. It is providing answers to two fundamental questions: first, whether the projects can act as good sources of venture capital in terms of assignments, organization and regional preconditions; second, whether this type of venture capital project can provide the results and outcomes in society which the EU and the government expects.

Ongoing evaluation should also contribute to a broader discussion in society over regional venture capital as a tool for increasing innovation through the supply of capital to small and medium-sized companies. Initially, the ongoing evaluation (Brulin and Svensson 2011) has focused on the mission of the projects, their organization and goal structure.

International research shows that this type of venture capital supply programme is difficult to organize. Different approaches must be related to the rules and cultural context of different countries. Murray (2007) notes that the state has historically played an important role in the emergence of venture capital markets in different countries. Nearly all countries which today have developed venture capital markets – amongst others, the USA, the UK and Israel – have had wide-ranging public initiatives focusing on building these up. At the same time, Lerner (2009) maintains, in his recent book with the memorable title *Boulevard of Broken Dreams: Why Public Efforts to Boost Entrepreneurship and Venture Capital Have Failed – and What to Do about It*, that it is easy to 'inflate' innovations with venture capital, but it is not easy to do it in the right way – it takes time and there are many pitfalls. Hence the central question is: how can such programme initiatives be more sustainable?

The 12 funds are managed by five different project owners in the eight regions. There are major differences between the regions in preconditions for venture capital investments as regards the number of relevant investment companies, the number of active venture capital companies and the number of active 'informal' venture capitalists (see Avdeitchikova 2008). This means that the challenges, as well as the expectations, differ. The most important factors in venture capital investments relate to finding good investment targets and competent private co-investors with strong capital resources.

A foundation stone for the initiative is that it should supplement the market and be operated in accordance with market principles. Nevertheless, there are no straightforward answers or precise definitions of what this means in practice. The market segment of the projects is difficult to identify. The investment targets should have a sufficiently high risk to deter private investors, but be good enough to be justified on commercial grounds. The main role of the public supply of venture capital vis-à-vis the private actor is reducing investment risk.

Operating in a way complementary to the market may be in conflict with working on commercial grounds. The fact that the projects are supposed to 'ignore' certain investments is a sign that they are complementary to the market. A pivotal issue is when the project should make its 'exit': when this is optimal for the project or for the company? A strict interpretation is when it is optimal for the project, if it is to function as a revolving instrument. This may, however, be difficult for such a public actor since there may be expectations of acting on behalf of the company or the owner, and/or taking into account regional factors such as not selling to an actor planning to move its operations from the region.

There are many different views on returns and what can be expected from projects of this type. For example, the Scottish co-investment fund has the explicit goal of achieving a 20 per cent annual return; but at the time of the most recent evaluation, the fund instead showed a decrease in value of 8 per cent (Scottish Government 2008). The actual return from the funds is difficult to assess today since not enough exits have been made. This relationship indicates that profitability in such funds follows a 'J curve', that is, the expected return in the early years is negative.

UNCLEAR GOAL STRUCTURE AND PROGRAMME LOGIC

It may be difficult to invest in companies in the early stages of development, and at the same time to obtain reasonable returns enabling the fund to rotate capital. There may also be a conflict between having a low management fee and being an active part in the investment process. Since experiences of this type of financing instrument are limited, there is no clear answer as yet on how these difficulties should be handled. The main direct mission of the projects is to act as good venture capitalists and make profitable investments in small and medium-sized companies.

An important part of the initiative is to test, in a joint learning process between the projects and the managing authority, how venture capital can be supplied in public–private partnership. In the long term, companies are expected to grow in terms of turnover, profit margins and number of employees, for example. Over an even longer time horizon, the projects are expected to contribute to regional growth through new jobs and new companies, by contributing to the development of the companies they have invested in. Ongoing evaluation should actively contribute to a broader discussion in society – via public debate – over financing questions, by addressing actors such as company owners, private investors, the Ministry of Industry, the Agency for Growth Policy Analysis, regional actors, researchers in corporate financing, and others. Parallel with ongoing evaluation, the Agency for Growth Policy Analysis is working on a commission from the Ministry of Industry with a broader evaluation, covering research reviews, international experiences from venture capital investments and evaluation of outcomes. Overall, this research aims to broaden the understanding of co-investment venture capital supply as an appropriate instrument for creating greater focus on innovation and regional growth. In *Investing in Europe's Future* (European Commission 2010: XV), it is argued that a new programming period should combine grants and loans and further experiment with revolving instruments such as venture capital:

> The EU budget review makes a strong case for increasing the leverage effect of the EU budget. New forms of finance for investment have been developed in the 2007–2013 programming period, moving away from traditional grant-based financing towards innovative ways of combining grants and loans. The Commission would like Member States and regions to make a more extended use of such instruments in the future … Financial instruments help to create revolving forms of finance, making them more sustainable over the longer term. This is also one way of helping Europe to increase resources for investment, especially in times of recession.

The ambition is the accumulation of experience and knowledge that has an impact in other parts of Europe and internationally when it comes to the provision of capital for small and medium-size companies. In other words, ongoing evaluation deals with developing methods and structures, and disseminating these, possibly within the framework of a new Structural Fund programming period in the 27 member states. As a result, this initiative could lead to multiplier effects of significance in terms of innovation-driven growth from small and medium-sized companies. But it may also be the case that this business model does not function outside Manhattan, Boston and Silicon Valley.

WHY IS PUBLIC VENTURE CAPITAL NEEDED?

Sweden is a country which has historically had relatively poorly developed venture capital markets. Just as in France and Germany, Sweden's financial system has been dominated by loan financing, in contrast to, for example, the USA and the UK, which both have a long tradition of providing venture capital. This relationship has led to limited access to both an institutional supply of venture capital and informal venture capital, that is, business angels. What problem is public venture capital supply intended to solve? A number of analyses come to the conclusion that there is a financing gap, both in Sweden and in other EU member states, in terms of an imbalance between financing solutions provided by the market and those that companies need. In particular, small and medium-size companies at early stages in the growth phase experience difficulties in obtaining financing.

As regards the lack of venture capital, it is difficult to determine to what extent this actually leads to market failure. International experiences and the literature on public venture capital often come to the conclusion that in reality it is market rationality which makes private venture capital inaccessible to the majority of small and medium-sized companies.[1] For instance, it is common that the investment risk is too high, growth potential in companies is not sufficiently large and the size of the investment is too small for it to be worthwhile to invest venture capital. In other words, the problem is not just that the market does not provide sufficient financing but that companies requiring capital are not sufficiently attractive for the actors in the market.

The industrial structure differs between the eight Swedish regions, not least in the existence of companies suitable for investing in and access to private equity capital. This means that the projects work under different conditions, which may be of pivotal significance when making investments, creating good development in companies and encouraging private venture capital markets. A national initiative with a number of regional projects functioning as venture capitalists is potentially advantageous. This is expected to strengthen regional

---

1   There is a growing number of evaluations of different public and private venture capital supply schemes: in an evaluation of Scottish experimentation, it is argued that a local structure of venture capital was created by means of the Regional Fund's initative: <http://www.scotland. gov.uk/Resource/Doc/209231/0055411.pdf>. In the West Midlands Risk Capital Study, there is more scepticism. In a study of European Regional Development Funding (ERDF)-funded venture capital and loan funds in England and Wales, there is less scepticism about the performance, whereas another study found 'divergent views among informants on whether the numerous funds associated with current publicly backed venture capital provision represent valuable diversity or inefficient "clutter"'.

involvement and provide opportunities for creating and experimenting with regional models based on the needs existing in regional markets.

How should the projects really work? Should they make profits, and in which case, over what time period? Should companies that receive relatively little interest from the private venture capital market – for example, companies run by women, young people with a foreign background – be given priority? Often women, immigrants and young business owners find it more difficult to get access to capital, which may be because they start companies more often in new and less established industries (Brulin and Svensson 2011). For example, how should the projects attract entrepreneurs and business owners with a foreign background? This could be solved, but then the projects will need to find cost-effective channels to identify the specific investment targets that they are interested in. This could be by cooperating with private actors focusing on investing in companies with, for example, a foreign ownership background. There is an investment company located in a suburb of Sweden's third city, Malmö, which has a large immigrant population, for example. The company is focusing especially on venture capital for entrepreneurs with a foreign background. Its goal is to contribute, on commercial grounds, to increased integration, more jobs and more entrepreneurs with an immigrant background.

More Innovations through Public Programmes?

The programming period 2007–2013 puts a lot of emphasis on greater innovation focus through the Structural Funds. Does this mean that we can expect to see more innovations? This critical review of what we can see so far shows, as mentioned, that it is very difficult to directly identify results in the form of commercialized knowledge. On the other hand, we can see effects in the form of new approaches to innovation systems and entrepreneurship. The Structural Funds have found a niche in creating structures and processes for knowledge spillovers between the scientific community and companies, and between and within companies. This can help in developing an 'entrepreneurial university' which does not value scientific knowledge and research as an end in itself, but looks at its usefulness in commercialization and industrial collaboration. In this respect, the Structural Fund has contributed to resolving the Swedish paradox, and might show a way for the rest of the member states to proceed to resolve the European paradox which we took up in Chapter 5.

Ongoing evaluation in Regional Fund projects should be carried out with a clear focus on innovation, commercialization, industrial collaboration and the comparative advantages existing in the region. The learning taking place between projects and regional development actors should focus on the mechanisms aimed at sustainable development – active ownership, collaboration and joint knowledge formation, as well as developmental learning. Case studies often reveal shortcomings in terms of the mechanisms which we believe lead to sustainable development. There are evident shortcomings in active ownership in a number of the projects. Project managements decide by themselves what activities and initiatives should be taken to increase cluster dynamics. Obvious shortcomings frequently occur in collaboration and joint knowledge formation. It seems that far too often the agenda of the scientific community and researchers steers projects. But what should be most troublesome for programme implementers, partnerships, regional development actors, evaluators, and so on is that experimenting to achieve greater innovation focus appears to be based to such a limited extent on past experiences. Far too often projects are initiated and given priority without project owners and management being required to provide a background description of what has been attempted earlier in the area. Reporting still does not provide a clear picture of what has been good and less good practice in projects. Knowledge feedback is conspicuous by its absence, even though experimentation should shape developmental learning to give rise to multiplier effects. Regional innovation strategies that put projects into a regional innovation and growth context would lead to greater clarity in the overall context of which projects are a part.

8

Owning, Steering and Evaluating Large Programmes

This chapter summarizes our results, analyses and reasoning on owning, steering and evaluating large programmes. We present a number of practical conclusions that can be drawn from the implementation of large programme initiatives. We also wish to highlight a few theoretical results and stake out areas where further research is needed.

Mechanisms for Sustainability

This book deals with how work on sustainable development can be organized. Is it possible that this can be done within the framework of large publicly financed projects aimed at innovation and inclusion in the labour market? Will project logic and short-term thinking make sustainability in the initiatives much more difficult? Can long-term effects continue after project completion?

The review of earlier programme and project initiatives in Chapter 5 indicates that sustainability has often been poor. Uncertainty about what projects lead to in the long term is great, since there is little research in the area and few evaluations study the long-term effects. The aim of this book is to try to understand the mechanisms for successful sustainable development work. What driving forces enable project results to continue, be integrated with other operations and be disseminated to other areas and lead to strategic impact? In the analysis, we take as our starting point the following three mechanisms:

1. *active ownership* within the framework of an efficient and transparent project organization;

2. *collaboration* between important actors and organizations, building on joint knowledge formation blended with action;

3. *developmental learning* that leads to multiplier effects.

When we used these analytical tools to examine different programmes and projects in Chapter 5, we saw evident shortcomings that could explain the difficulties of creating sustainable development through large projects and programmes. Active ownership has often been missing. Collaboration has been limited and learning adaptive. There has seldom been developmental learning that has led to multiplier effects. Feedback from experience and development of knowledge has not taken place.

What has the situation been in ongoing projects in the Regional Fund and the Social Fund? There is a more explicit aim here that project results should be disseminated and lead to strategic impact. A number of support projects and thematic groups have been organized within the Social Fund to raise the quality of projects and thereby contribute to greater sustainability. In the Regional Fund, there is substantial ongoing evaluation at the programme level. In both funds, learning through ongoing evaluation is an attempt to increase the efficiency and sustainability of projects. Have these comprehensive and partly creative initiatives meant that projects lead to sustainable development?

So far it has been difficult to draw overall conclusions from the ambitious attempts made through support measures and learning through ongoing evaluation. But we see a number of difficulties that are linked to the mechanisms for sustainable development work. Lack of active ownership is evident in many projects. This is a consequence of how projects are initiated, prioritized and steered. Projects are often initiated externally, from an intermediate level in the organization or from staff, which means that top management and line managers are not involved in taking long-term responsibility for them. It has also proved to be difficult to bring about learning collaboration between important actors and organizations, especially in large and complex projects that have been dominant during the current programming period. Innovation systems and Triple Helix also cover different actors with different traditions and cultures. The possibility of creating developmental learning leading to multiplier effects is limited by rules, routines and obstacles between projects, programmes and the system level.

What can learning through ongoing evaluation do to support mechanisms for sustainability? One conclusion is that learning through ongoing evaluation has been spread widely; knowledge about the approach has increased rapidly. It has started to function as a support for quality assurance in projects. At the same time, different follow-ups show a number of difficulties in getting learning through ongoing evaluation to function as intended: limited funding and use of results, lack of critical distance and of contributions to public debate, and so on. Learning through ongoing evaluation in itself is no solution to the sustainability of a project, but it is a part of the solution when appropriate conditions exist or are created.

Development Support Instead of Control

Growth and employment creation through programme initiatives involves getting individuals, companies and regions to have the ambition to grow and develop (Brulin and Halvarsson 1998: 98) by providing support for development. Different innovation, employment and competence development programmes are based on producing knowledge of how sustainable development can be created. Learning systems should ensure that experiences and knowledge are condensed, packaged and transferred to the programme implementing authority, decision-making partnerships, local and regional development actors, partnering organizations, participating companies, and so on.

There has always been a dream of total control and steering of programmes and projects. The Commission which studied regional organization in Sweden argued strongly for more evidence-based control and steering of regional development measures. There was a desire to mobilize forces into fewer, firmer controlled and better coordinated growth and development policy initiatives. The final report (Ministry of Health and Social Affairs 2007: 217) recognizes, however, that the question of what creates growth is not indisputable:

> *Growth and development policy are recognised as difficult to steer, and characterized by lack of consensus of what really creates growth in the long-term, and the difficulty of relating measurable results to individual initiatives. This makes steering by goals and results very difficult. It can easily happen that focus ends up on form rather than content, as the former is so much more understandable and concrete.*

The study argues in favour of the planning-steered developmental model in regional growth, despite the fact that the Commission recognizes that the prerequisites for measurement and control in areas such as regional development, health and medical care vary widely.

The alternative to the planning-steered developmental model was discussed in Chapter 2 – the development-supportive evaluation model. Instead of checking that development initiatives and projects really implement activities and follow the plan for achieving measurable and controllable goals in accordance with the SMART criteria, it involves learning through ongoing evaluation in order to provide support for development. The idea is to feedback experiences and generated knowledge by means of ongoing evaluation. It is through such systems for learning that the different professions which manage development processes – such as organizational consultants, venture capitalists, therapists and others – work. Putting together and combining insights and knowledge from a number of different organizations, companies and individuals in a similar development phase creates energy in programme and project implementation.

In this context it is important to consider profiles, competence and support from ongoing evaluators. One observation is that management consultants playing this role only have temporary responsibility. If the person is a qualified 'researcher', he/she possesses knowledge about the ethical conditions and critical role of research. Learning through ongoing evaluation can also be developed through clearer competence requirements from financiers and purchasers. It is important to reflect on how knowledge can be built up regionally through such efforts and how these efforts might contribute to affecting systems and increasing renewal in the long term. There are good examples of learning through ongoing evaluation, as well as interactive and action research, which have provided development support and thus played a strategic role for sustainable development.

Investing in Europe's Future (European Commission 2010: 257) argues that:

> *monitoring and evaluation systems need to be improved across the EU to track performance and to help redirect efforts as necessary to ensure that objectives are attained. This requires a clear strategic vision of what the programme aims to achieve and how success will be recognized and measured (proper target setting). It also requires a greater recourse to rigorous evaluation methods, including counterfactual impact evaluation, cost benefit analysis, beneficiary surveys, as well as a more rigorous use of qualitative methods such as case studies.*

To reach a more strategic and results-oriented approach to cohesion policy, the Commission wants to change the monitoring and evaluation systems in a number of ways (European Commission 2010: XV).

First, it is argued that 'the starting point for a results-oriented approach is ex-ante setting of clear measurable targets and outcome indicators. Indicators must be clearly interpretable, statistically validated, truly responsive and directly linked to policy intervention and promptly collected and publicised.' It might sound like an impressive ambition by the Commission to try to get the indicator system to work in a proper way. However, the Commission has not succeeded with it in the present programming period and will probably not in the next. The reason is that it is not possible to design an indicator system that can function as the Commission wants. There are a number of epistemological shortcomings behind its ambition, essentially of the same kind which can explain why a planned economy never worked. It is not possible to produce reliable and valid indicators of how complex programmes are able to achieve competitiveness, innovations and job creation. Achieving such objectives is a risky business, full of failures and surprises. They cannot be achieved in a smoothly working, linear development process, captured by clear-cut indicators.

This explains why the Commission's second aim also fails, where it argues that 'ex-ante evaluations should focus on improving programme design so that the tools and incentives for achieving objectives and targets can be monitored and evaluated during implementation'. As there are no such tools, the Commission would have to force programme managers and project leaders to organize programmes and projects in a linear way (often designed in line with the SMART criteria). It could be argued that the requirement to carry out programmes and projects in a linear way will hinder the implementation of those with the greatest potential, that is, the most innovative ones.

Thirdly, the Commission argues for greater use of rigorous methods in line with international standards in the control of projects. What methods in line with international standards can capture the many different types of implementation, the time lags in accomplishing results and effects, and the situation dependencies that characterize large public programmes and projects? Rather than trying to impose 'higher-quality, better functioning monitoring and evaluation systems', it is probably time to change the strategy on how to carry out large programmes. It is time to accept that they cannot be primarily monitored from above. A truly results-oriented approach is not about fine-tuning monitoring through remote control. On the contrary, a results-oriented approach has to be based on an iterative learning system. The main duty of the Commission should be to knit together member states, programme managers and project leaders in more horizontal learning structures. The implementation of large programmes would then be based on joint knowledge formation in a global context, and also on theory and practice, as well as being transparent. Such an epistemology would transform programmes in the Structural Funds into mechanisms for knowledge-based development processes that support sharing of innovative practices regarding growth and job creation. In this way, Europe could take decisive steps towards becoming the world's most competitive region.

It is time to establish a fifth-generation evaluation. Feedback from evaluation should be directed at a broader group – participants, users/customers, financiers, industry, managing authorities and other target groups, both during the implementation phase and on completion of the project. Seminars, conferences and other meetings with different actors can be identified as important for dissemination and strategic impact. Learning concerning regional growth and development processes involves finding ways of concretely looking at similarities and differences through different themes and questions, lessons to be learnt and successful examples, as well as finding forms that actively involve different actors (nationally and regionally). Learning can take place through different forms for the exchange of experiences, and also in networks through bench learning. Each region is unique and must find its own way of developing. Learning does not deal with copying what a specific region has already done, but rather providing opportunities for reflection, to draw lessons from the experiences of others.

Some Recommendations

What practical conclusions can we draw from the reasoning above in terms of administration, organization and management of programmes for the Social and Regional Funds? What can be done to strengthen sustainability of projects based on our research results? We have emphasized that sustainability is connected with the ability to resolve dilemmas and contradictions in a reflective way – and not just to look for simple solutions. Not least the experience of the worst financial and economic crisis to hit the world since the 1930s demonstrates the necessity of developing flexible and reflective implementation in programme initiatives. We summarize our conclusions in a number of recommendations and thought-provoking questions:

- Make a careful selection of applicants to determine if there are conditions for active ownership. Is the motive to develop operations, to obtain funding or just to demonstrate participation in a project? To what extent have project owners been actively involved in driving and developing projects over the long term? Does good collaboration exist with other actors?

- What does the project organization look like? Will there be a steering group that is competent, has a mandate and the capacity to work strategically, and will steer in the direction of long-term effects? What different and complementary competencies exist in the steering group? Has a gender and integration perspective been used to create dynamics in learning processes?

- Are there conditions for learning collaboration between important and relevant actors and organizations? Do applicants understand the need to build relationships of trust and confidence, and do they have the capacity for mobilizing and acting innovatively?

- Are there conditions for developmental learning that can lead to multiplier effects? How should interaction between actors at the local, regional and national levels work in practice? Are there ideas on using intermediaries – such as higher education, R&D centres, industrial development centres, learning centres, and so on – for dissemination and strategic impact?

Practical advice and recommendations may be good, particularly if they have a theoretical and empirical basis that can provide a stronger foundation and transparency, and function strategically. The recommendations are not intended to function as a checklist, nor a template for sustainable development work. Instead they should be regarded as a basis for dialogue between applicants, project case handlers and decision-makers on the rationale of a project and, above all, how it can be made better. A dialogue-based learning process of this kind can pre-empt problems and enhance the ideas underlying the project. This involves, amongst other things, the difficulties of managing programmes of this scope in a world where change has been and continues to take place at a rapid rate over a short period in the economy and society.

Development Opportunities

We have highlighted problems and difficulties in programme and project initiatives. We have taken as our starting point the high ambitions attached to the Regional and Social Funds in Sweden. We believe that there have been exciting developments in both programmes regarding learning through ongoing evaluation. Another innovative element is the close and ongoing cooperation that has developed between both the authorities, a feature that was lacking in the previous programming period. Why is this cooperation so important? If we regard competence issues as crucial, not just for a company's development, but also for a region's future and growth, then such cooperation becomes a necessity. Companies found it difficult to recruit skilled personnel even shortly after the downturn in the economy, which had led to a high level of redundancies. Competence and lack of personnel can rapidly become a bottleneck and an obstacle to growth and competitiveness. If both funds can jointly contribute to promoting the development of and an infrastructure for vocational education and training, as well as a system for the further training of employees, this would have an important strategic impact and provide multiplier effects throughout the economy and society, not least as regards regional innovation and growth.

Some Theoretical Conclusions

Our research has taken different starting points, with a number of perspectives and concepts originating from different disciplines. The questions deal with project steering, innovation, sustainable development work, evaluation, learning, collaboration, gender and integration. Our focus has been on identifying mechanisms for sustainable development work. A broad approach has been taken because of the types of questions involved and the combination of different research traditions used. An interactive approach has been the basis for our data collection and analysis. Both of us have had the opportunity of working within and outside the ESF Council and the Swedish Agency for Economic and Regional Growth, and because of this we have been able to combine closeness to operations with critical distance.

Figure 8.1 illustrates the three mechanisms which we have used to explain sustainability in development work. The first mechanism is active ownership, which is analysed by using a theory of project organization as an analogy to theories about work organization. The second mechanism is collaboration to generate joint knowledge formation, where theories on innovation systems, networks and cluster formation are covered. The third mechanism is developmental learning to create multiplier effects in a large project, where theories of learning are combined with theories on implementation, dissemination and strategic impact. Sustainability in development work can be studied as an interaction between these three mechanisms.

What theoretical contribution has our research made? What opportunities does the analytical model above provide for analysing sustainable development work? We would like to draw attention to some of the research findings, but

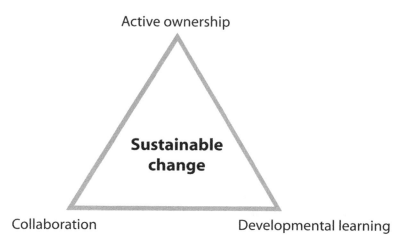

Figure 8.1   Mechanisms for sustainable change

at the same time emphasize the exploratory approach where results can be regarded as a 'pool' for further research. The most crucial result is that we have identified three mechanisms for sustainable development work. This is a research finding which we consider to be well substantiated through empirical data drawn from the different development programmes that we have studied. The foundations of the mechanisms are project steering, learning, collaboration and multiplier effects. These are terms used in different disciplines – in project and organizational theory, pedagogy, business economics, sociology and political science, as well as management research and activity theory. The terms are used in a generative and open way and thus they need to be defined more clearly in specific future studies.

The term 'sustainable development work' was part of our earlier research. Here we developed ideas on how project organization and learning need to be linked for projects to lead to sustainable development. The same applies to gender equality and integration. In one respect our research deviates from trends and praxis. Much of learning through ongoing evaluation deals with the development of ideas, initiation and planning, but very little with how to complete and leverage results from projects. The question 'what happens next' has been part of our focus, but since long-term effects are difficult to study and measure during a project period, the question of mechanisms and indicators of sustainability becomes crucial. From this perspective, vertical collaboration becomes important, between a local or regional level – where ownership and knowledge about specific conditions exist – and a national level – where there is an overall view and closeness to political power and regional development actors. A fundamental theoretical starting point is the inter-organizational perspective, which may be regarded as natural in large programmes where different organizations and actors collaborate. Collaboration does not occur spontaneously, but needs to be supported and organized. We have brought in the concept of intermediaries, that is, the function of a mediating link, as a critical factor for sustainability in development work.

We have also expanded the perspective of growth, innovation and regional development, and considered questions regarding welfare, inclusion and gender equality. If we are to understand how politics and economics can interact, the relationship between them must be viewed in terms of power, interests and resources, and this means that conflicts are to be regarded as both natural and as driving forces for future development. A development programme can contribute to strengthening the resources of established groups, which large system-oriented initiatives appear to do, but they can also contribute to evening out power differences by bringing in new groups and thereby creating greater dynamism in development, at the same time as more democratic starting conditions are established. Hopefully, our book will contribute to the latter.

A book which is not actively used in development work will not have an impact – either practically or in public debate. The ambition is that this book will be used in different projects and programmes, but also in different higher education situations. Training for project managers and steering group representatives is planned in the form of cooperation between different university colleges and universities, where this book will, we trust, provide a new perspective on sustainable development work.

How to Deal with Uncertainties and Extreme Events

It is tough to make predictions; especially of the future.

Yogi Berra

The strategies for discoveries and innovation are often organized through top-down planning systems. The literature on project management is often based on these scientific assumptions with a focus on linearity, planning, regularity, measurement and confirmation of facts. By using this verification paradigm, the project managers will not find the 'black swans' (Taleb 2010), namely rare and unforeseen events. Most projects are based on production logic, rather than developmental logic. Such a linear change paradigm can function in a predictable, controlled and stable environment, but not in an open and rapidly changing society. We cannot know the future by learning from the past. Taleb refers to the 'turkey problem' to illustrate the problem of induction. A turkey may be well fed for 1,000 days, but these experiences will not guarantee its well-being after Thanksgiving Day. This example illustrates the risk of naïve empiricism – the attempt to generalize from experience and customs. This risk is extremely high in a modern society which is dominated by rare and unforeseen events. In such a situation, the causes of a phenomenon may be difficult to identify from successful past experiences. To understand causality, it is often better to study failures in order to find traits and invisible patterns.

In a complex and unpredictable world with extreme events, the models for calculation and planning are less useful. An alternative change strategy would be based on identifying opportunities in situations that are recognized as being complicated, fuzzy, rare, inconsistent, random, unknown, improbable, non-linear and uncertain. The discoveries of the computer, the Internet and the laser have all been unplanned, unpredicted, and have remained unappreciated well after their initial use. They were all 'black swans' (Taleb 2010: 135).

A new scientific paradigm will be needed to conceptualize the uncertainties and unforeseen events in a complex system where chaos and order can be seen as complementary concepts. The critique of traditional linear thinking can be based on new findings in mathematics, evolution and computer science. We have been inspired by different thinkers:

- Poincaré's critique of the Bell curve as a single measure of randomness and uncertainty (with its ideas of standard deviation, correlation and regression);

- Turing's and Belusov's ideas of finding patterns and mechanisms for coordination and self-organization by using mathematics and geometry;

- Lorenz's chaos theory, in which small events can have dramatic effects in a system that is difficult to calculate;

- Mandelbrot's way of explaining variations and irregularities by fractional randomness (which is linked to the repetition of geometric patterns in increasingly small variants);

- Taleb's idea of a black swan, developed in this section.

A paradigm borrowed from the natural sciences has often been used to explain phenomena in the social sciences. This paradigm is often over-specialized and introverted with a reductionist striving for confirmation of well-defined objects. The ambition is to put knowledge in straitjackets (Taleb 2010: 211). This influence has been very detrimental to innovative thinking because it has been grounded in the old-fashioned paradigm of Newtonian physics. Complex projects aimed at sustainable change can learn much from natural science, but must be the modern variant presented above, not the old positivistic variant. It implies systems thinking which is based on incremental, asymmetric and random changes.

What does all this scientific and philosophical reasoning mean when it comes to project management? In a complex and rapidly changing work scenario, a project has to act fast and be innovative and flexible. Agile project management is a reaction to these demands from the market and growing uncertainties and ambiguities in society. Agility is the ability to both create and respond to change in order to profit in a turbulent business environment (Highsmith 2010: 13). The pressures for change and the abnormal are most pronounced in biotechnology, nanotechnology and information technology. Similar mechanisms for rapid change and transformation are going on in different – social, political, cultural – organizations. Agility implies a striving for innovation and exploration in response to new customer demands in the development of new products and services. The project organization has to be flexible, effective and dynamic in order to correspond to these new demands (Highsmith 2010).

In an agile project, the project manager has to be open-minded and have genuine curiosity. You must be careful where you are going because you might not get there. You need a variety of methods and views to be able to come to grips with the disorder. Randomness should be seen as a natural order and a dynamic mechanism for innovation. Be careful when you use statistics and models because they can give you a false sense of confidence. Always try to have a back-up system! Learn to love redundancy and simplicity, instead of trying to optimize a system.

Afterword

Cohesion policy, since its creation in 1989, has generated many positive effects across all member states. It has proved to be successful in providing investment for modernization, triggering growth, enhancing access to the labour market and social inclusion of Europeans, as well as acting as a catalyst for change. It is very encouraging for us to see that the evaluation approach in cohesion policy sets so large a footprint in the Swedish evaluation discourse. The current policy debate confirms, however, that further improvements in cohesion policy are much-needed to steer it more decisively towards producing verifiable results and to align it firmly with the objectives of Europe 2020. This creates a new challenge for evaluation, that is, to provide credible evidence on policy performance. This challenge has to be addressed in partnership: by the European Commission, member states and regions working together to capture and demonstrate the effects of cohesion policy.

Until now, cohesion policy has invested significantly in creating networks, facilitating exchange of experience and promoting evaluation. With the new challenges ahead, more should be done to organize reflective learning processes to enable ongoing critical and constructive evaluation of policies, programmes and projects. Managers and decision-makers need to continuously evaluate and learn in order to be able to steer development work appropriately. The authors of this book have named this new approach as development based on 'walking on two legs': learning and evaluation.

This book demonstrates how a constructive and productive learning framework can be established through ongoing evaluation and how a learning reflex can be embedded in administrative practice. The approach presented in the book encourages creativity among evaluators in order to generate an additional value and innovative approaches in cohesion policy programmes and projects. Learning from others' experiences, reflecting on evaluation needs, design and methods, pooling together and effectively using evaluation results, as well as drawing policy lessons would certainly benefit preparatory actions in the context of future programming.

There is a need to build on our experience so far, but also to explore new methodological approaches by referring to academic work and international good practice. For evaluation to be successful in delivering evidence on policy performance, there is a need to use robust methods adapted to specific areas of intervention. The idea of complementarity is important, where a mix of methods can be applied to answer different evaluation questions and, in particular, to address an issue of complex and multilayered causality in cohesion policy programmes.

The learning perspective is crucial in fifth-generation evaluation – named so by the authors of the book – and should take place both in and between projects/programmes, and cover both individuals and organizations. Learning should be a continuous process at all levels – in projects and programmes (including their beneficiaries), at the regional, national and, not least, transnational levels. Ongoing evaluation should target not only project leaders but also project owners, steering groups and funders. More theory-based and counter-factual impact evaluations should be presented in a communicative way and involve the partnerships, as well as regional actors in the public debate on evaluation evidence. The partnership approach is one of the key principles of cohesion policy. It has proven to be a crucial factor in helping to ensure the policy's effectiveness and successful implementation. Evaluation relies heavily on partnership, and our success in the future will depend very much on a joint capability to generate robust evidence regarding the effects and added value of cohesion policy.

In the next programming period, new demands will be put on the funds and programmes. The programmes will probably become more focused. They have to be carried through in a smarter way, getting rid of double work, partly overlapping support schemes which do not build on synergy effects and similar projects that do not learn from each other, and so on. European Regional Development Fund (ERDF) projects that focus on innovation should cooperate with European Social Fund (ESF) projects that support competence mobility and upgrade. This cannot be forced on the projects 'from above'; on the contrary, horizontal learning processes within and between projects have to be formed. Evaluations that produce solid narratives, backed up by firm quantitative and qualitative evidence on what is working (or not), how and in what context, are needed to maximize synergies, performance, and sustainable and inclusive innovation-based regional growth. Evaluation is a bridging tool for policy learning and innovation. This book highlights the necessity of using an open learning approach within ongoing evaluation.

Veronica Gaffey
Head of Evaluation Unit
DG Regio

Antonella Schulte-Braucks
Head of Evaluation Unit
DG Employment

References

Aagaard Nielsen, Kurt and Svensson, Lennart (eds). 2006. *Action Research and Interactive Research: A Way to Combine Practice with Theory*. Hamburg: Shaker Verlag.

Acs, Zoltan, Audretsch, David, Braunerhjelm, Pontus and Carlsson, Bo. 2005. *The Knowledge Spillover Theory of Entrepreneurship*. Discussion Papers on Entrepreneurship, Growth and Public Policy, Max Planck Institute of Economics, Group Entrepreneurship, Growth and Public Policy. Cheltenham: Edward Elgar Publishing.

Adler, Niklas, Shani, Rami and Styhre, Alexander. 2004. *Collaborative Research in Organizations: Foundations for Learning, Change, and Theoretical Development*. London: Sage.

Andersen, Erling. 2008. *Rethinking Project Management: An Organisational Perspective*. London: Prentice Hall.

Argyris, Chris. 1999. *Organizational Learning*. Oxford: Blackwell.

Avdeitchikova, Sofia. 2008. *Close-ups from Afar: The Nature of the Informal Venture Capital Market in a Spatial Context*. Lund: Lund Business Press.

Barker, Stephen and Cole, Rob. 2009. *Brilliant Project Management: What the Best Project Managers Know, Do and Say?* London: Prentice Hall.

Bjurulf, Staffan and Olsson, Anders. 2010. Regional Innovation in Värmland. *Journal of Nordregio* 1, 12–15.

Bjurulf, Staffan and Vedung, Evert. 2009. Do Public Interventions for Innovation Hit Their Targets? Evaluating Cluster Organisations in Northern Central Sweden. Conference Paper, *New Methods for Cohesion Policy Evaluation*, Warsaw, 30 November–1 December 2009.

Bourne, Linda. 2009. *Stakeholder Relationship Management*. London: Gower.

Briner, Wendy, Geddes, Michael and Hastings, Colin. 1998. *Projektledaren*. Stockholm: Svenska förlaget.

Brulin, Göran. 2000. The Third Task of Universities or How to Get Universities to Serve their Communities! in *Handbook on Action Research: Participative Inquiry and Practice*, edited by Peter Reason and Hilary Bradbury. London: Sage.

Brulin, Göran. 2002. *Faktor X. Arbete och kapital i en lokal värld*. Stockholm: Atlas and National Institute for Working Life.

Brulin, Göran. 2004. The Third Task: A Challenge for Swedish Research and Higher Education, in *Action Research in Workplace Innovation and Regional Development*, edited by Werner Fricke and Peter Totterdill. Amsterdam/ Philadelphia: John Benjamins Publishing Company.

Brulin, Göran and Ekstedt, Eskil. 2005. Forming Relations and Cluster Dynamics, in *Labour, Globalisation and the New Economy*, edited by György Széll et al. Frankfurt am Main: Peter Lang GmbH.

Brulin, Göran and Ekstedt, Eskil. 2007. Towards a New Work Organisation Contract in Sweden: The Need for a Legitimising Process, in *New Forms of Work Organisation and Industrial Relations in Southern Europe*, edited by Francesco Garibaldo and Volker Telljohann. Frankfurt am Main: Peter Lang GmbH.

Brulin, Göran and Halvarsson, Dan. 1998. Coalitions between University Colleges, Intermediaries and SMEs to Develop Regional Economies and Working Life (The Gnosjö Region, Sweden), in *Work Organization and Europe as a Development Coalition*, edited by Richard Ennals and Björn Gustavsen. Amsterdam: John Benjamins.

Brulin, Göran and Jansson, Sven. 2009. A New Programme Period, a New Evaluation Approach, in *Learning Through Ongoing Evaluation*, edited by Lennart Svensson et al. Lund: Studentlitteratur.

Brulin, Göran and Nilsson, Tommy. 1997. Productivity and Work Development, in *The Workplace: Volume 1, Fundamentals of Health, Safety and Welfare*, edited by Dag Brune et al. Geneva: CIS and ILO; Oslo: Scandinavian Science Publisher as.

Brulin, Göran and Nilsson, Tommy. 1999. The Swedish Model of Lean Production in Teamwork, in *The Automobile Industry: Radical Change or Passing Fashion?* edited by Jean-Pierre Durand et al. London: Macmillan Press.

Brulin, Göran and Svensson, Lennart. 2011. *Att äga, styra and utvärdera stora projekt*. Lund: Studentlitteratur.

Brulin, Göran, Hammarström, Olle and Nilsson, Tommy. 2009. Lean Production and Employment Relations in the Swedish Auto Assembly Industry, in *Globalization and Employment Relations in the Auto Assembly Industry*, edited by Russell D. Lansbury et al. Austin: Wolters Kluwer.

Cassin, Bryce. 2012. *The Social Infrastructure of Project Management*. London: Gower.

Cavanagh, Michael. 2012. *Second Order Project Management*. London: Gower.

Chen, Huey-Tsyh. 2004. The Roots of Theory-Driven Evaluation: Current Views and Origins, in *Evaluation Roots: Tracing Theorists' Views and Influences*, edited by Marvin Alkin. London: Sage.

Choi, Sang-Duk. 2011. Initiatives in VET and Workplace Learning: A Korean Perspective, in *The SAGE Handbook of Workplace Learning*, edited by Margaret Malloch et al. London: Sage.

Clemans, Allie and Rushbrook, Peter. 2011. Competence-Based Training and Its Impact on Workplace Learning in Australia, in *The SAGE Handbook of Workplace Learning*, edited by Margaret Malloch et al. London: Sage.

Collins, David. 1998. *Organizational Change: Sociological Perspective*. London: Routledge.

Collins, Mark. 2010. *Pro Project Management with SharePoint*. Avaliable at: www.apress.com [accessed: 14 May 2011].

Cooke, Philip, De Laurentis, Carla, Tödtling, Franz and Trippl, Michaela. 2007. *Regional Knowledge Economies: Markets, Clusters and Innovation*. Cheltenham: Edward Elgar Publishing.

Costley, Carol. 2011. Workplace Learning and Higher Education, in *The SAGE Handbook of Workplace Learning*, edited by Margaret Malloch et al. London: Sage.

Cronbach, Lee. 1982. *Designing Evaluations of Educational and Social Programs*. San Francisco: Jossey-Bass.

Dahlberg, Gunilla, Moss, Peter and Pence, Alan. 2003. *Beyond Quality in Early Childhood Education and Care: Postmodern Perspectives*. London: Routledge.

Dahmén, Erik. 1950. *Svensk industriell företagarverksamhet*. Stockholm: IUI.

De Herbemont, Oliver and César, Bruno. 1998. *Managing Sensitive Projects: A Lateral Approach*. London: Macmillian Press.

Delander, Lennart and Månsson, Jonas. 2009. The Type of Evaluation Chosen Depends on Which Questions Are Being Asked, in *Learning Through Ongoing Evaluation*, edited by Lennart Svensson et al. Lund: Studentlitteratur.

Descartes, René. 1637. *A Discourse on the Method of Rightly Conducting One's Reason and of Seeking Truth in the Sciences*. Edinburgh: Sutherland and Knox; London: Simpkin, Marshall and Co.

Dirkx, John. 2011. Work-Related Learning in the United States: Past Practices, Paradigm Shifts, and Policies of Partnerships, in *The SAGE Handbook of Workplace Learning*, edited by Margaret Malloch et al. London: Sage.

Doloreux, David and Saeed, Parto. 2004. *Regional Innovation Systems: A Critical Review*. Unpublished paper. Available at: www.urenio.org/metaforesight/library/17.pdf [accessed: 14 May 2011].

Edquist, Charles. 2010. The Swedish Paradox: Unexploited Possibilities. *CIRCLE Lund University*, 2010(5).

Ejermo, Olof and Karlsson, Charlie. 2005. Interregional Inventor Networks as Studied by Patent Co-inventorships. *CIRCLE Lund University* 2005(11).

Ekman, Marianne, Gustavsen, Bjorn, Asheim, Björn and Palshaugen, Öyvind. 2010. *Learning Regional Innovation: Scandinavian Models*. London: Palgrave.

Elkjaer, Bente. 2001. The Learning Organization: An Undelivered Promise. *Management Learning*, 32(4), 437–452.

Ellström, Per-Erik. 2001. Integrating Learning and Work: Problems and Prospects. *Human Resource Development Quarterly*, 12(4), 421–435.

Ellström, Per-Erik. 2009. The Use and Benefits of Evaluations: A Learning Perspective, in *Learning Through Ongoing Evaluation*, edited by Lennart Svensson et al. Lund: Studentlitteratur.

Ellström, Per-Erik. 2010. Organizational Learning, in *International Encyclopedia of Education*, edited by Berry McGaw et al. Oxford: Elsevier, 1, 47–52.

Ellström, Per-Erik and Kock, Henrik. 2009. Competence Development in the Workplace: Concepts, Strategies, and Effects, in *International Perspectives on Competence Development: Developing Skill and Capabilities*, edited by Knud Illeris. London: Routledge.

Engeström, Yrjö. 1996. Development as Breaking Away and Opening Up: A Challenge to Vygotsky and Piaget. *Swiss Journal of Psychology*, 55, 126–132.

Engeström, Yrjö. 2011. Activity Theory and Learning at Work, in *The SAGE Handbook of Workplace Learning*, edited by Margaret Malloch et al. London: Sage.

Engwall, Mats. 2002. The Futile Dream of the Perfect Goal, in *Beyond Project Management: New Perspectives on the Contemporary*, edited by Ingrid Sahlin-Andersson and Anders Söderholm. Copenhagen: Copenhagen Business School Press.

Eskelinen, Heikki and Maskell, Peter. 1998. *Competitiveness, Localised Learning and Regional Development*. London: Routledge.

European Commission. 2006a. Ex-Post Evaluation of Cohesion Policy Programmes 2000–06 Co-financed by the ERDF (Objective 1 and 2), Synthesis Report, European Union Cohesion Policy, April 2010.

European Commission. 2006b. Innovative Strategies and Actions: Results from 15 Years of Regional Experimentation. Directorate General for Regional Policy.

European Commission. 2007a. Innovative Strategies and Actions: Results from 15 Years of Regional Experimentation. Working Document. Directorate-General for Regional Policy.

European Commission. 2007b. Indicative Guidelines on Evaluation Methods: Evaluation During The Programming Period. Working Document No. 5. Available at: http://ec.europa.eu/regional_policy/sources/docoffic/2007/working/wd5_ongoing_en.pdf.

European Commission. 2010. *Investing in Europe's Future*. Fifth Report on Economic, Social and Territorial Cohesion. Luxembourg: Publications Office of the European Union.

Evalsed's web site. Available at: http://ec.europa.eu/regional_policy/sources.

Evaluation of the Finnish National Innovation System 2009. Available at: www. evaluation.fi.

Evans, Karen, Waite, Edmund and Kersh, Natasha. 2011. Towards a Social Ecology of Adult Learning In and Through the Workplace, in *The SAGE Handbook of Workplace Learning*, edited by Margaret Malloch et al. London: Sage.

Fenwick, Tara. 2011. Policies for the Knowledge Economy: Knowledge Discourses at Play, in *The SAGE Handbook of Workplace Learning*, edited by Margaret Malloch et al. London: Sage.

Fuller, Alison and Unwin, Lorna. 2011. Workplace Learning and the Organization, in *The SAGE Handbook of Workplace Learning*, edited by Margaret Malloch, et al. London: Sage.

George, Judith and Cowan, John. 1999. *A Handbook of Techniques for Formative Evaluation*. London: Routledge.

Government Communication (Regeringens skrivelse) 2009/10: 221 Strategiskt tillväxtarbete för regional konkurrenskraft, entreprenörskap and sysselsättning.

Greene, Francis and Storey, David. 2007. Issues in Evaluation: The Case of Shell Livewire, in *Handbook of Research on Entrepreneurship Policy*, edited by David Bruce Audretsch et al. Cheltenham: Edward Elgar Publishing.

Guba, Egon and Lincoln, Yvonna. 1989. *Fourth Evaluation Generation*. Newbury Park: Sage.

Gustavsen, Bjorn. 2010. Participation and 'Constructivist Society', in *Learning Regional Innovation: Scandinavian Models*, edited by Marianne Ekman, Bjorn Gustavsen, Björn Asheim and Öyvind Palshaugen. London: Palgrave.

Gustavsen, Björn, Finne, Håkon and Oscarsson, Bo. 2001. *Creating Connectedness: The Role of Social Research in Innovation Policy*. Amsterdam: John Benjamins.

Harrison, Frederick and Lock, Dennis. 2004. *Advanced Project Management: A Structured Approach*. London: Gower.

Hedlund, Gun. 2008. Partnership, Gender and Democracy, in *Partnership: As a Strategy for Social Innovation and Sustainable Change*, edited by Lennart Svensson and Barbro Nilsson. Stockholm: Santérus Academic Press Sweden.

Henton, Douglas, Melville, John and Walesh, Kimberly. 1997. *Grassroots Leaders for a New Economy: How Civic Entrepreneurs Are Building Prosperous Communities*. San Francisco: Jossey-Bass Publishers.

Hersey, Paul and Blanchard, Ken. 1972. *Management of Organizational Behavior*. New York: Prentice Hall.

Highsmith, Jim. 2010. *Agile Project Management: Creating Innovative Products*. Boston: Addison-Wesley.

Hopkinson, Martin. 2010. *The Project Risk Maturity Model: Measuring and Improving Risk Management Capability*. London: Gower.

Jaques, Elliott and Clement, Stephen. 2009. *Executive Leadership: A Practical Guide to Managing Complexity*. London: Blackwell.

Jenner, Stephen. 2010. *Transforming Governmental Public Services: Realising Benefits through Project Portfolio Management*. London: Gower.

Kerzner, Harold. 2009. *Project Management: A System Approach to Planning, Scheduling and Controlling*. New Jersey: John Wiley.

Kock, Henrik and Ellström, Per-Erik. 2011. Formal and Integrated Strategies for Competence Development in SMEs. *Journal of European Industrial Training*, 35(1), 71–88.

Laestadius, Staffan, Nuur, Cali and Ylinenpää, Håkan (eds). 2007. *Regional växtkraft i en global ekonomi. Det svenska Vinnväxtprogrammet*. Stockholm: Santérus Academic Press.

Larsson, Kerstin. 2008. Mellanchefer som utvecklar – om förutsättningar för hållbart utvecklingsarbete inom vård och omsorg. (Middle Managers Who Implement Changes: Prerequisites for Sustainable Development Efforts Within Healthcare and Caring.) Dissertation essay, Linköping Studies in Behavioural Science No. 127. Linköping University (in Swedish with an English abstract).

Lerner, Josh. 2009. *Boulevard of Broken Dreams: Why Public Efforts to Boost Entrepreneurship and Venture Capital Have Failed – and What to Do about It*. New Jersey: Princeton University Press.

Lewis, James. 1998. *Team-Based Management*. New York: Amacom.

Liker, Jeffrey. 2004. *The Toyota Way*. Stockholm: Liber.

Lindgren, Lena. 2011. If Robert Merton Said It, It Must Be True. A Bibliometric Analysis in the Field of Performance Measures. *Evaluation*, 17, 7–19.

Lissoni, Francesco, Llerena, Patrick, McKelvey, Maureen and Sanditov, Bulat. 2008. Academic Patenting in Europe: New Evidence from the KEINS Database. *Research Evaluation*, 17(2).

Lock, Dennis. 2007. *Project Management*. London: Gower.

Lundström, Anders, Almerud, Moa and Stevenson, Lois. 2008. *Entrepreneurship and Innovation Policies: Analysing Measures in European Countries*. Swedish Foundation for Small Business Research, FSF, 2008: 3.

Lundvall, Bengt-Åke (ed.). 1992. *National Systems of Innovation*. London: Pinter.

Malloch, Margaret, Cairns, Len, Evans, Karen and O'Connor, Bridget. 2011. *The SAGE Handbook of Workplace Learning*. London: Sage.

March, James. 1991. Explanation and Exploration in Organizational Learning. *Organizational Science*, 2, 71–87.

Markusen, Ann. 1996. Sticky Places in Slippery Space: A Typology of Industrial Districts. *Economic Geography*, 72, 293–313.

Maylor, Harvey. 2010. *Project Management*. New York: Prentice Hall.

Meredith, Jack and Mantel, Samuel. 2010. *Project Management: A Managerial Approach*. New Jersey: John Wiley.

Miettinen, Reijo. 2002. *National Innovation System: Scientific Concept or Political Rhetoric*. Helsingfors: Edita.

Ministry of Health and Social Affairs. 2007. Hållbar samhällsorganisation med utvecklingskraft (Sustainable Social Organisation with Development Power). Slutbetänkande av Ansvarskommittén (Final Report by the Responsibility Committee) SOU 2007: 10. Stockholm: Edita Sverige AB (in Swedish).

Moore, Simon. 2010. *Strategic Project Portfolio Management: Enabling a Productive Organization*. New Jersey: John Wiley.

Murray, Gordon C. 2007. Venture Capital and Government Policy, in *Handbook of Research on Venture Capital*, edited by Hans Landström. Cheltenham: Edward Elgar Publishing.

Nowotny, Helga, Scott, Peter and Gibbons, Michael. 2001. *Re-thinking Science: Knowledge and the Public in an Age of Uncertainty*. Cambridge: Polity Press.

O'Callaghan, Mark. 2008. Project Closure and Aftermath, in *Gower Handbook of Project Management*, edited by Rodney Turner. London: Gower.

Patton, Michael Quinn. 2010. *Developmental Evaluation: Applying Complexity Concepts to Enhance Innovation and Use*. New York: Guilford Publications.

Pettigrew, Andrew. 1985. The *Awakening Giant: Continuity and Change in ICI*. Oxford: Blackwell.

Pfeffer, Jeffrey and Sutton, Robert. 2000. *The Knowing–Doing Gap: How Smart Companies Turn Knowledge into Action*. Boston: Harvard Business School Press.

Popper, Karl. 2002. *Logic of Scientific Discovery*. London: Routledge.

Power, Dominic and Malmberg, Anders. 2008. The Contribution of Universities to Innovation and Economic Development: In What Sense a Regional Problem? *Cambridge Journal of Regions, Economy and Society*, 1, 233–245.

Pressman, Jeffrey and Wildavsky, Aaron. 1984. *Implementation*. Berkeley: University of California Press.

Reid, Alasdair. 2010. *Measuring Up: Evaluating the Effects of Innovation Measures in the Structural Funds*. Brighton: Technopolis Group.

Remington, Key and Pollack, Julien. 2008. *Tools for Complex Projects*. London: Gower.

Scottish Government. 2008. *Evaluation of ERDF Supported Venture Capital and Loan Funds*.

Scriven, Michael. 1998. Truth and Objectivity in Evaluation, in *Evaluation for the 21st Century*, edited by Eleanor Chelimsky and William Shadish. London: Sage.

Sjöberg, Karin, Brulin, Göran and Svensson, Lennart. 2009. Learning Evaluation – Ongoing Evaluation: A Synthesis, in *Learning Through Ongoing Evaluation*, edited by Lennart Svensson et al. Lund: Studentlitteratur.

Sölvell, Örjan. 2009. *Clusters Balancing Evolutionary and Constructive Forces*. Stockholm: Ivory Tower Publisher.

Stjernberg, Torbjörn. 1993. *Organisationsideal. Livskraft och spridning*. Stockholm: Norstedts juridik.

Stokes, Ian. 2009. *Training for Project Management*. 3 vols. London: Gower.

Storey, David J. 2000. *Small Business: Critical Perspectives on Business and Management*. London: Routledge.

Storper, Michael. 1998. *Regional World: Territorial Development in a Global Economy*. London: Guilford Publications.

Sundin, Elisabeth and Göransson, Ulla. 2006. *Vad hände sen?* (*What Happened Next?*). Stockholm: Vinnova (in Swedish).

Svensson, Lennart and Nilsson, Barbro. 2008. *Partnership: As a Strategy for Social Innovation and Sustainable Change*. Stockholm: Santérus Academic Press Sweden.

Svensson, Lennart, Brulin, Göran, Jansson, Sven and Sjöberg, Karin. 2009. *Learning Through Ongoing Evaluation*. Lund: Studentlitteratur.

Taleb, Nassim Nicholas. 2010. *The Black Swan*. London: Penguin Books.

Tamásy, Christine. 2008. Rethinking Technology-Oriented Business Incubators: Developing a Robust Policy Instrument for Entrepreneurship, Innovation, and Regional Development? *Growth and Change*, 3(38), 460–473.

Tarschy, Daniel. 2003. *Reinventing Cohesion: The Future of European Structural Policy*. Stockholm: Sieps, Swedish Institute for European Policy Studies, 2003: 17.

Tarschy, Daniel. 2011. How Small Are the Regional Gaps? How Small Is the Impact of Cohesion Policy? A Commentary on the Fifth Report on Cohesion Policy. *European Policy Analysis*, January issue 2011: 1epa.

Technopolis. 2009. FP6 *IST Impact Analysis Study*.

Tessmer, Martin. 1993. *Planning and Conducting Formative Evaluations*. London: Routledge.

Thomas, Janice and Mullaly, Mark. 2008. *Researching the Value of Project Management*. Atlanta: Project Management Institute.

Thomsett, Rob. 2002. *Radical Project Management*. New York: Prentice Hall.

Toulmin, Stephen and Gustavsen, Bjorn. 1996. *Beyond Theory: Changing Organizations through Participation*. Amsterdam: Johan Benjamin Publishing Corporation.

Turner, Rodney. 2008. *Gower Handbook of Project Management*. London: Gower.

Van de Ven, Andrew and Poole, Marshall Scott. 1995. Explaining Development and Change in Organizations. *Academy of Management Review*, 20(3).

Von Hippel, Eric. 2005. *Democratizing Innovation*. Cambridge, MA: The MIT Press.

Von Stamm, Bettina and Trifilova, Anna. 2009. *The Future of Innovation*. London: Gower.

Weick, Karl and Quinn, Robert. 1999. Organizational Change and Development. *Annual Review of Psychology*, 50, 361–386.

Wistus, Sofia. 2008. Birds of a Feather Flock Together: On Representation and Equal Relationships in Partnerships, in *Partnership: As a Strategy for Social Innovation and Sustainable Change*, edited by Lennart Svensson and Barbro Nilsson. Stockholm: Santérus Academic Press Sweden.

Index

For Product Safety Concerns and Information please contact our EU
representative GPSR@taylorandfrancis.com Taylor & Francis Verlag GmbH,
Kaufingerstraße 24, 80331 München, Germany

Printed and bound by CPI Group (UK) Ltd, Croydon, CR0 4YY
01/05/2025
01858377-0004